Old Geezer's

Memoirs

J. H. Ellison

Table of Contents

Chapter 1

OLD GEEZER'S MEMOIRS

Joe, an elderly gentleman in his eighties, sat listening to a speaker on TV. The speaker asked his audience, "Where has your journey in life taken you? What were your challenges? How did you overcome these challenges? What are your happy memories? Have you written down your journey for your posterity to enjoy? Or, will you become just a name in your family's history, unknown by the third generation?"

Joe had never thought about such questions. It caused him to realize that everyone born must take life's journey, like in the old song, "Life is like a mountain railway." Some will bear the scars of that journey. Some will meet the trials and experiences in life and overcome them. Others will look back at the "good old days" with nostalgia.

He could see the wisdom of writing down his journey through life, telling both pleasant and not so pleasant things, and how each situation was handled; that perhaps it might help his descendants as they face life's challenges. Going to his computer he began to write.

Old Geezer's Memoirs
My early years

I was a great depression baby. I was born on January 15, 1930 at the Oklahoma Baptist Hospital in Muskogee, Oklahoma. My father, Joy Hardy Marion Ellison, whose name was given to me, died of a ruptured appendix two months before I was born, at the same hospital.

My mother, Osie Ellison, went to a business school in Muskogee, Oklahoma to lean a trade. I was taken care of by my mother's married half-sister Emily Bennett and her husband George Bennett, whom I considered my grandparents, and my half aunts Lettye Bennett and Audrey Bennett. My grandmother, Emily Bennett, was the daughter of my real grandfather, William Hunter Oslin, by a previous marriage to Josie South. Upon Josie's death, Hunter married Fannie Bird Eubank. Hunter and Fannie were married by my great uncle S. J. Oslin, a minister. Hunter fathered my Uncle Bill Oslin and Osie Oslin, my mother. Fannie died in 1908, possibly due to complications stemming from childbirth. My mother was a one year old, and was reared by her half-sister Emily and her husband George.

My mother was nine days old when Oklahoma became a state. Before statehood, Oklahoma was plagued by lawlessness. Bell Star's gang roamed the area. My real grandfather, Hunter, had to testify in court against one of the Davis gang, a friend of Belle Starr. Expecting a raid from Bell's gang, my grandfather and his four sons, armed with Winchester rifles, stayed up all night to defend their property. The attack never came. My grandfather Hunter Oslin died two years before I was born and is buried in Fields Cemetery, Porum, Oklahoma.

Through family history research I learned that my mother's ancestors include Ministers, music teacher and hymn writer, Southern plantation owners, officer in the Revolutionary War and two English knights [Sir Robert and Sir Thomas Wingfield]. I have recorded my mother's family history on my computer Personal Ancestry File [PAF].

Emily and her husband George had lost their ranch in the great depression and had become managers of a Poor Farm in Muskogee, Oklahoma, run by the county. The County Poor Farm was a place of refuge for a few couples, until they could provide for themselves. They performed various farm tasks to help in their keep. Emily was in charge of cooking and housekeeping. George was in charge of the farm livestock and farming operations.

My half-aunt Lettye Bennett told me that their old ranch house was located at the foot of Warner Mountain, and that it was haunted. She claims she saw the ghost twice. She said a man had been killed in an upper bedroom of the house over a game of cards, by the ranch's previous owner. She claimed the dead man's spirit roamed the area. Both Emily and George claimed it's true.

Lettye told about Roy Graham, a member of our family, stopping by the ranch on a cold winter night. He was riding his horse to Warner and sought to get out of the snow and sleet storm. Roy had the reputation of being a "scraper", afraid of no one. He took a coal-oil lamp and went upstairs to bed.

Later George, Emily and Lettye, who were down stairs, heard a shout. They hurried up to Roy's room. He was standing up on his bed, swinging at the foot of his bed. He claimed he woke up and saw a man standing at the foot of his bed, and that he was trying to hit him. Roy got up, got dressed and rode on into Warner; never again would he spend a night at the ranch.

Lettye told how her father, my "Daddy" George, used to play his fiddle at local dances. She said late at night she could hear him returning home. While his horse walked along, he would be playing on his fiddle his favorite song, "Red wings."

My grandfather, "Daddy" George, gave me instruction on two things: Don't touch his fiddle that he kept under his bed at the poor farm, and don't ride the horse "Old Billie" without a farm hand along. I broke both rules. When I tried his fiddle it made such a high screeching noise I was sure it was heard by both "mother" Emily or "Daddy" George. I quickly put the fiddle back in its place and hurried out of their room.

Old Billie was noted for chasing the farm's mules in the pasture. I would take a short length of rope and walk out in the pasture to Old Billie. He allowed me to put the rope around his neck and lead him to a tree stump so that I could mount him — I was about four years old. I rode Old Billie around in the pasture and not once did he chase the mules. I then directed Old Billie through an unlocked gate into the farm's corn field. I was caught this time by "Daddy" George and given a stern lecture.

"Mother" Emily was a great cook. She knew my love for brown beans and cornbread, and her egg custard pies. She baked her cornbread in iron skillets that resembled ears of corn. I would help by setting out plates on a long table, for all those living there, and the food. She was always amused when she saw me placing my favorite foods close to my plate. The long table accommodated all those living on the poor farm, which was quite a few. I wanted to be sure I could reach my favorite foods.

During season, I was fascinated watching "Mother" Emily prepare peaches for sun drying. She would buy two or more bushels of peaches, peel and pit them. Then she placed them on a metal tray, cover them with cheese-cloth and place them on the roof of a low shed to dry by the sun. She would frequently check on them and turn them over to fully dry. They made great peach turnovers, pies and cobblers.

"Daddy" George was a kind, soft spoken man. He didn't drink but loved to smoke his pipe. He would take twist tobacco and crumble it up to fill his pipe's bowl.

In the early 1930s there were many gangsters. This was partly triggered by the great depression and the hard times that followed. Charles Arthur "Pretty Boy" Floyd's favorite hideout was in the Cookson Hills East of Muskogee. He was considered by some a Robin Hood. He didn't rob local people and was noted for generous "tips" for aid and food. He helped some from losing their farms. He teamed up with a vicious killer, Miller. When they were caught and convicted Miller was sentenced to die in the electric chair. "Pretty Boy" was sentenced to prison. He got an early release from Oklahoma Governor "Alfalfa" Bill Murray.

"Pretty Boy" then teamed up with John Dillinger, public enemy number one. When Dillinger was killed "Pretty Boy" became public enemy number one on the most wanted list. He was killed and buried in Akin,

Oklahoma cemetery. This was in October 1934. I mention this because "Daddy" George and "Mother" Emily took me to "Pretty Boy's" funeral. There was a large crowd. "Daddy" George held me on his shoulder so I could see. I vividly remember the experience, even to this day —seventy-seven years later.

Five armed deputies, in black suits, stood guard next to the casket. It was an open casket affair. The casket with "Pretty Boy's" body was under a canopy. People filed past, viewing the body. Sixty years later I visited Akin cemetery, with my wife Dorothy, and went to the spot where "Pretty Boy" Floyd is buried in an unmarked grave, next to his parents.

My uncle by marriage, Bill Moore, told me that in the early 1930s he owned a gas station in Muskogee, Oklahoma. He told how one day two men drove in and asked for a lube, oil change and to fill the gas tank. They then asked about the café across the street, if they served good food. He told them it was good.

My uncle said they crossed the street single file. Servicing their car, as requested, he noticed in their car's backseat were submachine guns, pistols and shotguns. When they returned they tried to pay my uncle more than their car's service and gas fees. He told them the correct amount, and that's what he wanted. Because he didn't call the police and charged the correct fee, only, his gas station was never robbed. Others in Muskogee were robbed. It was as though the two gangsters had spread the word to other gangsters that my uncle's station wasn't to be robbed.

My mother finished business school and became a postal clerk at the Warner Post Office. Her boss and Postmaster at that time was James Lacey. I remember that he was a nice guy about 5'9" tall, always wore cowboy boots and was pigeon toed, his feet toed in 90 degrees.

6

My mother rented a house on what is now 11th Street. In September 1939 she was appointed Postmaster by Franklin Delano Roosevelt. She held that position until 1969 when her health caused her to have to retire. She was recognized for her many achievements, and for being a regional trainer of other postmasters. Her clerk, Okemah Lloyd was promoted to Postmaster.

The house on 11th had tall bean trees on the west. Being five at that time, I loved to climb those trees to their top to be able to see Warner Mountain, much to the worry of my babysitter, my mother's housekeeper. She would scold me. Her favorite sandwich, one that I came to like, was iceberg lettuce, with sliced dill pickles and mustard on bread slices.

Since there wasn't any indoor plumbing, water was purchased from Joe Moore for fifty-cents per barrel. His well was the only well in town with soft water. All other wells had water so hard that soap wouldn't lather-up. The house had an outdoor "Johnny". "Thunder pots" were also used.

In the summer of 1947, when we lived in a rental next door to Judge Looper, Warner put in a water system to the town. Orrin Gillian was the boss over installation. I applied for the labor crew and Orrin hired me. The pay was fifty-cents per hour pick and shovel work.

Since Connors College was obtaining water from Warner Lake, the city was to tap into their system. A man with a team of horses, using a breaking plow, cut a furrow on the north side of the street leading to the college. Then, it was up to us laborers to get into the furrow and clean it out. The guy with the plow would keep doing this until he could plow no deeper. Then it became pick and shovel to get the ditch down six feet. A group would come along behind us, laying the water main pipe.

A classmate of mine, Ellsworth Harrison, boasted that if Ellison can do it he could. He was a rough and ready rodeo rider. He lasted two weeks; I finished out the summer. I had learned to arrive at the work area pick-up early, and grab a long-handled shovel. It was less tiring on one's back.

One day, after lunch, Orrin announced to his work group, "Time to go to work. It's 109 in the shade, and there's no shade." After the second week, hard labor made me feel good. I felt I could whip anyone, not that I wanted to or ever tried. I rigged up a shower in the shed above a useless cellar; this was at our rental house on 8th Street. The shower was a large hanging can with tiny holes in the bottom. Standing in a galvanized wash tub, I'd pour a full can of water in the top, and it would give a tiny spray for me to shower in.

When I had to quit the crew to go back to school, Orrin confided to me that when he hired me he thought I wouldn't last a week. He was surprised at how long I had lasted, and told me I was a good worker.

I've always had a love for flowers. Back of the house on 11th Street, when we lived next door to Trimm's house, was a patch of wildflowers. This was to be my flowerbed. I took a hoe and scraped a dirt bare spot around them. In the process, I unearthed a dime —I was rich. My playmates at the time were Bob Trimm and Ramona Gilliam. Bob's father, Roy Trimm, owned a car repair garage downtown. Ramona's father, O. C. Gilliam, owned a gas station and bait shop.

The year I entered first grade, my mother found a better rental on 8th street. It was closer to school and a block from downtown. It had a cistern with crank up water cups on a chain track. House gutters funneled water off the roof through a purifying bed of charcoal into the cistern. Like the first house, it had an outdoor toilet, a very cold place in winter. It also had a shed above a cellar that always had standing water, making the cellar useless. The neighbor to the west was Judge Looper. The house across the street from us was first owned by teachers, Wheeler's, and then by the local sheriff, Bill Howland. The neighbor to the east of us was Boyd Campbell, owner of the local drug store.

I was nine when my mother was appointed by FDR to be Postmaster. I felt I was too old to have a baby-sitter and house keeper. I convinced my mother to let me not have a baby-sitter and let me take care of the house. I suppose she reasoned that with our surrounding neighbors I was reasonably safe and let me try my idea. We had a four room house— master bedroom for mom, living-room, dining-room with my built-in single window seat bed for me and a kitchen. The living-room and master bedroom had area carpets. The other rooms were vinyl.

My mother would fix our breakfast and leave the dishes for me to wash. She left for work a 7:45 AM, walking a block to the post office. I'd leave fifteen minutes later and walk to school. The only danger I faced was crossing state highway 64, which was never busy.

Our school was a combination of high school and grade school. It was a WPA project and was built of native flagstone. The lower grades were on the north end of the building. The Principal and Superintendents offices and library separated the lower grades from high school classrooms. A basketball gym with stage formed the building into a T shape. There were two double doors on both the north and south entries to the gym, and stairs going down to the basketball court. Coke and candy bar machines we located along the wall between the gym doors.

9

Since the town didn't have running water at that time, toilets were outhouses. The boy's toilet was located about 300 feet northwest of the grade school section. The girl's was about 300 feet northeast of the grade school section. Both toilets had four-hole seats partitioned off. There was a six foot high fence around the front for privacy.

The north end of the school building had swings and teeter-totters. The south end had a soft-ball diamond. A baseball diamond was adjacent to the school grounds. During recess, kids would play ball on those diamonds or small clusters would gather to talk, or look for four-leaf clover or a weed we called sheep-shank. When sheep-shank stems were chewed, it had a sour taste.

In grade school, I would get to school early. I would take my fishing-pole and bait along. In the pasture northwest of school was a pond that had perch and catfish. I'd bait my hook, check the depth I wanted for my bobber, cast out my line, place a large flat rock over the end of my cane-pole and run to school. During recesses I would run and check my pole. If I caught a fish large enough for the table, I'd use my pocket knife to cut a thin limb from a willow tree, string the fish and bury the end of the willow into the dirt pond, below the water line. After school I'd pick up my fish and take them home for my mother to clean and cook. This helped with our small income.

When in the sixth grade, Billy Joe was the lower grade school bully. A cute girl, Mary Ann Bullard, had joined our class. Her parents had moved to Warner from New Mexico. Mary Ann had her blond hair done in a Shirley Temple style set of curls.

Billy Joe was set on her being his girl. Mary Ann seemed interested in my regular fast trips to the pond in the field. One day when I went to check my fishing pole, I found my pole floating in the middle of pond, my bait can and my anchor rock gone. Passing Billy Joe on my way to the pond and seeing his sarcastic smile, I had a good idea of the culprit.

Billy Joe was standing next to Mary Ann by the school swings. When I accused him, he decided he might win Mary Ann by whipping me. He grabbed me, intending to throw me to the ground and pound on me. Falling, I managed to twist my body in mid-air. Billy Joe hit the ground first, on his back, and me straddling him. When he tried to hit me, I pinned down his hands.

He had to say, "Uncle" before I'd let him up. This happened two more times. The madder he got the more amusing to me. He finally gave up and went into the school building. Mary Ann and I became good friends. It saddened me when her parents and she moved back to New Mexico.

I appreciated growing up in a small town of 300 people. Downtown was a block long north, west and south. It was a town where people were friendly, ready to help others in times of need.

In May, on Decoration Day, my mother and I, and family members from Muskogee, Checotah and Dallas, Texas would get together to decorate the graves of our departed loved ones. I especially loved when we met at Mount Nebo, three miles or more west of Warner, on Warner Mountain.

Every family brought a pot luck dish. All would work hard cleaning around our family's graves. I would sometimes use a hoe or help carry away brush and weeds. Then all sat down on the ground to eat a pot-luck lunch. I always hoped our distant cousins Jim and Virgie Steen, with their daughter Juanita from Checotah, would attend decoration. I had a crush on Juanita and Virgie would always bring strawberry shortcake, my favorite. This family gathering was a time for getting acquainted and kids meeting cousins they hadn't seen in a long time. It brought families close, something that isn't seen very often today. Aunt Ella from Dallas was my favorite. She lived to be 103. One of her sons was a professional boxer.

A small town isn't a place for those who wish to do wrong things. If you did, you can rest assured that the whole town would know in minutes. People in small towns are friendly and willing to help others going through difficult times. If I had a sore throat, the druggist would take me into his office and swab my throat with Mentholatum, at no cost. That coated the throat and did away with my sore throat.

In the hot sultry summer months, people would sleep on cots in their yard, without fear. Most of the people didn't have air-conditioning or even fans in the 1930s. Many nights I remember going to sleep in our yard, looking up at the stars and listening to night sounds.

Warner businesses consisted of a drug store owned by Boyd Campbell, where Trailway bus tickets could be bought, and it had an attached tiny doctor's office [8' x 12'] in back for doctor Burns. Entering the drugstore, there were glass cases for store items. Next to the counter where bus tickets were sold was a soda fountain. Boyd and his wife made some of the best sodas I've ever enjoyed. My favorites were cherry or strawberry sodas. Boyd always put two large scoops of ice cream in my soda.

In front of the soda fountain were about five small tables and with chairs, so one could sit and enjoy their soda. The rest of the store had medical supplies typical of a drugstore. Boyd had a tiny office in the back of the store.

Warner had two small grocery stores owned by L. B. Brown and "Shorty" Gilliam, Post Office, barber shop owned by Frank Shinn and large general merchandise and grocery store owned by Maurice Finklea. Every year, as a youth, I'd go to Finklea's store to buy a cane fishing pole, bobber, hooks, sinkers and some bait. My mother bought all her major appliances from Finklea's. In later years the drugstore, Gilliam's grocery store, the old post office and Frank's barber shop was destroyed by fire.

The café diagonal and across highway 266 from Finklea's store was owned by Sara Hale, a small gas station was located across 8th street, north of her café. Next door, to the south was a beer/pool hall, L. B. Brown's grocery store with IOOF lodge above and ice house owned by Joe Moore.

Telephone central, managed by the Cargels, was south of the drugstore and saddle shop. A blacksmith shop owned by Melton was located south and behind of the old Post Office and Frank's barbershop.

A small two story wooden hotel was located diagonally southwest of Trimm's garage. A Stable owned by Dutch Schaublin, who was also a veterinarian and mail carrier, was located a block northwest of Trimm's garage. The two major auto repair garages, in Warner were owned by Roy Trimm and Hub Davis—Davis also had a gas station in front. Hub's daughter, Emma Ellen was in my class.

"Shorty" Gilliam's store was next door to the Post Office, on the east side. It was a small store. Frank Shinn's barber shop was on the west side of the Post Office. I received my first haircut from Frank. Frank was also a good gunsmith. In my teen years he repaired the firing pin on my father's scout .22 rifle. There wasn't any air-conditioning in his shop, making tiny bits of hair going down one's back uncomfortable.

The Post Office had interesting town visitors. I worked as a temporary clerk one summer while my mother, the Postmaster, searched for a full-time clerk. The mail truck from Muskogee brought the mail down in the morning and picked up town mail, being sent, to Muskogee on their return.

A little old lady in town would come in several times a day, asking if she had any mail —general delivery. On her first trip I'd check general delivery to see if she had mail. On her next trips I didn't have the heart to remind her that mail only came in once a day. I would sort through the general delivery mail and politely let her know she didn't have any mail. I think her trip to the post office filled in her lonely days.

Irene Vore, an elderly lady who lived in a small house west of Finklea's store, made a great cheese-cake with gram-cracker crust. She would bring two to the Post Office and my mother would buy them.

There was a gentleman who came to the post office to get his daily newspaper, mailed from Muskogee. The post office had a bench seat running the width of the office, backing to a full glass front. This gentleman would begin looking over his newspaper. When a postal customer came in for their mail, this gentleman would tell the customer, "It says here...", and read the whole article to that person. He would read different newspaper articles to others for over an hour, before leaving.

For postal customer services there were two windows, one large one for mailing boxes; the other for buying stamps and general delivery. The stamp window had small heavy wire bars —the money drawer was below that window. My mother heard many funny stories, as Postmaster for 39 years, being told by town members in the lobby. I told her she should write an Erma Bombeck type book, and title it "39 Years Behind Bars." She never did.

Sara Hale, owner of the downtown café, knew my love of pinto beans and corn bread. When I entered her café she'd let me know that "brown" beans and corn bread was on the menu that day. That would be my lunch.

Across 8th Street, north from Sara's café, was a gas station. Many times I would stop there to purchase an RC [Royal Crown cola]. I'd give my nickel to the station attendant, go to his outside pop cooler, lift up the lid and get my RC. I'd use the opener attached to the cooler to pry off the cap. Then, I'd use my pocket knife to remove the cork from the pop lid to see if I was a lucky winner, to get another free pop. I was pretty lucky, at times, and would get another free RC.

Along state highway 64 were three gas stations. The owners were Hub Davis, O.C. Gilliam and Washum's. The Texaco station also has a café, owned by Nellie Washum and her husband, and was a favorite hangout for school kids. We school kids called Nellie Washum, Aunt Nellie. She was always friendly to us kids.

Nellie told me that one day Nedra Kay Finklea brought some of her school friends in for lunch. It was to be put on her parent's, Maurice and Margaret Finklea's, bill. Nellie checked with Margaret Finklea who said to go ahead and put the lunches on her bill.

One of the other stations, owned by O. C. Gilliam, had an attached bait shop. Nearby was a small beer hall called Blue Moon? This beer hall was located behind the sheriff's house. One night two men were causing trouble at the place and word was sent for the sheriff, Bill Howland.

The men got wind that the sheriff was coming and jumped into their car. As their car spun gravel in the hall's parking space, sheriff Howland appeared around the corner of the building. He drew his .45 pistol and shot out both rear tires. The car, running on flat tires, continued onto the highway. By the time the sheriff ran back to his home for his car, the culprits had disappeared.

At this time, Oklahoma was a "dry" state. However, Warner had its known bootlegger. Several in town would buy from him on the "cue-T." The bootlegger drove a dark green Hudson Hornet, and would pick up his "goods" in Texas.

One night he was stopped in Checotah, a town fifteen miles west of Warner, by their local sheriff, who demanded he open the trunk of his car. The bootlegger said he had lost the key to the trunk. The sheriff got on the running board of the bootlegger's car and told him to drive to the local blacksmith shop.

When the bootlegger slowed down, as if to turn for the blacksmith shop, he shoved the sheriff off the running board of his car and floor-boarded the gas pedal. The Checotah sheriff went to the nearest phone and placed a call for the Warner sheriff.

Since the Warner sheriff didn't have a home phone, most others in town didn't own phones either, a runner was sent from telephone central to get the sheriff. The sheriff and runner then walked back to telephone central. The sheriff was told to stop the bootlegger's car. When the sheriff stepped out of telephone central, the bootlegger's car zipped past.

Warner's sheriff hurried home and got his car. He headed north out of town in the direction he had seen the Hudson Hornet headed. At a beer hall three miles north of town he spotted the parked Hudson. Going in, he found the bootlegger casually sipping a beer with friends. The sheriff demanded to have the trunk key. It was given to him. He searched the car and other possible hiding places. No liquor was found. Town gossip had it that the bootlegger pulled into the beer hall and got the many patrons to help him hide his "goods."

One summer a gypsy looking wagon, pulled by a team of mules, stopped where the highway to town and the state highway met. His totally enclosed wooden wagon had people images holding a bottle of elixir painted on it, a traveling medicine man had arrived.

Dropping down the back of the wagon, it became a platform. He sat out gaudy pillows and decorated tapestry for sale. Taking a seat on a strait-backed wooden chair, he began playing a banjo. When a sufficient crowd had gathered to hear him play, he then "Pitched" his elixir. For one dollar it was guaranteed to cure all sorts of ills. I would guess it probably had lots of alcohol with bitters to make it taste like medicine. When he had sold what bottles he could, he then tried selling his bright gaudy pillows and tapestry. Next morning he hitched up his team and left for the next town.

On another occasion a young man parked his car by Campbell's drugstore and got out his guitar. Sitting on his front fender, he began playing and singing western and popular tunes. When he had a nice crowd, he let all know they could buy his song book of lyrics for only one dollar. I got my mother to buy me one so that I could learn the words to my favorite tunes.

The sixth grade was a rebellious year for me. A coat closet formed the back of our classroom. There were no dividers the length of the closet. A few class members, myself included, brought comic books to school. When the teacher's back was turned a few of us would quietly go to the coat closet, go inside and close the door, sit on the floor and read our comic books. I was also guilty of day-dreaming. Our classroom windows ran from the ceiling area to desk level. Many times I would look longingly towards Warner Mountain, seeing in my "mind's eye" my favorite places, there.

About that same time my teacher and my mother had angry words. What it was about I never knew. My mother hinted it was about postal matters. My teacher flunked me the sixth grade. Others who had similar grades were passed. I was devastated and my classmates saddened.

Word of my not passing sixth grade spread rapidly around town. I was the only kid in town to ever fail a grade. Our neighbor across the street, Mr. and Mrs. Wheeler were teachers. They heard about my dilemma. They told my mother they were holding summer school at Buckhorn and that I could make up the sixth. When my mother told me about it, I jumped at the chance to rejoin my classmates in the fall.

Buckhorn country school was about eleven miles north and east of Warner. Eight miles was on paved road and three on dirt. I rode to summer school with the teachers. The teacher's car wasn't in the best of repair. Their son, Heber, sat on the front seat between his mother and father, pliers in hand. When his father saw a bump in the road ahead, he'd tell Heber to pull up the foot-peddle, while he applied braking. This occurred frequently, due to rainwater run-off making washes in the dirt road.

The schoolhouse was built of wood and had one room. Desks were lined up in twelve columns, one for each class. Mr. Wheeler taught classes seventh through twelfth. His wife taught the lower grades. The first thing each morning was the teachers going to each grade class and making assignments for the day. This time I worked hard at learning. My failing a grade had taught me a valuable lesson. I had failed myself, my family and my classmates. I felt the sting of shame.

Each morning we traveled down the dirt road to school I was impressed by the early morning beauty. With the car windows down the air was cool and refreshing. Here and there along the road were small farm homes. Trellises in front had morning glories in full bloom. The Wheeler's car kicked up huge clouds of dust. I felt sorry for all those homes plagued by the car's dust.

Students at this summer school were from the local farming community. During recess it took a majority of the older kids, both boys and girls, to make up a baseball team. The only member on either team to have a glove was the catcher. It amazed me that girls, playing infield, would catch hard hit balls, bare-handed.

At noon, each student would take his brown-bag lunch to a cool shady place to eat. My favorite lunch during summer school was a baloney sandwich, a whole tomato and a small thermos of milk. Since Buckhorn country students tended to be clannish, I sat alone in the shade formed by the schoolhouse to eat my lunch.

One day going home from Buckhorn, Mr. Wheeler's car blew a right rear tire. We were climbing up the northern part of Warner Mountain, south of Dirty Creek. He pulled to the shoulder and all got out. He put large rocks under the three good tires, to keep the car from rolling backwards down the mountain road.

Getting out his spare tire, he learned that his jack was inoperative. He told us to find some flat rocks and stack them by the rear tire, while he searched for a lever. Someone had cut down a small tree and trimmed it, preparing it to be a fence-post. Mr. Wheeler brought it back to the car. He told his son to loosen the lug-nuts.

Placing the gathered flat-rocks, and tree post to use as a fulcrum, all of us but Heber pushed down on the tree, lifting the car's rear end up while Heber changed the tire. It was a great lesson in physics.

That fall I enrolled in Warner's seventh grade. I was happily greeted by old classmates. Our teacher was an older lady. She introduced herself as being Pennsylvania Dutch. If she had to leave the classroom momentarily, she'd tell the class to be quiet and study. We didn't do that. We'd talk and laugh among ourselves. One day when she left the room she stood outside the door, listening. She re-entered the room and asked for a show of hands by those who were talking. Since I was guilty, I held up my hand. Sixteen had done as I. We were lined up at the front of the class and spanked. Again, I learned a good lesson. The spanking didn't hurt that much, but the embarrassment did.

Chapter 2

My mother made sure I spent some time with my grandparents, to bond with them. My father's parents were Francis Lafayette "Jack" and Maude Estella [Goodall] Ellison. From family history research I learned that the Ellison's raised good riding horses and was land owners in Tennessee and Missouri. They are mentioned in White River Valley quarterly and in Taney County history. A Street in Branson, Missouri is named Ellison, and a bend in White River is called Ellison's Elbow.

When I was very young they had a farm located between Warner and Checotah, where my grandfather raised watermelons on a commercial scale. When my mother took me for a visit, Papa Jack would set me in the shade of trees along his melon patch, bring me a melon, cut it open and leave me to enjoy it. Later, they moved into Checotah, Oklahoma, fifteen miles west of Warner. My mother would put me on a Trailway bus to

Checotah, telling the driver to be sure I got off there, and I was met by my grandparents. The driver would have me sit behind his seat.

"Papa Jack" and Maude were always there to meet me. We walked back to their home, talking along the way. Talking was done more by Maude. I quickly learned that Maude prattled a lot and whatever "Papa Jack" said was worth hearing—wise words.

When visiting them, I slept in a back bedroom, next to an enclosed storage room filled with books. Several of the books belonged to my father, who I never got to meet. In this room was an old overstuffed chair. I would spend hours in that room, looking through my father's books, reading some.

When I got tired reading and looking through books, I would go to my bedroom and play old records on my Grandparents old floor-model, crank-up Victrola. Their Victrola model was made around 1906-1925. Their records were 78 RPM—some were impregnated paper type and very warped. I played such tunes as "Home Sweet Home", "Turkey in the Straw" and "Banjo Medleys."

My grandfather, who I called "Papa Jack" in my pre-teens, had an orchard. My favorite fruit tree was his yellow plum. I'd climb up in the tree to enjoy its fruit. He had two yellow plum, two red plum, two peach and two cherry trees. Over the chicken house was a huge mulberry tree. I had free rein to eat any of the fruit.

"Papa Jack" also raised a large garden. When vegetables or fruit ripened, my grandmother would can them, and then stored the jars in their storm cellar. They put up enough food to take them into another season.

Neighbor kids next door, the Emerson's, used to get into corncob fights with me. Sometimes they would throw just the empty cob at me. Other times they would throw a full cob of corn. I would pick up these corn cobs, loaded with seed, and throw back at them, hiding in their barn loft. When the cob hit their barn wall, it would splatter corn kernels back into "Papa Jack's" garden. One day at the table he remarked he couldn't understand why corn was coming up in places he hadn't planted. I kept quiet.

For meat he'd raise a couple of pigs and some chickens. In the fall he'd slaughter the pigs, cut them into desired cuts and salt them down in his smokehouse. Salt preserved the meat. A black walnut tree next to the smokehouse helped keep it cool. Chickens supplied meat and eggs. This kind of lifestyle didn't require much money to get by year after year, and it was nourishing.

Grandmother loved the movies. She would take me to the theater in Checotah. Movies were only shown in the evening. The movie let out about ten. About that same time the passenger train "Blue Bonnet" went through the edge of Checotah.

To get home we had to cross those tracks. The train roared through Checotah at 60 MPH. The train would blow its whistle as it approached town. It was like the wailing of a banshee. A few people heard the wailing, thought the train was far away and safe to cross the tracks. They didn't make it. By the time they heard the train's wailing sound the train, traveling at 60 MPH, was much closer than they thought. Several people were killed at that crossing. The one most talked about was a mother reaching back for her daughter. The train killed both.

In 1938, my grandmother and I were taken, by my uncle, to Noel, Missouri to watch the filming of Jesse James. It stared Tyrone Power and Henry Fonda. I was eight years old and too small to see over the crowd gathered to watch the filming. I climbed up an outside stairway to where I could see, and sat down to watch. A person put his hand on my shoulder, saying, "Pardon me." It was Tyrone Power.

My grandparents would occasionally tell me about Crazy Snake, a full-blood Creek Indian. They said Crazy Snake got together a following of other tribesmen and several Negros. He sped a blanket on the ground and asked for donations to make war against the whites who had violated their treaty. The Checotah sheriff and a posse went to break up the gathering. One of the posse members was the sheriff's son. In an exchange of shots, his son was killed. Papa Jack and Maude said this happened when they lived in the country near where the battle was fought. They said wagons carrying dead bodies would go past their house. This account was told to me by my grandparents who lived in Checotah. This account isn't mentioned in the history of Crazy Snake, only the verbal account by my grandparents.

A story told to me by my uncle by marriage is about an incident in Checotah. It gives another picture of life in the early 1900s. He told of the time when he was a young boy in Checotah. Where two main state highways cross in Checotah, forming the center of town, he had stepped inside a store to get an ice cream cone. When he came out a man grabbed hold of his arm, held him at arm's length, drew a pistol and fired at a man on the opposite corner. Holding my uncle at arm's length kept him out of the line of fire. My uncle said he still remembers the sound of passing bullets.

I idolized my grandfather, Papa Jack. At one time he was McIntosh County Chairman of the Democrat party, and personally knew Oklahoma Governor "Alfalfa" Bill Murray. Papa Jack was also a member of the IOOF lodge. He and my father had many friends. He said it was a sad time when my father died of a ruptured appendix at the age of twenty-five.

When Papa Jack introduced me to people in Checotah, he would introduce me as "Joy's boy." These people would say how sorry they were that my father had died so young; that they loved and missed him. Since I was given his name, I became determined to try and never disgrace his name.

If grandmother served ham, eggs and biscuits for breakfast, Papa Jack would pour a little coffee into the skillet grease and use a biscuit to sop it up. One would think that would clod-up his arties. His doctor said he had the heart of a man half his age. He died at the age of eighty-eight of pneumonia, from getting soaked outside in a winter rain.

Grandmother made me some special treats. For breakfast she might serve me crumbled up biscuits with coffee, sweetened by adding sugar and cream. She would make up some pie-dough, roll it out flat, coat it with plenty of butter, sugar and cinnamon, roll up in a log form, cut the roll into two inch lengths and bake. It tastes good. When my grandmother made pumpkin pies, she did it from "scratch." She always placed on top of the pie a white topping of whipped egg-whites and sugar. It was a tasty treat.

It was pleasant to be around my grandfather. He never said much. It was great to have so much quite moments with him. When he did speak his wisdom was shared with me. His comments have stayed with me throughout my life and been my guide. They are, "Son, if you don't stand for something, you'll fall for anything."

Each day of my life I've seen the wisdom in this statement. He could have used "core values" instead of "something." If we don't have strong core values we can be swayed down a bad path. His other word of advice, when I was a teenager, was, "Son, a baby can drink and get drunk. It takes a man to drink and stay sober." I was told he did drink, but I never saw him drunk or smelled liquor on his breath.

From conversations with him, I also realized the importance of doing nothing to bring shame on the family name. It was difficult to live up to that standard, but I did. My peers were always pressuring me to do things that were risqué and against my grandfather's guidance.

I was visiting my grandparents on August 15, 1935 and remember hearing about the plane crash that killed Will Rogers and Wiley Post, the pilot, at Point Barrow, Alaska. Will Rogers was Oklahoma's favorite son, and liked by many worldwide. His death spread like wildfire throughout the state.

My grandfather and I were great "buddies." When I was older, we'd slip away from grandmother to go to the beer tavern to compete against granddad's old friends in a game of dominos. Grandmother had forbidden grandfather's going to a beer tavern. I never told of our going there to play dominos. My grandfather learned that I was good at the game. The loser in the game had to pay the nickel for the next game—we never lost. He would also take me with him fishing. He would put on his hook a substance he called Asphidia. It seemed to draw fish.

One summer I found him up on his barn, coating the galvanized roof with zinc oxide. I asked for a brush to help him. We quickly finished the roof. When we were walking to the house, he told me I was like my father, always volunteering to help. That really pleased me.

When I visited him one summer, in my early college years, he told me he had some work in town to finish before he could visit with me. I told him I would go and help him. The job turned out to be loading heavy 100 pound bags of feed onto a railroad boxcar. I lasted about a half-hour and could do no more. He quickly finished the job and we walked to his home.

On another occasion I went to pick cotton with him. I learned that cotton hulls can really do a number on my fingers. Their sharp edges dug into my finger's cuticle. How he managed to do that day in and day out, without complaints, I'll never know. One day was enough for me.

I usually visited him about twice a month. One day I got him to let me give him a haircut and trim his mustache. He was a little hesitant the first time. When I finished he liked the work I had done, telling me I did a better job than his barber. He would then hold-off on a haircut until my next visit.

When the war ended in 1945, I was fifteen. My uncle, Willard— granddad's youngest son, served in the eight Air Force in England. When a crated-up glider arrived, he'd take the empty crate and convert it into living quarters for himself or a friend. He'd wire the units and put in plumbing. When he returned to Checotah, he and "Papa Jack" ran in plumbing and electrical outlets into the granddad's house.

Grandmother would talk to me about her father, Hardin Goodall and his family, saying they came on the Mayflower. Grandmother's sisters are Myrtle, Bertha and Ella. When I asked her about her mother's family, all that I could get out of her was, "No damn good." That was her way of telling me not to ask that question again. I and some of my cousins have come to the conclusion that Grandmother's mother, Rebecca Delilah Combs, was a full blood Cherokee, and she didn't want it known. She preferred to tell of her father's side.

My grandfather had traded a cow for a Smith & Western .38 caliber revolver before moving to Indian Territory around 1906. My grandparents, aunt Gussie and my father traveled in a wagon to Henryetta, Oklahoma. He had a trading post in Henryetta, Oklahoma. When his older daughter, Gussie, by a previous marriage to Minta Hicks, became interested in an Indian boy, Papa Jack sold his trading post and moved to Checotah. A few years later oil was discovered at his old trading post.

I was always fascinated with his guns. One day while visiting one of grandmother's sisters, Bertha Knoblesdorf, Papa Jack and I went fishing at Bertha's pond. A snapping turtle was caught on Papa Jack's line. When he saw what was on his line, he told me to take his .38 and shoot it. I fired two shots. When he looked where the bullets hit, he told me that was good shooting. Both bullets were about an inch apart. He told me that when he passed on, he wanted me to have his pistol and shotgun. My uncle sold both. I managed to buy back his shotgun, but could never find his pistol. His double-barrel 12 gage "thumb-buster" shotgun now rests in my gun cabinet, among my several guns.

On one visit, when I was young, I brought along my airplane model kit that I was working on. I used a straight-edge razor-blade to cut the wing struts and fuselage frame from balsawood, glue together, mount propeller and rubber windup band, and cover with colored tissue paper. I flew this from Papa Jack's roof. It was a long and good flight.

In 1940, Willard "Bill" Ellison, wanting to become an actor in the movies, moved to southern California. He didn't make it as an actor but went to work at North American Aviation. His roommate at the time did make it in the movies; he became the assistant of Joe Friday on Dragnet. Bill would tell me how Ben Alexander and he would take turns washing dishes at a large nearby restaurant, to be able to eat.

He met Beverley Belle Thamplin at North American and they were married in 1942. Shortly afterwards he was drafted into the 8th Army Air Corp. He was sent to Lincoln, Nebraska to be trained in engine repair on the B-24 Liberator bomber. I visited Beverley and uncle "Bill" in Lincoln. I'll never forget the elevator ride in the state capitol building. The three of us had ridden the elevator to the observation deck. When we got in to go down the roughly twenty stories, it was like the floor had dropped out from under us. It was scary.

While in Lincoln, "Bill" introduced me to a guy about my age. The guy's father had a pool table. I was asked by the young guy if I'd like to play pool. Being fond of playing pool, I accepted. I was thoroughly beaten. I later learned that the guy's father was a mathematician. From the angle shots made by my young shooter, I figured his father had taught math.

"Bill" told of his harrowing flight to England. He had been assign as crew-chief on a C-47 transport plane. In route they had to jettison some of their equipment and clothing to make it to Europe. Once in England "Bill" said he became a clerk in the orderly room.

He told me about the horrible drowning of a group of paratroopers, flown by his unit. When the troopers bailed out the Germans blew up a dam, flooding the area as they were landing. Hundreds of American troops were drowned.

In 1945 my Uncle Willard "Bill" Ellison, my father's brother, returned from WWII. He had been part of the Army Air Force's eight Division. He and I were more like brothers. The age difference between him and my father was the same as between he and I. I looked up to him as I would an older brother. He brought me a gift of a thermal flight cap and a small crank-up record player, when he returned home. Being a lover of music, the small crank-up record player was a treasure to me. He also gave me some records of WWII big band songs. Because it was a small portable player, kids in my class would ask to borrow it for a party. I wouldn't let it out of my sight. I became the disc jockey at all parties.

One night my friend Eugene Ross came by in his dad's pick-up truck. He asked me to come along with a group of kids from our class, to bring my record player and some records. The plan was to dance on the mountain by Warner Lake. His dad's truck had a stock rack in back, all but the rear end. There were so many of us that we had to stand. The bed of the truck was full. I stood near the truck cab.

Bill Underwood was in the very back of the truck bed. Everyone was making so much noise that it irritated Eugene. By Trimm's garage he put the truck into a lower gear and gunned the engine. The sudden jerk causes us in back to shift backwards. Bill was tossed off the rear end onto the street. We pounded on the cab, yelling stop. We thought he was hurt. He got up, unhurt, and ran to the truck, and we continued on to the lake

In 1946 "Bill" bought Papa Jack the second television in town. It had a small oscilloscope type round screen, powered by vacuum tubes. It had only one channel and the picture had a greenish look. People from blocks around would visit "Papa Jack" to view this marvel. I was sixteen.

My first experience at driving was to drive Bill's Buick. Beverley, her younger sister Thelma and "Bill" were visiting "Papa Jack". Driving the Buick was quite a thrill. I was a gangling and bashful kid who had just reached 6'2". Bill had me stand next to Thelma and put my arm around her shoulder, while he took our picture. Thelma was a very attractive blond girl probably around 19. I felt very uncomfortable.

I've admired my aunt Beverley from the time my uncle brought her to visit "Papa Jack" and Maude in Checotah. She's a tall brunette and looked like the actress Ann Miller. What was even more remarkable, her dance instructor also taught Ann Miller?

Uncle Bill said that on several occasions individuals would come up to Beverley, thinking she was Ann Miller, and ask for her autograph. To please them Beverley would sign their autograph books —Ann Miller.

When Bill and Beverley were getting started in life, Bill worked at North American Aviation. Beverley also worked there as a private secretary, and taught dance lessons to kids.

I watched Beverley put young ballet dancers through stretch exercises on an elevated bar. It looked so simple and the kids did it easily. When they left, I thought I'd give it a try. I couldn't do a tenth of what they did, and my leg muscles were sore for a week.

Chapter 3

I was fortunate enough to have close family relationships. Strangely all my favorite uncle's first names were Bill.

Bill Oslin was my mother's only brother. He and my aunt Lizzie lived southeast of Pampa, Texas near Lefors. Uncle Bill worked for an oil refinery company. They lived in company supplied housing. Their older son was an ordained minister living in Arkansas. Bill, Lizzie and their daughter Frances would stop by and visit my mother and me, when they visited their son Owen in Arkansas. Both Bill and Lizzie were devout members of the Assembly of God Church. In all the times I knew them I never heard them quarrel.

One summer my mother let me go visit them. They picked me up at the Pampa bus station. That day a misty rain was coming down, bringing oil from asphalt highway to the surface. Bill told how slick the road gets under these conditions. There wasn't any traffic on the road. He said, "I'll show you how slick it gets". Lizzie yelled, "No"! Too late! Bill touched his car's brake and we did a 360 degree spin in the middle of the road. I was eleven years old at that time and vividly remember my visit with my uncle Bill.

My first cousin, Frances, was about twelve and I was about eight. It was nice having a close cousin to share thoughts with. While she was helping her mother, I used to explore the dry-wash near their house, looking for interesting pebbles. I would bring them back to the house to show Frances.

My visit was in July. On the fourth Uncle Bill and Aunt Lizzie took me to Pampa. They and Frances did some shopping and I bought a few fireworks. When we got back to the house, I wanted to try my Red Devil racers. Uncle Bill was working in his garden. I sat the racer to run in the opposite direction from the garden area. When I lit the red racer it began a loud screeching noise, scooting along on the ground. It hit a croquet wicket that deflected it down the garden row my uncle was working on. It went between his legs and blew-up. I was horrified. He just turned and smiled.

That night I wanted to shoot of a sky rocket. I anchored the rocket stick in my uncle's chain-link fence. I pointed the rocket towards the sky and lit it. When it took off it headed for the oil refinery, not the sky. I stood yelling, "No, no, no!" I had the horrible vision of it hitting the refinery and causing an explosion. To my relief, the rocket burned out before reaching the refinery. These two incidents caused me to not want to set off anymore fireworks.

Frances, me and sometimes Bill and Lizzie, played plenty of croquet. It's a fun game.

My uncle, aunt and daughter's religion prohibited them from going to movies, and females were prohibited from wearing make-up. All my life I've enjoy movies. They would take me to Pampa to do their shopping and let me go to a movie.

One Sunday I went with them to their church. The sermon was on the evils of beer, wine and whiskey. It reached the point where the preacher began pounding the pulpit. He said, "If I had all the beer, wine and whiskey in the world, I'd dump it all in the river"! He then turned towards the choir and said, "Sing choir sing"! They sang, "We'll all gather at the river". After services I mentioned this to Uncle Bill. He just chuckled and said, "He should have checked before hand with his choir director." One night a bad storm hit the area. Aunt Lizzie woke us all up, telling us to get dressed. She said, "If we're going to be blown away we must be dressed."

That summer Bill drove all of us to Carlsbad, New Mexico to visit the cave. Bill didn't make much money. Driving up to a traveler's cottage's office, he told Frances and me to duck down below the front seat, so the cottage manager couldn't see us. When we went into our cottage there was only one double bed. That night all four of us slept crossways on the bed. I was on one end next to Uncle Bill. Lizzie slept next to her husband and Frances on the far end.

At the time we visited Carlsbad Caverns, we didn't use the elevator to the bottom. We followed a park ranger down a narrow trail. The ranger would point out various interesting sites and tell us about them. When we arrived at the bottom of the cavern, we were told to be seated around what he called the Rock of Ages. When we were all seated, he showed us how dark it is in the cave when the lights are turned off. With the lights off, I touched my hand to my nose and still couldn't see it. As sections of lights were turned back on, all sang the song, "Rock of Ages." I enjoyed the caverns.

While on that trip, my uncle stopped for gas at a station that had a small zoo of caged wild life. There was a circular walled pit with lots of rattlesnakes. There was a screened in coyote and Bobcat cages. One large screened in cage held two full grown bald eagles. The zoo owner asked my uncle if he would like to take a picture of me with one of the bald eagles perched on my arm. My uncle and I agreed on the idea. I gave my browning box camera to my uncle and with the zoo owner stepped into the cage. The zoo owner brought one of the eagles over and placed it on my arm. Mature eagles have a strong grip. Years later we learned that the station/zoo owner committed suicide by getting into the rattlesnake pit.

Uncle Bill's son Owen Oslin was the minister of a large congregation in Fort Smith, Arkansas. He would go on trips to the Holy Land and report his findings. Later in life he ran into hard times, but never gave up his love of preaching. He wrote several books.

In doing research on the Oslin family history, I found that the first Methodist minister to America was John Oslin, who was born in England in 1627. The Oslins are all from the south. Jesse Oslin was messenger for the Georgia House of Representatives for almost twenty years. John Henry Oslin and Jesse Fletcher Oslin were Revolutionary War soldiers from South Carolina.

Parents of some of the women who married into the Oslin line were well to do plantation owners. The Oslin line is rich in history, much of which hasn't been recorded by me.

Chapter 4

I joined our local Boy Scouts of America troop 51 when I was twelve. To this day I think the scouting program is one of the greatest training for boys. It instills leadership and confidence in boys, many of whom will become future leaders. If a scout commits himself to live up to the Scout Oath, Scout Law and Scout Motto, he'll stand out in his community. He'll be looked-up to as an upstanding citizen. One might wonder what is so great about the Scout Oath, Law and Motto. What makes a person who lives up to these standards so different? That's easy to see.

From reading James Fennimore's books about early America, I became fascinated by statements about Indians moving through the forest without making a sound. I wanted to be able to do that. I bought moccasins made by Cherokee Indians in Tahlequah, and quickly learned how they could travel through the forest without making a sound.

Moccasin soles are thin, one can feel objects before putting weight on it, when stepping. Dry twigs on the ground can be felt and avoided. I could now move through the forest without making a sound.

There are those who would destroy boys getting such a firm foundation of core values. So what is the Scout Oath? A boy gives the following oath: "On my honor I will do my best to do my duty to God and my country, and to obey the Scout Law; to help other people at all times; to keep myself physically strong, mentally awake and morally straight."

What is the Scout Law: "A scout is Trustworthy, Loyal, Helpful, Friendly, Courteous, Kind, Obedient, Cheerful, Thrifty, Brave, Clean and Reverent."

What is the Scout Motto? "Be Prepared."

To strive to fully live up to the Scout Oath, Law and Motto establishes a strong core value that will serve a boy well in manhood.

"The scout merit badge program has 120 areas of knowledge and skills. Each scout can explore topics from American Business to Woodworking, as he has interest in. The only limitations are his ambitions and availability of adult merit badge counselors to offer instructions." Consider the few merit badges I list here and how it might interest and help a boy on his way to being a man: American Business, American Heritage, Archaeology, Architecture, Atomic Energy, Automotive Maintenance, Camping, Chemistry, Electronics, Dentistry, First Aid, and the list goes on and on. I would recommend scouting to any young boy. Don't let those who would distract you from reaching your Eagle Rank. Scouting is the thrill of a lifetime.

I took to scouting like a duck to water. I quickly advanced through the ranks and merit badges. I became an Eagle Scout at sixteen and earned a

Bronze Palm a year later. I was ready for my gold Palm by the time I was eighteen, but couldn't get an available counselor to past-off my last two merit badges.

Our scoutmaster, E. A. Grantham was also our school Superintendent. Working on our Camping merit badge, he took the troop on an overnight campout on the shores of Warner Lake. Warner Lake was a state project to provide needed water to Connors College. Before the lake was built I used to walk the valley, following a small spring fed stream. On the far end of the lake, near where the stream entered, was a sheer rock face. The rock face was about thirty-feet high. It had a small crevice which I'd use to climb up to the top.

I would walk to the mountain and watch the construction crew cut down the trees and haul them out of the small valley. Then a bulldozer would clear out the stumps. This was followed by a dirt mover, to build up the dam.

Our scoutmaster chose the only small sandy beach, near the spillway, as our camping spot. In those days sleeping bags had not been invented. Scouts would ask their mother for an old comforter. He would roll up the comforter and a ground cloth, and tie it onto his backpack. On most campouts scouts carried food, matches and a change of clothes, in case they got wet, in their backpack.

A few, like me, had scout axes that they carried in a holster attached to their web-belt. Most carried a scout flashlight that clipped onto their belt, and a scout knife in their pocket. We fulfilled our scout motto: "Be Prepared."

Our scoutmaster found himself a nice spot on the tiny beach. He carefully put down some small evergreen branches to make his bed softer, and then he spread out his blanket. We scouts just put down our ground clothe and blanket. When night came and we lay down to sleep, we would lie on half our comforter and pull the other half over. Those of us working on a Cooking merit badge made our meal and got it checked off by the scoutmaster. Later we gathered around the campfire to enjoy its warmth and to talk. Talk would soon dwindle and all head for their beds. More wood was added to the campfire.

In the early morning hours the fire had burned down to red embers. A chilling breeze blew off the lake. Otto, a creek Indian in our troop, got cold and went to look for firewood. Going up the incline from the lake, he found an old tree stump that dozers had pushed there.

The exposed roots were dry. Using his axe he cut off a dry root. That was the root that was anchoring the stump to the hill. In camp we heard the rumble of the stump coming down. All, including our scoutmaster, quickly left our beds and got out of the way of the rolling stump. The stump missed our scoutmaster's bed by only a foot. He thought that his scouts were out to do him harm. He never went camping with us again.

Water from the lake spillway formed a small branch below the dam. Along the branch were some large trees. On many of the trees a small vine attached itself to the tree trunk. The vine was about thumb size and had tiny roots that attached the vine to the tree. When the vine reached the tree's canopy it would branch out, grow leaves and mix with the tree's leaves.

We guys would use a pocket knife to cut the vine near the base of the tree, pull the small roots loose, leave the leafs in the canopy attached and use the vine to swing back and forth over the branch, playing like we were Tarzan. On one occasion when I was swinging, the vine came loose and dumped me in the branch. My two friends, with me that day, helped me build a fire and dry out my clothes. They were wrinkled but my mother didn't notice it.

On the mountain is a small ravine. On the north side is a rock overhang. Previous scouts of our troop had used flat rocks to wall in a room. We referred to it as our scout cave. On a shelf in front of scout cave were some rock seats built by previous scouts, and a rock fire-pit. To get to the rim from scout cave, we used a large tilted rock slab that was covered by wild grape vines.

On the south rim of the ravine a small spring- fed stream spilled over onto a large rock slab below. Even in the summer, the spring-fed water was very cold. We scouts, in our nature's bathing suit, would try to see who could stay the longest under the waterfall. I don't remember who won that challenge. I know it wasn't me. This small ravine, made for privacy, had a beautiful sitting.

Trying to finish off our camping merit badge, myself, Goy Lee Jackson and the Clays decided to go to scout cave on a Friday afternoon, and spend all day Saturday camping out. Jack and Mignon Clay, brothers, hitched up a team to their country wagon, and we four rode to the mountain. We took an old road, which weeds had reclaimed, to a meadow on top. Jack halted the wagon among some trees with plenty of grass for the team to graze.

We took our packs and camping gear, and headed for scout cave. When we arrived at scout cave we found a troop from another town, Webber Falls a small town east of Warner, camped in our spot. Goy Lee Jackson, of our troop, tried to talk the other troop into leaving our camping place. Goy Lee was a great talker. Later in life he became an attorney. The other troop became belligerent, spoiling for trouble.

They were about double our number. We left and chose a campsite around the rim, under a huge rock overhang, to keep dry incase it rained. We laid out our beds, built a campfire and prepared our meals. We grumbled a bit about the other troop taking over our scout cave, but went to bed.

Sometime in the dark early morning hour, the other troop paid a visit. From the top of the overhang a member of their troop dropped dynamite caps into our campfire. The explosion instantly awoke us, blowing our campfire apart and setting the mountain near our campsite on fire. The other troop began throwing rocks at us. Jack who had a bean-flip fired back and drove them away. For the next hour or so we fought the mountain fire and put it out.

In anger for what they did to us, we paid them a visit. To get to the top of the rim from scout cave could only be down by either the slab with the grapevines or a young pine tree. Goy Lee with rocks guarded the rock slab and I the tree. Jack and his brother went to the south rim of the small ravine. Jack had collected small pebbles for his bean-flip. His brother had collected dry sticks to build a small fire. When the sticks were burning good, Jack's brother would throw them at the door entry to "scout cave". This would light up the room's interior and give Jack a target. This didn't last long before the troop from Webber Falls broke out of the room, running in different directions, intent on doing us harm.

Goy Lee couldn't hold his position and fled. I did the same in a different direction. In the darkness of pre-dawn, I spotted a cluster of scrub bushes and dove in, hoping there were no snakes. About a minute later several scouts from the neighboring town came searching. I stayed still and they continued searching.

After they had gone, I cautiously made my way back to our campsite. There I was met by the rest of our troop. We checked our gear and found out that the opposing scout troop had stolen all our food supplies. We gather our camping gear and went to our concealed wagon. We threw our gear into the wagon while Jack and his brother hitched up the team to the wagon. Jack asked Goy Lee and me to be the wagon brakemen. The wagon braking system were small poles sticking up above the bed of the wagon. These poles, when pulled back, caused a wooden brake to be applied to the rear wagon wheels. Jack said if he yelled we were to apply the brakes.

Our intent was to move quietly back to the grassy road and down to the county road without waking the other scout troop. As we were making our way to the grassy road, the other troop ran to try and cut us off. Jack whipped the team into a run. Approaching the grassy road entrance, Jack yelled. Goy Lee and I applied the brakes. The wagon made a sliding turn onto the grassy road. Jack called for brakes a couple more times going down off the mountain. Once on the county road the horses were pulled to a walk. I was left off in town.

Monday morning we were called into the Superintendent's office. Apparently the scoutmaster from Webber Falls had called our scoutmaster, telling of the incident. Our scoutmaster grilled us on the incident. Hearing the full story he scolded us, and the other troop's actions. He told us we weren't acting like scouts and dismissed us.

Much of my early teen years were spent exploring Warner Mountain, my favorite place. The meadow on top of the mountain must have been an Indian campsite at some time in the past. A careful scrutiny of the meadow would usually turn up an arrowhead. On the mountain edge facing town was a large rock shaped like an overstuffed couch. From this rock one has an awesome 180 degree view of the valley below. When I was troubled by things happening in my life, I'd walk to the mountain and go to couch rock. I'd sit there in that peaceful setting and think out my concerns, and clear up my thoughts —getting my mind put back in order, again.

On a northwest curve of the mountain was a shale slide. We fellows would put down a piece of cardboard box to slide down on the shale, using our heels as brakes, or to guide our decent. It was great fun.

Roaming the mountain top, I came across what apparently was a smoke vent hole. Below the ground someone had made a square room about 10'x 10'. I was small enough to wiggle through the small opening into a short descending hallway that led to the room. In the middle of the room was a pile of campfire ashes. The main entry to the room had been closed off due to a cave-in, or blown shut. Small dead trees, to be used as firewood, were piled near that area. I often wondered if the room had been used by robbers. Then there was the story of a guy believing there was gold on the mountain, making a large cave in his search. No one knew the answer.

I located a grove of persimmon trees on the mountain and enjoyed their fruit. I also found a wild plum tree. I would take these fruits, plums and grapes, to my mother who made them into jelly.

A mile north of town was an old abandoned coal strip mining site. Parts of the area had filled in with water. It became our swimming hole. Some areas were too deep to reach the bottom, other areas were shallow. On the piled up rubble from the mining operation wild Poke-salad plants grew. Cooked, the leaves tasted somewhat like spinach. I would gather a batch of these for my mother to prepare for dinner. In the fall I'd go to George's Fork, a stream two miles south of town to gather wild onions and pecans.

From my scout training I knew which plants were edible. I learned to navigate by the stars at night. Passing the hiking merit badge, I learned how to cover long distances without tiring. This training would go good for survival, if ever needed.

Each year I would save up money from mowing lawns and attend scout camp near the small hamlet of Welling, Oklahoma. This area was part of the old Cherokee lands. Scout camp was located in a mountain setting along Baron Fork creek. Baron Fork is a clear running stream, fed by underground springs. Scout camp's main dining room and a few out buildings were built of native stone slabs, very rustic. From the dining-room one had a good view of the valley between the mountains.

Arriving at scout camp, I was assigned a tent, with another scout, near the trail to Baron Fork Creek. A purser had me turn in all my money to him and receive that amount on a hard paper ticket. Any purchases I made were deducted from that card. To pass some merit badges I spent some of my money on craft material. Much of my money brought to scout camp was spent on "Junk" food—candy, chips and pop. We were given canvas mattresses and pillows, and told where to get straw to stuff them.

With a rough sketch to guide us, we took our stuffed mattresses and pillows and went to our tent. The tents had wooden floors and single metal frame beds with metal laced springs. We placed our mattresses, pillows and bedding on the beds. If the day got hot, we rolled up the sides of our tent. After a short break of "settling in", the call went out for swim time.

Each scout and his tent mate were issued separate tags with the same number. We were told to take those small number tags with us when we went swimming, and they were to be hung on the same nail head, on the swim board. This was a quick way to tell if a scout was still in the water, when swim time ended. If a scout left the swimming pool and forgot to take his number with him, it caused a search of Baron Fork creek for a drowning. A scout who was negligent in not removing his number from the swim board, causing a search was given a stern lecture.

My first year at scout camp, I didn't know how to swim. I, and some others like me, paddled around in the shallows. A senior scout would offer suggestions on swimming. I passed my swimming requirements that year. It was scary. I realized I was jumping into water over my head. A scoutmaster and two senior scouts who had their Swimming and Life Saving merit badges spaced themselves to rescue me, if necessary. I had learned how to "dog paddle", and I passed the swimming requirement. I was thrilled.

At scout camp meals, four scouts were assigned to a single table. At meals each table had an assigned "table-boy", one of the four boys at that table. It was the table boy's task to keep his table supplied with food from the kitchen, while trying to also eat. The game for the non-table boys were to eat fast and keep the table boy on the run. Each meal had a new table boy—all joined in the fun.

At one meal my friend Bob Trimm was table boy. He knew the game. At breakfast one morning he had put a platter filled with pancakes on the table. Before beginning every meal a blessing is given on the food.

Unnoticed by us, Bob was prepared with fork in hand. The moment "amen" was said there was a loud clank of fork on the plate of stacked pancakes. Bob got his share first. Our scout executive smiled and said, "I can tell someone's hungry."

In my second year at scout camp, another scout and I teamed up to have fun with a bunch of Tenderfoot scouts. From the kitchen we took two small cans, polished up their unopened bottoms and placed them slightly apart on top of a boulder, alongside a hiking trail.

That night my friend gathered a few Tenderfoot Scouts together for a hike. I hid behind the boulder. My friend, using his flashlight, came down the trail with the Scouts in-tow, telling them a tale about mountain lions in the area.

Approaching the boulder where I was hidden, my friend flashed the light on the cans that gave a reflection. I gave my best imitation of a snarling mountain lion. The young Scouts let out a yell and ran for camp, like a stampede of young colts.

Next morning at breakfast our Scout Executive, with a smile, said, "I understand we had a mountain lion scare last night." He was aware of the prank we had pulled. The young scouts were never told it was a prank. They now had an exciting story to tell when they got home.

Scouting has always been an important and helpful part of my life. In high school there was a "thing" between town and country kids. Country kids were intent on putting down town kids as softies to be "shown up."

One day a few country guys came up to me, inviting me on a night snipe hunt. That alone made me suspicious. I agreed and that night we went on the hunt. We left town walking west towards Warner Mountain. Reaching the mountain, we took the old grass-grown road north to the top. They made sure to make several confusing turns, before finding "the spot" for the hunt.

I was given a gunny-sack and flashlight. They said if I pointed the light from the flashlight into the bottom of the sack, snipes would fly into the sack and be caught. When I saw the light from their flashlights disappear. I turned out my flashlight.

From scouting, I searched the skies for the north-star. Finding it, I stretched out my arms sideways—like compass needles. Knowing we had walked west and north from town, I faced southeast and took off at a scout pace for town. A scout pace is twenty-steps walking and twenty-steps running. One can cover a lot of ground without tiring. I was the first to arrive back in town, enjoying a milkshake at the local café. When the country guys walked in, they were shocked.

They said, "You're supposed to be on the mountain catching snipes."

I replied, "Do you think I'm that dumb?"

Two of their group did get lost on the mountain and didn't find their way out until the next day. From that time on, I was accepted among their group as an equal.

From scouting I learned to be a good tracker, learned First Aid to be able to help someone injured, Swimming, Life Saving, Survival Techniques, how to tell edible plants, map making, and so many more things that can be useful in life.

In high school I raised a Poland-China piglet into a mature hog, as training for a 4-H project. One day I came home from school to find the pig had broken out of his pen. I studied the tracks he made, got a piece of rope and began tracking the pig. I tracked him for over two miles in the country before catching up to him. I put the rope around his neck and led him back home.

At sixteen I was selected to attend the Philmont Scout Ranch in New Mexico. I had received my Eagle badge in the spring of 1946. I later earned my Bronze Palm. My grandmother, Maude, asked me to accompany her to visit my Uncle "Bill" Ellison in Los Angeles. I chose the trip to California instead of Philmont. Although the trip had several interesting sights, I've often regretted that choice.

My grandmother, Maude, and I caught the Katy flyer, a diesel power passenger train to Dallas. That was my first time on a train. We had coach seats. It was exciting. In Dallas we were put on a Santa Fe steam powered locomotive passenger train. We had hoped it would be the Santa Fe Chief, a diesel powered train.

The trip to Santa Fe was a thrill to me. I was seeing parts of our nation I had never seen. At the stop in Santa Fe, Indians walked up and down alongside the train offering passengers, looking out their open coach windows, various items for sale. Across the aisle from me was a young girl who tried to strike up a conversation. I was 16 and thought, by her looks, that she might be 10 or even younger. I wasn't interested in talking to a child. On the outskirts of Los Angeles passengers used restrooms to clean up, to get off the coal dust grim that blew back in the open windows. When this girl came back to her seat, all dressed up for her Los Angeles departure, I realized I had been a fool. She was pretty and my age.

Uncle "Bill" and Beverley met grandmother and me at the train station, and drove us to their home in Inglewood. "Bill" was studying to be a mortician and was on call to a drive an ambulance. One day he invited me to come to the mortuary to sit out in the waiting room while he finished his work, saying he would take me to a movie, afterwards. He said I could listen to some music while I waited.

When we got to the waiting room, I could see into the other room and saw the feet of a corpse. I told my uncle I'd see him later and went to the movie by myself. Later that evening Uncle "Bill" and Aunt Beverley showed grandmother and me Hollywood. They also took grandmother and me to see a live radio broadcast. I was fascinated with the sound effects guy, as he made sounds needed for the program script. When the main actor mentioned to his guest to come into his sunken living-room, the sound effects guy crushed a small balsawood strawberry box against his chest. The actor said it's still sinking.

It was a magical world seeing Grumman's Chinese Theater with huge searchlights fanning the skies, announcing a newly released movie; the fabulous restaurants of Ciro's, Trocadero, Coconut Grove and the famous Brown Derby where movie stars hung out. We saw the entries to MGM, RKO and Universal Studios. California in 1946 was exciting. At night powerful searchlights would stab a black sky, an indication of some advent. It's a shame today, 2012. It's not safe at night to walk there, due to drugs and gangs.

In later years, 1968, I would serve as Cubmaster in Broken Arrow, Oklahoma. I wanted my two sons, Jeffrey and James to be able to experience the thrill of scouting. In cub scouting it's difficult to get men to volunteer as drivers, councilors and general helpers. Mothers readily volunteered as Den Mothers for the boys.

At one meeting I was trying to get male volunteers. One of the men said he was too busy. I said, "If I can match or best your busy schedule, will you volunteer?" He said yes. He told me what his regular job was. I told him I was a management analyst at Tulsa division of Rockwell. He told me of another job he "moonlighted" doing. I told him mine was importing women's wigs from Hong Kong. I told him I was also putting together a corporation to build apartments for married college students. He said, "Where do I sign to help with the cubs?"

Our Cub Scouts had a booth in a Regional Cub Scout Fair. Our booth was African Safari. A 2" x 4" frame and shelves were set up. The cubs, with help of Den Mothers, cut out small pictures of African animals, about three inches high, from magazines. These were glued to a similar sized poster-board for support; then to a small piece of balsawood, so they would stand up. All the cut-out animals were then placed on the two 2 x4 shelves. The gallery shooter's rail, 2 x 6, was about eight feet in front.

Our Den purchased two small cork-stopper rifles. If a kid knocked over an animal we had tiny two cent prize rewards. Our booth was the most popular at the fair. There was always a long line of kids waiting to get their turn at shooting. It really kept our Den Mothers and me busy.

In 1969 Rockwell moved me and my family back to California. I became Scoutmaster in Walteria, California. A wise scoutmaster places a junior scoutmaster over the boys. Being 18, too old to be a scout, his closeness to their age got him respect from the younger scouts.

One of our scouts, Corky, was noted for being unruly. He was selected to bring in the American flag and post it; he came in dragging the flag on the floor. I quickly got out of my seat and sternly lectured him. I told him too many men had died while serving under the flag, and that I'd best never see him do that again. I got his attention.

On another occasion, when corky was cutting up, my junior scoutmaster called him up before the group and had him do 50 pushups, telling Corky, "Make sure your forehead touches the toe of my boot each time." As scoutmaster I was "drummed out" to become a member of the Order of the Arrow honor society.

To be "drummed out", an undisclosed person had secretly put in my name. Order of the Arrow scouts, in Indian costumes, have fellow scouts and their leaders seated in a circle by a campfire. They begin an Indian dance while drums are being played. Suddenly one of the dancers goes to the seated group and selects a person. This is being drummed out.

Those that are drummed out are then put through a test. I and about a dozen others drummed out were driven to Big Bear Mountain, and put on a work detail. Suspended around our neck's, by stout cord, was a small wooden board. We were sworn to silence for 24 hours. If during that time you spoke, and were caught doing so, a niche was carved on your board. Three niches and you were removed from becoming a member of the Order of the Arrow.

I managed to remain silent the whole time. One guy was asked a question during lunch, and he answered—one niche was carved on his board. Another guy was caught sneaking a smoke by his son—one niche. When I made my bed that night it was soft and comfortable. In the middle of the night I was awaken and told to put my bed on a pile of sticks. I did this without saying a thing. When the 24 hour ordeal was finished, I had no niches on my board. I was awarded the Order of the Arrow sash.

While scoutmaster, our troop went on a regional campout. Two adults and I drove our troop to the event. The actual campsite was in a large field. All cars had to park about a quarter mile from the campsite and walk in. That day I saw the most impressive sight I have ever seen. As our Walteria Troop was getting our gear ready, I saw the Palos Verde troop, marching in single file over a ridge, to the campsite. Each boy, in full scout uniform, had identical red knapsacks on their shoulders and wore red berets. Each squad of eight boys had a person carrying their squad guide-arm flag. What a beautiful sight.

Chapter 5

My early years were fun years. I had convinced my mother that I, at nine, didn't need a babysitter, and that I would do the housekeeping chores. With my mother at work, I would come home from school and listen to our radio. I sat up a work pattern where I could do all the housekeeping chores in thirty minutes. That gave me two hours to listen to my favorite programs, or music. I would listen to Jack Armstrong—the all American boy, Amos and Andy, the Green Hornet, Inner-Sanctum, Old Ma Perkins and Jack Benny.

The sheriff's wife, who lived across the street from our house, told my mother that a "whirlwind" hit her house every day, about a half-hour before she got home. That "whirlwind" was me clearing house. The first thing I did upon arriving home from school was crank up water from the cistern and put it into two small galvanized dishpans on our kitchen gas stove. I learned the right level of flame for the one that held dirty dishes and soap, and the one to rinse them with. Then I'd listen to my programs.

At 6 PM my mother closed the Post Office, did some book work and walked home. At that same time I began my housekeeping chores. Dishes first and throw out the water in the field behind our house, sweep with a broom the two rooms with area rugs—we didn't have vacuum cleaners in those days. I'd then oil-mop the wooden floor areas, wet mop the dining area and kitchen floors. I'd finally use an oil rag, with O-Cedar polish, to clean dust off furniture and then I'd sit down on couch, trying to look causal. By this time my mother would be entering our front door. What really made my day was when I overheard a friend of my mother say, "Osie your house is so clean and neat. Who's your housekeeper?" My mother told her, "My son."

On Saturday's I had the whole day to explore Warner Mountain or roam the fields around town. The mountain was my favorite place. I would pack a small lunch and canteen of water or Dr. Pepper, and spend the day there. I knew the mountain well.

One Saturday a dog with rabies was found roaming our neighborhood. The sheriff shot and killed it. My mother was afraid I might have come in contact with the dog. She and our local doctor, Dr. Burns, decided that I should take the Rabies shots, to be on the safe side, and not get lockjaw. Each day for fourteen days I'd go to his tiny office to get the shots in my stomach area, telling him where I wanted the shot.

I and my two friends, Jack Campbell and Junior Addy, owe our life to Dr. Burns. We had been having fun jumping down onto a pile of cotton seed hulls at Jess Shinn's cotton gin. This stirred up dust and cotton fibers. We began having trouble breathing. Dr. Burns gave us sulfur drugs for pneumonia. This cleared up our lungs.

On another occasion I was playing tag at our neighbor's house. Being chased I ran up on their porch and jumped off its edge, to escape being tagged. In jumping a rusty nail head punctured my left arm below my elbow, pulling out a small piece of muscle from my arm. Dr. Burns cut off the protruding bit, gave me a tetanus shot, sprinkled sulfur power on the wound and bandaged it, telling me to not get the bandage wet or dirty. I later learned, after it healed, that he had told my mother if my arm became infected it would have to be removed.

Some Saturdays I'd play football in the vacant lot between the Judge's house and ours. In the southeast corner of that lot was a patch of blackberry bushes. One day, when I was quarterback, I threw a pass to my older friend Jack. He hadn't watched the blackberry patch. Both he and his tackler fell headlong into the patch. Jack's father, a pharmacist, treated the many scratches on both.

If the weather got hot, several of we guys would walk the mile to the open coal pits for a swim. After learning how to swim at scout camp, I found this a pleasant way to cool off on a hot summer day. We fellows didn't use bathing suits. Since the pits were near a country dirt road, we'd keep a sharp lookout for any cars. The coal pit water was very cold. We'd swim for awhile and then get out on the bank to sun and get warm. If a car was spotted, someone would yell out the alarm and about twenty guys made a dash for the water and dove in.

The water was very deep. Rumor had it that a railroad boxcar lay on the bottom, in this area. Several guys would take a large stone and jump in, trying to see if they could touch the boxcar before letting the rock go and surface. I tried it once and almost drowned. When I finally let go the rock, not touching bottom, I had to fight to get to the surf to get air, almost not making it. I couldn't have lasted much longer without fresh air. I never tried that again. None of our group ever reached the bottom.

One day my friend Bob and I were paddling around in the shallow end. We didn't know how to swim at that time. A young couple, in their bathing suits, joined us. We were trapped. We didn't have bathing suits and couldn't leave the water. We hung around in water chest deep for a long time. We thought the couple would never leave. Finally, as dusk was setting in, they left. Bob and I had been in the water for hours; our skin was wrinkled. We hurriedly got dressed and ran back to our homes, fearing a lecture from our parents—it didn't happen.

Jack and Junior were my friends. They were three years older than me. They allowed me to go with them on hunting trips and taught me gun safety. They told me to never be in front of the muzzle end of a gun, the killing end, and always assume a gun is loaded, until you check it out yourself.

I asked my mother for a .22 rifle to hunt squirrel and rabbits for our dinner table. It took the help of "Cap", a friendly game ranger, to finally convince my mother. She bought me a used .22 single-shot rifle for $1.50. I was eleven. Rabbits were easy to get. Squirrels were hard—they would hide behind the tree trunk. I learned that fried bullfrog legs tasted good. Once the outer skin is stripped off, the meat is white and tastes like chicken. There were many farm ponds around Warner and many frogs. I would use my .22 to kill the frogs. My mother would fry the legs for dinner.

My friend Eugene lived in the country, about two miles south of Warner. I found that by going through the fields I could shorten the distance by a half mile. Owners of the various farms knew me and asked if

I saw any jackrabbits or crows to shoot them because they were destructive of their crops.

Crows would never let me get into range. Jackrabbits would jump up and run a short distance. When they felt it was safe they would stop and look back at me. I would take direct aim at them and fire my rifle. I'd look were the bullet hit, kicking up some dirt. I'd then elevate my rifle barrel and shoot again, seeing where that bullet hit. If the rabbit was foolish enough to not move, my third shoot was a fatal one.

When visiting Eugene, I would occasionally go to George's Fork Creek. I would sit on the railroad trellis, over the creek, and shoot at snapping turtles and water moccasins swimming in the creek. These two killed fish in the creek

When I was thirteen, "Cap" and I convinced my mother that it was time for me to have a shotgun. When trying to decide on the gage, "Cap" told me to use a 20 gauge, it was a better gun and more sporting for the bird—the bird had a better chance to escape. A hunter had to be a good shot. "Cap" was the game ranger for our area. He would stop in the Post Office to visit with my mother and her rural mail carrier, Harry Smith. Through them he learned much about the local people. My mother, at "Caps" assurance, bought me a single shot 20 gauge shotgun. In season, I'd supply quail to the menu.

"Cap" took an interest in me. I think he enjoyed teaching me to be a good sportsman. All this blended well with my scouting interest. When he dropped by the Post Office, he would hear from my mother about my hunting stories.

When I was about sixteen "Cap" asked my mother if she'd let me go on a quail hunt with him and a guy from Muskogee. He told her he'd like for me to see a good birddog in action. With much coaxing from me, my mother finally agreed. "Cap" and his friend came by the house to pick me up. "Cap" had his English-Sitter birddog, Jake, along. The other guy had a Pointer birddog.

What a day! We drove to the bottom-lands near Webber Falls. There was plenty of cover for quail. Getting out of "Cap's" car, we loaded our guns. "Cap" and I would hunt together. The dogs were let out. "Cap's" dog, Jake, waited for his master to direct him to hunt. The other guy's dog took of with his master following and cursing. When "Cap" pointed to the open field, Jake took off in a back and forth searching pattern, nose to the ground. If "Cap" spotted a likely hiding place for a quail, he'd whistle. Jake would look up and see where "Cap" was pointing. He'd run over and check it out for quail, then resume his hunting pattern. He would check often to be sure he wasn't too far ahead of us. It was beautiful to watch.

When we reached a grove of trees "Cap" went around one edge. I went through the middle. The other guy and his birddog took the opposite edge. The guy's birddog went on point. The guy kept telling his dog to hold. Suddenly the dog jumped and a covey of quail flushed, coming in my direction. When I saw the other guy's gun come up, pointing towards me, I flattened on the ground as he shot. I still remember the sound of birdshot going through the trees just over my head. From that time on I wouldn't hunt near the guy.

In the afternoon the sky suddenly turned a dark blue. It was a northerner blowing in. We hurried back to the car. The northerner hit just before we reached the car. The temperature suddenly dropped from a balmy seventy degrees to thirty-two, in less than five minutes.

When going hunting I'd wear old Jeans, cotton shirt and my boots that I used for hunting. I'd wear a beat-up old leather jacket with a box of lose shells in the pockets, and a pouch for carrying game.

One beautiful fall day I had walked several miles in search of game. Finding none on the mountain, I began my two and a half mile walk back to town, with my shotgun across my shoulders and my arms dangling over the gun. I was very tired. As I approached the one mile section from town, I saw a school bus approaching that intersection. It was running late and dusk was settling in. A young girl I knew got off the bus. She was two years my junior. She lived a mile back from which I had just traveled. I knew it would be dark before she could reach her home. I volunteered to escort her home and she accepted.

She was a nice girl and thanked me. As we walked and talked, she said, "You look very rugged in your hunting gear." I thanked her for the compliment. Leaving her at her home, I again headed for town. When I got home I was met by my worried mother. I told her what had happened. She said that was a very chivalrous deed that I had done for the young girl. Anyway I felt good about escorting home the young girl. I was an avid reader of Zane Grey novels and felt I had lived up to the code of heroes, in his books.

On one hunting trip with Jack and Junior, we were slipping up a pond dam to see if any ducks were on the pond. We went single file up the bank. Jack was in the lead. Peering over the bank he didn't see anything. As we straightened up, a Mallard duck swum out from under a thick growth of weeping-willow trees, taking to wing.

Jack, being in front, should have been the only one to shoot. Junior, in his excitement, tried to cock the hammer on his dad's old "thumb-buster" double- barrel twelve gauge shotgun. His thumb slipped off the gun's hammer, and the gun went off. Mud splattered Jack's legs. Jack thought he had been shot. Junior thought he had shot his friend Jack, and so did I. All three of us froze for a moment. The duck flew off without a single shot fired at him. Shaken from that experience, we decided to go home.

On a hunt with Jack, I had borrowed "Papa Jack's" double-barreled "thumb-buster" twelve gauge shotgun. Coming to a small brush covered wash, Jack said it was a good place for quail. He told me to stand on the bank and he'd flush out any quail in the wash. When he went into the wash, a huge covey took to wing. I cocked one hammer of the gun, sighted them and pulled the trigger. Nothing happened. Too late I noticed I had cocked the hammer on one barrel and was pulling the trigger on the un-cocked barrel. Again, we called it a day and went home.

When Jack left for military school my classmate, Allen, became my hunting companion. He and his family had a farm about a mile and half southwest of town. Allen began his bird hunting days using a 410 gauge shotgun. To be able to bring down a fast moving quail with that gun, you had to be good. Later Allen's father gave Allen his semi-automatic 20 gauge shotgun. With that gun, Allen had to wait for the quail to get out far enough before shooting. When a covey was flushed, Allen would look for crossing birds and bring them down with one shot. He was that good.

On one hunt with Allen, I took along my grandfather's old "thumb-buster" double-barrel 12 gauge shotgun. A covey, out of range, flew up. Allen and I saw where a single landed. Approaching the area and knowing how fast Allen was with a gun, I cocked both barrels of my gun. When the bird took to wing, I pointed my gun in that direction and fired, from the hip, both barrels. The bird went down—one pellet had hit him. Allen declared that wasn't fair, shooting from the hip. I let him know that was the only way I could get a shot before him.

Maurice Finklea, owner of the largest general store in Warner, would host members of state and federal government for quail hunts on his ranch south of town. I was about seventeen at that time.

Maurice would ask me to go along to drive the car. It was a double pleasure for me. I got to drive a car, and Maurice would loan me a semi-automatic 12 gauge shotgun, and plenty of shells. He would have me drive to a departure point for he and his guests. I'd let them out and Maurice would tell me where to park the car in the next section-line road. Then I was to hunt back until I linked up with the group. If I jumped a quail I was to shoot it.

On one hunt I jumped a quail, but, it was out of range. I didn't shoot. When Maurice came up, he said, "I loaned you that gun and gave you plenty of shells. Why didn't you shoot?"

I told him the bird was out of range. He said, "I shoot until they are out of sight. Give me the gun and I'll load it like mine."

The first shell was a #2 normally used for geese. The next was a #4 usually used for ducks; next came #6, followed by #8 bird shot. Later that day I again jumped another quail that was also out of range, and flying a crossing pattern. Remembering Maurice's statement, I empted the gun. Maurice, with a big grin on his face came up saying, "Now that's what I like to see." Maurice was a great person, and so was his wife Margaret. They were so outgoing, and loved by many.

Margaret would take a bunch of us kids in her car to a movie in Muskogee —a seventeen mile drive. On one occasion she had twelve of us packed into her car, a Buick. She told us if she spotted a police car half of us were to duck below the seats. She was such a kind person.

On one Saturday each month, Maurice would hold a drawing for an item from his store. When people bought goods from his store, they were given tickets based upon the amount purchased. Stubs from the ticket were then placed in a box. Maurice would shake up the box real good and then have a young child draw out a stub. The person holding the correct ticket won the prize. I won my mother a cedar chest from his store.

The Finklea's had a nice size concrete cellar. On one occasion my mother and I hastened to their storm cellar one night. It was raining hard. The clouds were dark and looked ominous. The wind was high and caused tree branches to sway and bend. My mother and I hurried to their cellar, a block away. When I rounded the corner of their house, I caught the full force of water running down their gutter. I pounded on their cellar door, and they let my mother and me inside. From all the many spring storms, I learned to sleep sitting upright in a chair in someone's cellar.

On Warner Mountain Lake someone had a flat-bottom boat that they chained to a tree and was pad-locked. I learned that if I held the pad-lock against the tree and struck it with a fist sized rock, it would pop open. I'd then take the boat and paddle around the lake. When finished, I put the boat back as it was when I borrowed it.

Warner had a cotton-gin owned by Jess Shinn. In the early evening a bunch of us kids would play tag on the rows of stacked cotton-bales. The bales were about six-feet tall. They stood about five rows wide and thirty feet long. The space between the rows was about three feet. Whoever was "It" would chase and try to tag someone, who would then become the new "It." Trying to not get tagged meant jumping and running between the rows of cotton bales. Sometimes there were boxcars parked nearby, on a railroad spur. Being pursued by the "It", I would quickly climb to the top of the boxcar, running and jumping between boxcars and then back to the cotton bales.

Another favorite game was *Go-Sheepy-Go.* The game is played in the evening. In this game a referee is chosen. To start the game he chooses an "It" person and a home-base tree. The "It" hides his eyes and begins counting to one hundred. The referee goes with the "Sheep", the kids playing the game, to see where each one chooses to hide from the "It".

The object of the game is when a "Sheep" is discovered, they out-run the "It" back to touch the base tree without being tagged. If tagged they become the next "It". If the referee, who accompanies the "It", feels the "It" is far enough from those hiding, he yells "Go Sheepy-Go". All those hidden run to tag the tree and not get tagged by the "It". Going back to the tree, the referee would let the "It" know when all are now hidden and the game begins, again.

Another favorite game was "Anti-over". In this game a group of kids are equally divided and go to opposite sides of a house. To start the game a rubber ball about the size of a soccer ball is given to one of the teams. He or she yells "Anti"! The team on the opposite side of the house yells "Over"! The ball is thrown over the roof-top to the opposing team. Whoever catches the ball will run with his team, trying to conceal the ball, to their opponent's side of the house, and try to hit one of the opponents with the ball. If he or she is successful in hitting one, that person is out of the game. The winning team is the one that has the most players left.

On hot summer nights it was fun for kids to get together and tell ghost or other scary stories. Each one would try to tell their story in such a way as to make it suspenseful. My favorite was "Night Monster."

When I was about nine I saw the movie "Night Monster" in the auditorium at Connors College, a quarter mile west of town. Movies for the town had been shown in the IOOF hall above the L. B. Brown grocery store, until stopped by a fire marshal. To see the movie cost me a quarter. Mr. Schaublin was a veterinarian who had a stable in back of his house and bought feed for animals he was treating.

During the week I'd go by his place and ask if he had any gunnysacks he would give me. I could cash in the sacks at Finklea's store and get five cents each. For five sacks, I'd get a quarter and could go to the movies on Saturday.

When too many people in town began going to the IOOF hall to see movies, the Fire Marshall closed it down. Movies were then shown at the college, while a new theater was being built. This happened about 1939. The last movie I remember seeing in the IOOF Hall was the newly released "Snow White and the Seven Drafts." I sat next to Billie Jean Cargill, a cute girl that I liked.

The local movies were shown by the Tarkingtons. Movies were sent by mail truck, with all the other mail, from the area post office in Muskogee. They came in large metal cans. Once the movie was shown the Tarkingtons would mail them back to their sender. I loved movies, still do, and would go to the movies each Saturday, if I could get the money. If I couldn't get gunny-sacks or a lawn to mow, my mother would offer me a penny for each fly killed inside our house. If I couldn't find twenty-five flies inside our house, I'd fill in by swatting them on our front porch.

The theater the Tarkingtons built in town was located south of the old Cross Telephone Company building. It was a single story building, resembling a barn. It was a wooden clapboard structure facing state highway 266. It had a narrow covered porch with ticket booth. Doors on each side opened to a small inside foyer, about five feet wide.

On the south end of the foyer was a popcorn machine. The foyer ran the length of front. Midway of the foyer was the middle isle doorway that led to the theater. Each side of that main isle was rows of wooden seats, whose seats would fold up. The screen was at the far end of the building.

To the right of the screen was a pot-bellied stove that burned coal, to heat the building in winter. When the attendant went to stroke-up the fire or add more coal, movie goers would miss a few minutes of the movie, due to glare from the fire. For summer cooling, the theater had a huge squirrel-cage evaporator cooler in back of the building that added cool air through a vent above the screen.

One night, while I was a junior in high school, I saw a scary movie in this theater. Young kids like to sit on the first row seats, close to the screen. I always sat in the back rows. The movie was about a man who at times appeared to have died. He asked family members to be sure he had really died, before burying him.

One night the family thought he was really dead this time. To be sure they placed his body in a casket, and placed the casket in a cave, until they were sure he was dead. The cave had drops of water that dripped onto the casket. The drama and suspense was increased by music and scene. Suddenly and unexpectedly a scream comes from the casket.

Four young boys sitting on the front row jumped up and ran down the main isle, heading for the exit doors. A teen age girl sitting next to me was so frightened that she jumped onto my lap and gave me a bear hug, then sheepishly retook her seat and apologized to me.

The night I saw "Night Monster" at the college auditorium, I remember it was a nice balmy night. About a third of the way from town to the college was a large pond on the right. Bullfrogs there were making quite a noise. Night lights, mounted on telephone poles, were evenly spaced from the edge of town to the college. College students had knocked out all the lights from the edge of the college to the edge of town.

The movie began about an older man, without arms or legs, inviting several doctors to his remote country home. He secretly hated them for the condition he was in. At night that hate was so intense that it caused him to temporally grow arms and legs, giving him enormous strength. When he went out to kill one of his doctor guests, frogs would stop croaking. He killed his victim by twisting their head off, told not shown. At that age my imagination was very healthy.

After seeing the movie and thinking about it, I began my walk home. When I neared the pond all the frogs suddenly stopped croaking. I bet I would have broken the Olympic record in my sprint to town. I was motivated.

Warner was hit by a tornado before I was born. It had ripped the local bank off the floor above Maurice's store. Growing up in Warner, before the present warning system, people would go to their storm cellars, if they had one, when severe weather threatened. On real stormy days or nights, my mother and I would go to the Judge's cellar, a small one, or Maurice's, a large cellar. I learned to go to sleep sitting up in either storm cellar.

One day my school friend, Eugene, was visiting with me. A bad electrical storm hit. Lightning bolts were instantly followed by a loud bang. We decided it was time to go to the storm cellar. To get to the Judge's cellar, we had to cross a vacant lot. At a lull in the lightning strikes, we began a run for the cellar. I stumbled and fell at the same time a flash of lightening lit the whole sky. Eugene thought I had been hit. It was the fastest I had ever seen him run. He quickly entered the cellar. I laughed all the way to the cellar.

My mother had an operation in 1945 and was recuperation at her "Parents" home in Muskogee, on the corner of York and Hays Street. A lady from Warner was taking care of her. I was fifteen. My grandmother Maude came to look after me while my mother was healing. My friend Bob Trimm and I caught the bus to Muskogee to see a Tarzan movie. In the middle of the movie it stopped and the lights came on. A loudspeaker was turned on and we were told to leave the theater. We were told to pick up free passes for a future movie. We grumbled as we left the theater.

Mary Wanda, a cousin of mine, was in a parked car in front. She called me over to tell me President Franklin Delano Roosevelt had died. That came as a shock. Then she said the eastside of Muskogee had been destroyed by a tornado. This was April 12, 1945.

I became concerned. My mother was recuperating from an operation on the eastside. I managed to get her on the phone. My mother said the tornado had lifted off the ground a block before passing over where she was. She said she saw horses and cows swirling around in the air.

She said she had heard that Warner had been destroyed. Knowing my mother was okay, I began worrying about my grandmother, Maude, in

Warner. Bob and I hitchhiked to Warner and I learned to my great relief no storm had hit the town.

On a Saturday Eugene Ross, Bob Trimm and I had gone to Warner Mountain Lake, to fish. I told Eugene and Bob about the boat and how to unlock the chain holding it to a tree. They decided to go get it and meet me across the lake. To get from where the boat was secured to the point where I was fishing, they had to cross the main body of the lake.

They were midway in their crossing when an electrical storm hit. Sheets of rain were followed by numerous lightening strikes on the hills surrounding the lake. I was under the shelter of a rock ledge overhang. With a fury, Eugene and Bob frantically paddled the boat to where I was, and safety. Huddled under the rock ledge, we waited until the storm passed over and then went home.

Eugene and his parents would sometimes go fishing on the Illinois River, and ask me along. They would fish. Eugene and I would use a flat-bottomed boat to paddle around in. There was only one paddle and I was usually the one "elected" to use it. It was fun gliding around on the river on a hot summer day.

One day Eugene talked his father into letting him and I go along on a fishing campout on Piney Creek. We were told they only had a two man tent, and that we'd have to sleep in the pickup cab. We agreed. Due to the cold, it was my most miserable night. I don't care for the taste of coffee. If I drank it, it had to have cream and sugar. I was so cold the next morning that when I was asked if I'd like a cup of hot black coffee, no sugar, I took it.

For a small town of 300, Warner had vets that had experienced the dangers of WWII. Stanley Synar was an Army Air Corp fighter pilot and

Ace, Bob Jahrman was a B-17 pilot that was shot down over Germany and held as a prisoner and Chick Looper, a Judge's son, was part of the Normandy landing on Omaha Beach. I would be their attentive listener.

Bob Jahrman was an American of German parents. He was fluent in the German language. He told me of his war experiences. He said when they were hit over Germany; he was trying to "nurse" his plane back to England. He said his right wing had a hole that a man could drop through. He said suddenly a MS-109 German fighter pulled alongside. He said he and the German pilot looked at each other. The MS-109 did a banking turn and strafed his plane. He said it sounded like a snare drum. Bob said his instrument panel exploded; it was time to bailout.

When he was captured he spoke to his captors in German. They declared he was a spy and would be shot the next day. Each day, for three days, his German captors planned to execute him. Each day he managed to talk them out of that. He was finally put in a prison camp, located near a German war factory. The camp had two fences and used German Sheppard dogs to patrol the area between them. One of the dogs was vicious. If it caught a prisoner in that run, it would kill.

Bob told of his trying to escape. While in the run he heard a dog coming. Lying flat, face down, he heard the dog approach him. He wondered if it was the killer or not? He said the dog sniffed him and went on. Bob said that short time was the most terrifying time of his life. Bob escaped and got to the border with Switzerland before being caught. He said the Germans put him under guard by two of their soldiers. He was then put on a civilian train to be returned to his prison camp.

Bob said that a German girl sat on a seat across from him. While the train headed towards his prison camp an American pilot in a P-51 strafed the train. Again there was the snare drum sound. A bullet decapitated the girl; her head hitting in his lap. When I asked what did he do, he said, "I parted my legs and let her head drop through.

People on the train wanted to lynch Bob. His guards had to take him to the engine to keep that from happening. He said when the Russians to free the prison camp, he and a few others had broken out and took over a German plane. Bob lined up the plane for takeoff. Russian soldiers demanded they kill the plane's engines. He motioned for them to get out of the way and took off, getting his passengers to England.

On the lighter side was the stories told by Don Jalbert. He said his was stationed in an Army camp outside Nashville, Tennessee. He said that on a Fourth of July he and a couple of buddies "commandeered" an army jeep, got some firecrackers, cigars and a bottle of bourbon. They got drunk and were having a great time celebrating the holiday. He said an army jeep of MP's began chasing them.

Don in the backseat of their jeep would use his cigar to light a string of firecrackers and toss them back over his head at the pursuing MPs. He said the guy driving his jeep accidentally turned into a blind alley. The three bailed out and ran in different directions. Don said he ran through a door and found himself on a lighted stage. He said he did a graceful bow, jumped off the sage and ran out the front door.

To put this in proper perspective, Don is about 5'9" tall and was thin. He was a native of Maine who married Doris, a local Warner girl. Both were talented in music and play writing. Don was also an architect with an office in Muskogee.

Don was the life of any party. Once a month my mother and I would ride with the Don and Doris Jalbert to a square-dance in Muskogee.

Maurice and Margaret Finklea would also take a carload from Warner to the dance. We had lots of fun. In one of the dances a very stout lady was in their group. When the dance ended, we asked Don what happened when the square-dance called for "swing your partner", did he do that? In his French-Maine brogue he said, "She swung me." We would tease him about his inability to say wasp. No matter how hard he tried, it was "Asp."

One month, after square-dancing, someone of our Warner group said, "I bet the fish are biting this morning." Maurice invited the group to fishing party at his ranch's large pond. All went home, got their fishing gear and bait and got to Maurice's pond early in the morning. My mother and I got a ride. That day would see the end of my fishing, forever.

On that day 119 fish were caught and I never got a nibble on my line. I had people fishing close by on each side of me, catching fish. I used the same bait they used, and set my hook to be at the same level as theirs. Still I didn't get even a nibble. I made a vow at that time I'd not go fishing again. I've kept that vow. I was about seventeen at that time.

Chapter 6

In my mid-teens "Cap", the game ranger, would occasionally visit
Warner. He worked out of Muskogee. He'd stop by the Post Office to visit
with my mother and Harry, her rural mail carrier. When he learned from
my mother that I didn't have a dog, he said, "No boy should be without a
dog."

On his next trip to Warner he brought me an English screw-tail
bulldog puppy. A bulldog won't win a beauty contest, but they're very
loyal. I named the dog MacArthur but called him Mac for short. He
became my constant companion.

When out of his puppy stage, "Cap" dropped by to see how Mac was
doing. Seeing him, "Cap" said it was time for Mac to have a swing.
Needless to say I was puzzled —a swing for a dog? "Cap" got a length of
rope from his car and tied it to the low branch of our yard's bean tree. He

called Mac over to him, judged for height and tied a large knot. With a little coaxing, Mac got the idea. He'd make a short run, jump and grab the rope's knot in his jaws. He'd swing back and forth, and then drop to the ground. He's do this over and over until he tired of the game. A bulldog's jaws are very powerful.

Mac would lay around on the floor, always keeping his eyes on me. If I got up from my chair and began putting on my hunting boots, he went on an excited alert. I'd let him go along. He'd happily trot along behind me.

I found him useful, when quail hunting. If I saw a clump of bushes that looked like good quail cover, I'd pick up a stick, show it to Mac and throw the stick over the cover. Mac never went around the clump of bushes. Like a charging tank, he'd burst through the bushes. If quail were hiding there they would take to wing and I'd get a shot at them.

If I went fishing, Mac would tag along. He would calmly sit beside me. Both of us watched my bobber. If it went under I'd pull out the fish. Mac excitedly made sure the fish, if loose, didn't make it back to the water.

One winter Lucinda Finklea, a girl from Muskogee, visited her cousin Nedra Finklea in Warner. I had a crush on Lucinda. She was a nice soft-spoken girl, and kind. She was pretty.

She liked my friend Eugene. He was nice looking, had a smile similar to a cross between Frank Sinatra and Elvis Presley, wore a scarf causally around his neck without a jacket; he never lacked for girlfriends.

Lucinda knew Eugene and I were friends. She asked me if I could get a message to him that she was in town for the weekend and would like to see him. The day was cold and dreary with sleet coming down. Because I liked her, I agreed to let Eugene know. Donning my hunting boots, winter coat and gloves I made ready to walk the mile and half through the fields of snow and sleet to Eugene's house.

Mac was excited and ready to go with me. I told my mother to keep him inside, that with the sleet and cold it was too cold for him to go with me. About half way on my hike to Eugene's house, I looked back and here came Mac with his nose to the ground, following my trail. When he reached me I could see that his paws were bleeding from cuts made by the sleet.

I picked him up and carried him, all forty-five pounds the rest of the way to Eugene's house. Eugene, Mac and me rode back to town on Eugene's father's John Deere tractor. Lucinda was pleased to see Eugene. She never knew that I had threatened Eugene that if he ever took advantage of Lucinda's affections, I'd use him to wipe up the highway. He treated Lucinda well. Nedra and she gave a party for several of us.

When I went squirrel hunting with my .22, I'd leave Mac at home. His running around made it hard to get a shot at a squirrel. When I got back home I would find Mac had shown his displeasure of being left behind. He had pulled the mattress off my bed.

One day when I again left him behind to go to Eugene's house, he again followed my trail, when he was let out. It was a warm fall day. Eugene and I had gone to George's Fork Creek bottom to look for pecans and persimmons.

Eugene's mother told us that she saw Mac coming through the field on my trail. One of their cows spotted Mac and tried to hook him. Mac would dodge the attempt. Mac put up with this for a while. When the cow tried again to hook him, he grabbed the cow by the nose and "bulldogged" her, throwing the cow to the ground. That accomplished,

Mac continued on his journey. The cow, having learned her lesson, went the opposite way.

When I went blackberry picking, I would come home and take a soda bath to get rid of chiggers and ticks. Since our house didn't have indoor plumbing, I stood in a wash tub and bathed. I never succeeded in getting off all the chiggers. The ones I missed would burrow into my skin. It caused itching and then infection.

I found that the only solution to cure that was rubbing alcohol, which stung like the devil. I would go out in our yard, dab some alcohol on the sores, set the bottle down and run laps around the house, to take my mind off the stinging. Mac thought this was great sport. On one occasion I made the turn at our house corner—Mac didn't. Like a professional football player, he knocked my legs out from under me.

One summer day my aunt from Muskogee paid my mother a visit. She brought along her two female cocker-spaniels. She and my mother sat on one end of our front porch with the cocker-spaniels, Mac and I sat on the opposite end of our porch. Every time Mac looked around my leg at the two cocker-spaniels they would growl. Mac would then hide behind my leg.

Two birddogs came trotting down our street. The two cocker-spaniels went charging towards the two birddogs, barking. The two birddogs turned to give chase to the fleeing cocker-spaniels. Quick as a flash, Mac charged the two birddogs, knocking both of them over. The two dogs ran and hid under the neighbor's porch, across the street. Mac trotted back to our house and again began the game of growl and hide behind my leg.

One day our school Superintendent came by our house to ask me a question. When he knocked on our front door, I went to answer. As usual,

Mac was behind me. When I opened the door, Mac came around to see, through our screen door, the superintendent. When our Superintendent spotted Mac, he put his hand and foot against the door, saying, "Don't let him out!" He didn't realize Mac was huge "teddy bear" at heart, and wouldn't hurt anyone.

In my early teens, Warner had no town water. Those in town that had water in their home came from a water-well. This and a septic tank allowed for indoor conveniences. Most people, like my mother and I, had an outdoor toilet, called outhouses. One didn't stay very long in an outhouse on cold winter days. Many people also used what was called "Thunder-pots", or "Slop-jars", indoors, emptying them later in the outhouse.

Come Halloween, several guys would get together to go turn over people's outdoor toilets. I never did join this bunch. I didn't want ours turned over and my having to push it upright. I was intent on keeping ours from being turned over. Previous to Halloween some of our neighbors had been doing some pruning of trees, and brush clearing. They piled all this in a neat stack on the vacant lot next door to us.

Armed with a flashlight, I opened our rear door and sat on a chair in our dark kitchen. Looking through our screen door, I listened for anyone headed for our toilet. Mac sat next to me, also watching. When I heard their muffled voices I switched on my flashlight and yelled, "Who's There?" In a flash, Mac charged through the unlocked screen door, heading towards the group. Someone yelled, "Bulldog!" There was a loud crash as some collided with the brush pile. Not having anyone to play with, Mac trotted back to be with me. Next day at school it was easy to tell who had been in the group, by scratch marks from the brush pile.

It was a sad day when my mother and I learned that someone in town had fed Mac food with ground up glass in it. We had to have him put to sleep. I've never forgotten the sad look on his face as we left. It was as though he knew we were parting for the last time. It would be a long time before I'd ever take in another dog.

Chapter 7

I've always loved music, and still do. While I was in High School the
band director from Connors State College visited our high school, asking if
any of us would be interested in becoming members of the college
marching band. I was interested in learning to play a guitar. Since that
wasn't part of a marching band, I chose to play the clarinet. To play the
clarinet and keep from screeching one has to use a razor blade to scrape
the reed to adjust it to where it's right for you.

Since I was fourth clarinetist I would fake playing and let others do the
songs in a concert. I was always afraid of making a screeching
embarrassing sound. I loved marching and wearing a band uniform.

In high school most of my friends were Methodist. I joined that church
to be with them. I never believed their teachings. Their choir director,

London Howard, got me interested in singing bass in a southern gospel quartet. I really loved the music, words and rhythm. Hymns and gospel music was uplifting to me.

In high school I had a heart runaway and blacked out, while practicing basketball. I thought I might die young. From hymns and gospel music I gained a better idea of the savior, and the life I needed to live to be with him.

London would take our quartet to area gospel singing conventions, and we would perform. Some Sundays I would ride with him and his wife to an all day southern gospel singing event at the Singing Cathedral in Muskogee.

Everybody attending was met at the door by two men who handed out song books to each person. These men then asked what part each one sang. We would then be directed to that part of the church for our voices. I remember bass, the part I sang, was along the east wall. Baritone and women altos were along the west wall. Tenors and sopranos were on the stage.

When all were seated the singing began. The director would tell us the page number and song title. To this day I remember the two songs I liked best were "We're made to weep and wonder why" and "Bend way down low, lift your heavy load", with its deep bass lead. At noon everyone broke for a pot luck lunch on the lawn. It was great fun.

London tried to get our male quartet to sing "Rocking on the Waves." In the song the first Tenor and Bass sing a back and forth musical word "Rocking", depicting an ocean wave. To get the rocking part in rhythm is tricky.

We were to perform this song at a singing convention east of Warner at a place called Poke Chapel. London gave up on us getting the "Rocking" in sink and said he'd take the girl's quartet instead. That made us angry. Our second tenor, James Van Landingham, borrowed his father's car and drove us to the convention.

When we went in we informed the convention director that we were a quartet and wished to sing. He put us down below those that had already signed in. We tried to ignore the girl's quartet. When their time came to sing the "Rocking on the Waves", they did well. After about seven other quartets sang, it became our turn. We sang the same song as the girls. We did well. We had vindicated ourselves. London and the girls, being good sports and knowing how we felt, came over and congratulated us. All of us were now on good terms.

Southern gospel music and words always lift my spirit. If I'm "down", really depressed, I can listen to the music and words, feeling uplifted again. The songs helped me to clear up my mind from worldly troubles or physical problems, and give me peace of mind. J. D. Sumner is listed in the Guinness book of Record as having the lowest bass voice. I can get within one note of him—low B flat. I loved hearing J. D. sing and would sing along with him, trying to reach his low bass pitches. I really enjoyed his "Sailing down the river of memories."

During high school, I would frequently visit my friend Eugene on their country farm. It was quite an experience for me. They used coal-oil lamps and the cook-stove burned wood. Their house was heated by a pot-bellied coal burning stove. Mrs. Ross would wake all of us at 4 AM. While Gene and his father milked and fed hay to the cows, and fed the pigs, I chopped wood for the stove. The wood was dried young persimmon trees, cut to proper lengths for the stove.

When I was called in for breakfast, I was confronted with a platter filled with eggs over easy, ham slices, sausage, bacon, biscuits, jelly or honey and mashed potatoes. Eugene and I drank milk. His parents drank coffee. Sitting down at the table, I thought, "What a waste of food." It was then that I realized that chopping wood for an hour builds up an appetite. I did my share at making the food disappear.

Sometimes when I visited Eugene I would take along my quart-size ice cream maker and powered ice cream mix. Eugene and I would get into his mother's milk-laden cream in her ice chest. We'd mix up the ingredients, take some of her ice and head for the barn loft. There we'd hide among the hay and turn the crank on my ice cream maker. When it finally turned to ice cream, we'd sit and eat the whole quart. We thought we were getting away with our stealth, then Eugene's mother let us know she was aware of what we were doing. She had missed the cream and ice.

Sometimes Eugene and I would go for a walk along George's Creek, seeing what we could find. One hot summer day, Eugene suggested we go for a cooling swim in the creek. I told him no; that there were too many snakes and turtles. He teased me as being chicken. The water was very murky.

Having shot at snapping turtles and water moccasins from the train bridge above, I didn't like the idea. But, with teasing and coaxing, I agreed. We stripped to our nature's bathing-suit and slid down the muddy bank into the water. We'd swim for awhile then use a downed tree to get back on top the bank again. The mud slid was great, but, I kept a wary eye out for snakes and snapping turtles. I was glad when Eugene suggested we get out and go to his house for fishing gear, and then try our luck fishing in the pond near their house. I would never swim in George's fork again.

On our senior year trip we went to Hot Springs, Arkansas on a school bus. While some of us waited for the rest of our senior class to return to our bus, I decided to run back in and by my mother a souvenir. I told my friend Eugene to be sure to tell our teacher and chaperon to wait for me. Eugene, more interested in the girl he was sitting next to, acknowledged my request. When I let the gift shop, I saw our school bus going around a distant corner.

I hitchhiked until it began to rain; then caught a Trailway bus heading for Fort Smith. When the Trailway bus passed our school bus, I got off and flagged down our school bus. Our teacher was shocked that I had been left behind. I was angry at Eugene. I walked back to where he was sitting with the girl and said in an angry voice, "Get over!" He quickly did as I asked. He had learned years before he couldn't whip me. He once tried and I blocked each blow, laughing at him, which made him madder. The ruckus had been over who would peddle my bicycle, and who got to ride on the seat. I won and rode on the seat.

In High School our quartet was asked to sing "Rock of Ages" at our class graduation baccalaureate service. The quartet consisted of Eugene Ross as first tenor, James Van Landingham s second tenor, Brown Johnson as baritone and me as bass.

Graduating from Warner High, I considered attending Northeastern State College in Tahlequah, Oklahoma. I went to the campus to take an aptitude test. They sent me a letter telling me I had achieved the highest aptitude score in Music ever received at the college. I was flattered but chose Connors State College in Warner, because neither my mother nor I could afford the college tuition and dorm fees at Northeaster State College, at that time. Going to Connors I could save money by living at home and walking to school.

In college I joined the Glee Club. Our Director, Mrs. Jeanne Parker, asked me what part I sang. I had always admired Nelson Eddy, a baritone. I told her I was a baritone. She gave me the sheet music for the song "Bali High", from the musical South Pacific, and asked me to sing it. She saw I was having difficulty hitting the high notes.

To determine my vocal range, she asked the pianist to take me step by step up and down the musical scale. As I took the seven note practice scale, going up from one basic note to the next, our director stepped outside for a moment.

I didn't get very far on the higher scale. The pianist then began the downward scale runs to determine my lower range. As I keep going down and down the scale, our director stepped back inside and stood by the door for a moment. When I hit my lowest pitch, the director came up to me and said, "Baritone my foot! You have the lowest bass voice I've ever heard!"

I enjoyed the two years I was in the glee club. A talented member of our group, Oliver Lusk, wrote Excerpts from the musical play, Oklahoma. Our glee club director and our college music director took the play on a tour of high schools in our area, sort of a promotion to come to our college, Connors State College.

The presentation became easy for the cast. Our play director, Mrs. Parker, was young. When we put on the play at various high schools, our cast would try to come up with some clever prank to pull, to see how it would affect Mrs. Parker.

At one school we found backstage an old model wheelchair and rusty shotgun that apparently had been used in one of their school plays. While a love scene between Curly [Bill Graham Dickerson] and Lorie [Pauline Jackson] was being enacted on stage, the comedian, Ado Annie [Gwendolee Haraway], got seated in the wheelchair. The comedian, Snookie [H.C. Snook], a roly-poly guy who played Ali Harkin the traveling salesman, hurriedly pushed Ado Annie across the stage; her supposed father [Tracy Folks], shotgun in hand, was in hot pursuit.

The cast not on stage were peeking through the curtains to see Mrs. Parker's reaction. She went pale. Curly and Lorie, on stage, adlibbed the event as though it was a part of the play. The audience loved it.

At another school we presented the play on their auditorium stage. In part of the play Ali Harkin, Snookie, was to say to Ado Anne, "Once I was free as a bird", in a sweeping open-hand jester. Apparently a bird had gotten into the auditorium. When Snookie made his speech and jester, there was a plop in his hand. The expression on Snookie's face as he looked at the bird dropping in the palm of his hand caused both cast and audience to burst out laughing. It took a bit of time before the play could resume. All of us had to fight back snickers every time we thought of what happened.

At another school we were having trouble making a tiny fake picket fence stay up. Our cast's bus driver always liked to take a nap while the play was going on. He knew of our fence problem from our play at other schools. We concocted up an idea. While the stage was being set for the Virginia reel, one of our cast members hurried to the bus driver, asking for his help with the fence. As he hurried onto the stage another cast member opened the drapes. He had to join us in the Virginia reel. He never took a nap again when the play was on.

The play was such a success that the college took all the cast members to dinner and a tour at the Will Rogers museum in Claremore, Oklahoma. When the museum heard about us they asked us to sing the song Oklahoma for those touring the museum.

Our college Dean, A. B. Childress, Music director and our Play director asked if we'd do that song a cappella. Out of sheer devilment we sang, "Our Dean wears a pair of BBD's. He wears them in the summer and he wears in the fall, and sometime he doesn't wear them at all." Our Dean, A. B. Childress, burst out laughing and our play director's face got beet-red. Then our cast burst out in a rousing rendition of the song Oklahoma. We received a great round of applause.

The second year in the Glee Club, I joined the Cowboy Quartet as their bass. We dressed in our western ware that we had used in the play Oklahoma. Snookie on bass fiddle and our baritone guitarist accompanied us as we sang songs made popular by the Sons of the Pioneers.

For my final grade, before graduating from Junior College, I was to sing a solo before an audience, on a Saturday at the local Baptist Church. I was to pick either "Asleep in the Deep", or "When Big Profundo Sang Low C." "Asleep in the Deep" has a very low note at the end. To sing solo was a great concern of mine. I didn't want to make a mistake. I chose the Great Profundo song. It went well and I got a good grade.

All of my life I've sung in quartets, glee clubs, church choirs, and in Montana the Big Sky Singers.

The big Sky Singers was a semi-professional group that gave concerts. The songs I liked the most was "Just a closer Walk with thee", a southern gospel song, and "Elvira". Like the Oak Ridge boy's quartet, I can hit the same low note as their bass singer.

When singing "Elvira", Jerry a baritone in our group, would take out a big comb and pretend he was combing his hair—Jerry's bald as a bowling ball. It always got a laugh from the audience. Our group's costumes were floor-length blue dresses for the women and light blue tuxes for men. My wife Dorothy, a soprano, and I sang in the group for two years.

One year, at our church's Stake Conference in Helena, Montana, I was asked to sing solo the second verse of "How Great thou Art." That was scary for me. I'd never sung a solo before about two thousand people, before. To make matters worse, the choir director made sure another member held the microphone close to me. Giving a silent prayer before hand, all went well with my solo. After conference several people came up and complimented me.

Our church, Church of Jesus Christ of Latter Day Saints—Mormons, would have a talent show on a few selected Saturdays. On one occasion our quartet sang a barbershop song. I'm not all that fond of barbershop type singing. I think the song was Ida Rose, like the Buffalo Bill's quartet sang in Music Man. However, we four did well. On another occasion, our quartet sang "Elvira". Our Bishop came up and told me he didn't realize I had such a deep bass voice. I thanked him for the compliment.

During one church choir practice, I noticed a young girl, Michelle Scheck, had an exceptionally good voice. She hit her note pitches exactly on tune. After practice I told her so and asked if she had taken voice lessons. Tears welled up in her eyes as she thanked me. She told me she's never had lessons. Again, I told her that her voice was great.

Later she competed in the Miss America contest as Miss Helena. In the talent part she sang. She won Miss Helena. My wife Dorothy and I were among the crowd at the airport to greet her. Spotting me in the crowd, she invited me over to have our picture taken together, by the many reporters. Before the picture was taken she put on her crown. Through her vocal talents she went to Vienna, Austria to take professional vocal lessons. I've always felt that my simple and sincere compliment gave her courage. She's a very nice young lady and certainly deserved the compliment.

I have a large collection of CDs and cassette music. It ranges from country/western to classics. I loved the music of my era. To be a success then, one had to have a good voice and a song that carried a good message. The music played by bands was more soothing. It was the time of big bands. Only Laurence Welk's orchestra has kept this era alive, and after seventy-two year it's still popular today.

Music today is more sound effect. It seems the louder the sound, the more the effect on youthful audiences. It takes an outlandish dress of the band members to succeed. To me that doesn't show talent, just big noise.

Chapter 8

Hard times during the great depression and WWII caused me to take an interest in political activities, and happenings around the world. At the time of WWII, America was in an isolationist mood. This was brought about by the horrors our nation suffered in WWI.

Americans felt our nation was protected by the Atlantic and Pacific oceans. Americans wanted no part of another European war. Our president, Roosevelt, was trying to get our nation out of the great depression. He was also watching Hitler's army gobbling up nations in Europe, their resources and looting their treasury. This fed Hitler's war machine.

Britain was already engaged in the war. Churchill sought our help. Our congress voted to not get into the war, but did agree to lend-lease —

supplying war materials to the British. With the bombing of Pearl Harbor, America entered WWII.

I've often wondered what would have happened if Japan hadn't attacked our fleet at Pearl Harbor. I think they would have conquered all of Asia. Then with all the raw materials they now controlled, they would have been much stronger and would, along with Hitler, try to conquer our nation.

I was eleven when war was declared. We were now at war on two fronts, Japan and Germany. Germany had as allies Russia and Italy Millions of Americans were drafted into the military. "Rosie the riveter" posters were everywhere. American women went to work in our factories, doing fantastic jobs. Military hardware, planes, tanks, trucks and ships were being turned out in record numbers. No other nation in the world could match our production.

Ration cards were introduced. Gasoline, butter and sugar were heavily controlled. Margarine came with a tiny plastic coloring pill to make margarine look like butter. For gasoline, if you had an "A" packet of stamps you were not allowed to buy much gasoline.

Bob Hope, on one of his shows, kept repeating "She'll be coming around the mountain." When his comedian, Jerry Colona, asked why Hope didn't finish the song, Hope said, "She only had an "A" card."

As a Boy Scout, our troop would go from house to house collecting scrap metal for the war. People would give old pots and pans that could be melted down and be used in the war.

It was a time in which all movie theaters showed Movie News about what was happening in the war. Before the news was shown the American Flag was displayed on the screen. Everyone in the theater would stand and clap their hands. Many movies based on the war were produced in Hollywood. It fired up the patriotic spirit in Americans. I could hardly wait to join the military. The war ended when I was fifteen—too young to join. Five years later I would join the Air force, due to the Korean War.

Our family members were Democrats and great backers of Franklin D. Roosevelt. My mother was appointed Postmaster by him. Local people were stunned by his death.

An Oklahoma U. S. Senator, Robert S. Kerr, told my mother he would appoint me to West Point, if I would accept. I turned it down. I had gone through a heart runaway in high school one night at basketball practice. My heart rate was so fast that everything went black. I thought I was dying. Also, I didn't like math and figured that it and physics would play a big part at West Point. I would probably have flunked out of West Point, and I didn't care to be in the army. The air force academy hadn't been built as yet. I did like ROTC in college.

When FDR died, Harry S. Truman, a Democrat, became President. He brought the war to an end by dropping the atomic bomb on Japan. This act got world anger. Truman determined to drop the bomb would save many thousands of servicemen's lives. Much of his belief came from what happened on Saipan Island. Many national Japanese men, women and children committed suicide rather than be captured by Americans. Truman figured that by attacking the Japanese mainland, millions of American troops would be killed.

When I was eighteen I attended a President Truman rally in Spaulding Park, in Muskogee. Many were pleased with the no-nonsense brashness of Truman. I and other family members voted for him. When Khrushchev got up in the United Nations, pounding his shoe on the podium, declaring to America, "One day we'll bury you", many were heard to say if Harry had been there he would have punched Khrushchev.

Harry Truman was an interesting President. He purchased mailing stamps from his own pocket and drove himself home when his term of office ended. On his desk was a sign that said, "The buck stops here." He and General MacArthur clashed over tactics in the Korean War—MacArthur was fired.

President Eisenhower, a highly respected General during WWII, became the next President. He was responsible for getting built our present interstate highway system. Although a Republican, he was elected in a landside.

John F. Kennedy was the last Democrat to run for President that I voted for. In his inaugural speech, his saying, "Ask not what your country can do for you. Ask what you can do for your country" will live on through history. JFK, and our race to be first on the moon, brought in our personal computers and micro-circuits. He also forced the Russians to back down on placing missiles in Cuba.

When JFK was killed in Dallas, Texas on November 22, 1963, I was working at Rockwell's Tulsa Division. At night I helped work on Senator Robert S. Kerr's (D) platform. Two things caused me to leave the Democrat party. While working on Kerr's platform, I suggested workfare to replace welfare. Others on the committee really got on to me for suggesting such a thing. That's when I got angry and told them that I was in the wrong party, and stormed out. The second was when I heard LBJ say, "I'm going to take from the haves and give to the have not." From then on I became a very active Republican.

In the 1980s I was elected Jefferson County Precinct Committeeman. Later I formed the Family Republican Club, and was elected its President. I served two terms. My wife Dorothy and I put out a monthly newsletter for the club. I wrote the articles and she did the art work.

Our club was fortunate enough to have the Speaker of the House of Montana as a member. Our Governor, Marc, would occasionally attend our Saturday morning meetings. Governor, Marc, and I became friends.

I heard him speak at a luncheon and was greatly impressed. He was serving as Attorney General for Montana, at that time. We had a Republican Governor that was up for re-election.

After Marc's luncheon speech, I told him he should run for governor. He said he was satisfied being Attorney General. When the governor, Stan Stevens, got ill, Marc was drafted to run for Governor. He won two elections by a wide margin—a landslide.

He remembered that it was I who first suggested he run for Governor of Montana, in a heavily Democratic state. When we had our Lincoln Day dinner, Marc would attend as a guest. At these fund raising dinners we'd auction off pies and cakes donated by party members. Our auctions were rather unique. Montana's Speaker of the House, Bob Marks, was always the auctioneer and our Governor handed out the pies or cakes to the winning bidder.

I then ran for county chairman on the Republican ticket, and won. My grandfather, Papa Jack, had served as county chairman of the Democratic Party in Oklahoma; now I was county chairman of the Republican Party in Montana.

It was interesting being the County Chairman. I got to personally meet important political people, the "Movers and Shakers" of State and Federal government. I would lead our county delegates to State Political Conventions. I would serve on committees that drafted our state political platform. I always chose to be on the Human Rights and National Defense committees.

There were several members of the Republican Party that were Pro-Choice. A lady who served as a Montana National Delegate got into a heated discussion we me over pro-life and pro-choice stances. She was a Catholic and I knew what the Pope's view was on that subject. I thought I could convince her to change to pro-life. She came back at me with, "It's the women's body. She should have the choice over whether or not to have an abortion." I told her, "How many choices does a woman need?"

She asked, "What do you mean?"

I told her the woman chose to have a relationship, knowing she didn't want to become pregnant. That was her first choice—how many does a woman need? That catholic lady has never spoken to me since.

At this convention it was clear that a battle was going to be fought over this issue on the convention floor. Attorney General Marc told us what position could be upheld in a court of law. He said that only in a case in which there was danger to the mother's life, rape and incest could an abortion be upheld in a court of law. Both sides agree on this solution and a floor battle was averted.

Our U. S. Senator, Conrad Burns, enjoyed mixing bits of humor into his speeches. On one occasion he was giving a speech when someone in a portioned off-room dropped a load of dishes. This sounded as though many dishes were broken. I had to laugh when Conrad turned towards the sound and said, "Don't wash those" and returned to where he had left off in his speech.

I used to send him one-liners in Washington. Some that I remember sending him are: "The way to tell if it's real cold, it's when congress goes around with their hands in their own pockets." Another one was the definition of an Ingrate: "A person who bites the hand that feed them and complains of indigestion." I also sent him a W. C. Fields quote: "If at first you don't succeed, try, try, try again. Then give up. No need being a damn fool." Or, the Art of Diplomacy, "Saying nice doggie until you can find a good rock."

Many of my quotes and quips came from a book of that title. There are 14,000 in that book. Conrad sent me a four glass set with the gold Senate seal on them. I served two terms as county chairman.

As previously stated, in my grandfather's time he was the Democratic chairman for McIntosh County. In my time, I was elected county chairman of Republican Party in Jefferson County, Montana, and I won re-election for a second two year term. I tuned down running for a third term.

I've always had a great love of my country. In high school we were taught American History. We were required to memorize famous statements made by such national leaders as Patrick Henry, John Paul Jones, Nathan Hall and George Washington, to mention a few. Years later I learned that one of my Goodall ancestors served as an Ensign under Patrick Henry.

I was an avid reader. My favorite authors in my youth were James Fennimore Cooper, Zane Grey and James Oliver Curwood. Cooper's books were basically fictional adventure stories about our nation in the 1700s. Zane Grey was about the American west in the 1800s. Curwood's books were about the Canadian Rockies.

I read slowly, converting the story into a movie in my mind. This allowed me to remember in detail the story. These books also gave me a love of my nation. They were stories of brave men and women forging a great nation out of the wilderness. It told of their hardships, dangers that they faced and how they overcame those obstacles.

In my adult years I spent time reading my books on the Civil War. My great grandfather, Francis Marion Ellison served with the south in the Civil war —Company E, 3rd Calvary, Missouri, CSA. He was written up in Taney County Missouri History. A bend in White River near Francis Ellison's lands was called Ellison's elbow. There's a street in Branson called Ellison. Francis gave some of his land to College of the Ozarks. The rest of his land has now gone to the college, when my cousin Lenore Hurley died, on condition that the college maintains the Ellison cemetery located on the given land.

I enjoyed my many books on the west. My favorite authors are Zane Grey, Luke Short and Louis L'Amour. I have books about the Mountain-men, Indians, the cattlemen and a shelf of books on the American Civil War. I have shelves of leather-bound books — Harvard Classics Editions, International Library Collections, American Classic Editions, and Time/Life Collections.

My library book "Lost mines and Hidden Treasures", written by Leland Lovelace and "Coronado's Children", by J. Frank Dobie portray the adventurous spirit of Americans, and bits of history. This is but a short list of my many books in my personal library. Books are a great source of information and reusable references, more permanent than computer data that can be removed or lost without notice.

Chapter 9

COLLEGE YEARS

In my college years, I was an average student. The summer before going to Connors, I worked various jobs at the college. I worked in the college's vegetable garden; plaster's aid, painter and furniture placement laborer in girl's dorm, for fall enrollment. Plastering the ceilings, I learned the proper consistency of plaster, to keep it from falling back in one's face. I attended Connors State College in Warner, Oklahoma, and class of 1948-1950. I received my Associate of Science degree at Connors. In the fall of 1950, I enrolled at Oklahoma A & M, now Oklahoma State University, in Stillwater, Oklahoma.

Subjects that held little interest to me caused me problems. Subjects that I disliked were math, physics and English courses. Those that I enjoyed were history, civics and chemistry.

I tried hard in math. My teacher, Claire Harrison, had taught my father. I felt I needed to uphold my father's name, which is also my name. Claire was kind, but, I had no interest in the studies.

In Physics our teacher, Mr. Martin, always spoke in a monotone. On warm summer-like days his droning voice would make me drowsy, and I had to fight off sleep. His test had only four questions. To miss one question entirely amounted to a low grade score.

English, under Mrs. Muncie, wasn't interesting to me. I tended to daydream. One day she saw I wasn't paying attention. She asked a question and said, "Is that so Mr. Ellison." I was caught but felt I had a 50/50 chance of guessing the answer. It turned out I was lucky and gave the correct reply. She then told me to pay attention. I never saw her smile. Determining what was an adjective, verb, predicate and conjugating a sentence didn't excite me. Thank goodness for the modern day computer.

I enjoyed civics under Professor Boatman. The study of how our Republic form of government works was interesting, and still is to this day. I learned how congress wrote bills, that bills had to be approved by both House and Senate.

If there was a disagreement it had to be worked out in a subcommittee comprised of both houses, and then sent to the President. If the President didn't like the bill he could veto it or use his Pocket Veto option, not taking any action and letting the allotted time to sign expire.

Chemistry was also very fascinating to me. I was always asking my Professor, A. Q. Polk, such questions as, "What are the chemicals in black powder?" Or, "What does TNT stand for."

I learned how to do chemical formulas, well. One day in lab we were to make soap. From the soap making process a gelatin is filtered out. My instructor came to my table, checked off my results and told me to dump the gelatin down the drain.

He stood by to be sure I did as he said. He then said, "Had you added nitric acid, in the right proportion, you would have had nitroglycerin, which you've been trying to figure out all semester." I got an A for a final grade.

The study of history was interesting. For our finals, we were asked by our teacher, Mrs. Lura Rimmer, to write a "blue book" essay on one of three topics. They were: [1] The French Revolution, [2] The American Revolution or [3] The American Civil War.

When trying to remember dates and happenings of the first two events, my mind went blank. I chose the Civil War because I knew some of the Generals and battles.

After writing only a page and a half in my "blue book", containing about 20 pages, my mind went blank. I decided that since I was going to flunk the course, I might as well have fun.

As fast as I could write, making up fake battles with lower grade officers in a historical General's command, I finished a "blue book" and a half. I was writing so fast that I hadn't noticed the teacher was beside my desk, looking over my shoulder. She said, "Very interesting Mr. Ellison." I surmised I had been caught.

I turned in what I had written. A few days later she called each class member to her desk to pick up our graded "blue books." On the way to her desk I was trying to figure out how to keep the other students from seeing the "F" I was sure I'd get.

To my shock and amazement, my blue book had an A+ on the front. Mrs. Rimmer told me I must have really read up on the Civil War; that she would need to study that war, because she couldn't remember some of the battles I mentioned. I didn't say anything. Years later at a school reunion, my conscious got to me and I told her what I'd done. She burst out laughing and said, "Well, it was good writing."

Mr. Charles Willis was my Zoo teacher. I found the course interesting, but, not as interesting as Chemistry. One day a few of us fellows caught, in a jar, what we thought was a baby rattlesnake. We took it to Mr. Willis. He carefully studied the snake, and opened the lid of the jar, saying the snake was harmless. He pulled the snake out of the jar and let it bite him. Giving the snake and jar back to the guys, he left.

One of the guys had the bright idea of putting the snake in someone's bed. At the boy's dorm they found that a guy had gone for a shower. They carefully put the snake between the guy's sheets, at the foot of his bed. They said the guy came back and got between his sheets. They said his eyes got big and he exploded out of bed, to the glee of the perpetrators.

Realizing the prank pulled on him, he threatened he'd kill the guilty guy. He calmed down when it was decided they would turn the snake loose in the girl's dorm. It turned out that one of the girls, who spotted the snake, was a zoo major. She picked up the snake and put it outside.

As stated previously, I joined the college glee Club and enjoyed many exciting things, putting on excerpts from the musical play Oklahoma, being a part of that cast and my bass solo before an audience was the tops.

My Spanish class was frustrating. Our teacher, Mrs. Eaton, encouraged 27 of us to enroll in her Spanish class. Before the class ended, she had flunked out 20 of the class. The best grade that semester was given to her daughter who received a C. The next highest grade was her daughter's friend who received a C minus. I was third highest with a D. Mrs. Eaton would write the test sentience's on the black-board. The class was to translate these sentences to English. We never saw the end of a test. Mrs. Eaton would be still writing test sentences why the ending class bell rang.

On one occasion, during a test, a wasp crawled up my pants leg and stung me on my left knee. While I tried with my left hand to kill the wasp, I was writing as fast as I could with my right hand the English translations. That year, 1950, I was a member of the Los Amigos club.

I don't know how Mr. Long, drama teacher, talked me into doing a live radio skit. I'm not into drama and didn't perform well in reading my script. I talked too much in an unemotional monotone.

Our Dean, A. B. Childress, taught Speech Class. Needing some extra credits, I enrolled in that class. I was also dating his secretary, Ouita Covington. When the Dean wasn't in his office, I'd stop by and visit Ouita.

One day in speech class Dean Childress called on me to give a pantomime speech. He said I was to pantomime singing to Ouita in her upstairs dorm window. I told him I wouldn't do that. He said the pantomime carried a lot of weight towards my final grade. I still refused. He finally gave me another subject to pantomime. A student wouldn't be able to get away with that today.

At the time I was going to school at Connors State College they had a football team. I love football and tried to not miss any of Connor's games. One year the team had a quarterback we called "Jumping Jack" Murray.

He stood about 5'6" tall and was slender built. He was good at both passing and running.

On one rainy day, with a muddy field, Murray was tackled by heavy tacklers and line-backers. I thought they had surely hurt Murray. When the last man got off Murray, he reached down and got Murray by the belt, setting Murray on his feet. Murray trotted to the huddle. On another play, Murray tried an end-run, was cut off, reversed his end-run and outran a defender. The defender was tall. The defender got so mad that he pulled off his helmet and threw it at Murray.

Another good man on our team was halfback W. G. Hamby. We called him "Hambone." When he got the ball and hit the line, you'd see a defender go head over heel into the air. We had a full-blood Indian tackler called by his friends, Chief. If the other team played fair, he would. If they played dirty, he would tackle high and use his shoulder pad to clip the opposing player's chin, while falling to the ground, knocking them out. He never got caught by the referee.

In one game a tackle of ours keep letting an opposing team member get through. Our coach put our fullback in that spot. He told me later that he found out why the opposing team member got through. It was a cold winter day with sleet coming down. When the ball was shifted, the opposing team member hit our fullback in the face, with his fist. Our fullback told me it really hurt, being made more so by the cold weather. Our fullback was determined to get back at this guy, even it he was kicked out of the game. On the next play our fullback gave the guy a hard uppercut to the jaw. The opposing team player never hit our fullback again.

Our football field had a few rows of seats for spectators. They were along the back wall of our basketball field house. Along the far side of the football field, several people would park their cars and watch the game in comfort. I used to walk up and down the football field watching each play at the line of scrimmage.

My good friend in High School, Wanda "Cokie" Ward was chosen as a campus queen attendant. She was such a nice person and well liked by all.

Oklahoma A & M

I transferred all of my credits from Connors State College to Oklahoma A & M, beginning my Junior year in the fall semester of 1950. Going from the smaller class numbers at Connors to large class sizes at Oklahoma A & M took some getting used to. Connors smaller class size allowed more help from teachers.

I chose Oklahoma A & M above other colleges because my father had gone to school there. As previously stated, my father died two months before I was born of a ruptured appendix. I was given his name. Going to Oklahoma A & M, I felt it was a tribute to him. I was seeing and doing things that perhaps he had done.

To earn my school tuition, I had worked that summer at three jobs. My uncle Bill Moore had helped me get hired as an oil rig worker. He told me to back date my birth by one year. To meet company insurance requirements I had to be twenty-one. The oil company was Socony. I didn't like doing that, but, I needed the job.

The oil drilling rig was mounted on a KR-11 International truck. It weighed twenty-two tons and folded down over the cab, when it was moved to new test drilling sites. Because it was so top heavy, only my uncle was permitted to move the rig to a new site. The oil company was following a hard rock, Blain, formation. Once the drill penetrated this hard rock formation, the pipe-string was removed, the well was capped and the rig moved to a new location.

I was hired to drive a K-7 International truck with a one hundred gallon water tank mounted in back. The tank had an auxiliary power unit and hose attached, to suction up water into the tank from a nearby stream. A small stream of water, from the truck mounted tank, was used to flush-out drill-hole samples.

The head driller would use a small strainer to catch samples, and record what formation his drill was going through. When I had to go for more water, the driller had to reduce the drilling speed. Speed in getting back with the needed water was important. Driving the empty truck over dirt wash-board roads, it would start "dancing" and I'd have to slow down. With a full load of water it rode like a Cadillac. With the heavy load I had to work the truck thru its gears, from compound to over-drive, requiring double-clutching. I loved the job.

At each new sight I'd help a guy dig a "mud pit." The pit was about four foot wide by fourteen foot long and five feet deep. Water flowing out of the drill hole was channeled into this pit. Rock sediments would remain in the pit and the water drain back into the soil. When I wasn't needed to go for water, it was my job to use a shove and stir the mud pit, helping the water-part leach back into the soil.

Being an oil-crew member was exciting. I kept asking crew members if they ever accidentally struck oil. One night while I was stirring the mud pit I saw a small stream of black oil appearing. I dropped my shovel and ran back to the drilling platform to tell what I'd seen. I was met by a smiling crew with one still pouring old engine oil in the stream going to the mud pit. We all had a good laugh on me.

One day when our shift had ended our crew went to a local bar for a cool drink, after a long hot summer day on the rig. We lined up at the bar. Since I didn't like beer, I got a cold coke. The rest of the crew ordered a mug of beer.

At a table in back of us, two men were talking. One had a heavy foreign accent. A member of our crew who was known for being good-natured turned and smiled at the two men at the table, then turned back to the bar and his refreshing beer.

Sudden the guy with the accent was behind us. He said, "If someone don't like the way I talk, they know what they can do about it." Our crew member set down his beer, turned and slugged the guy. He hit the guy so hard that the guy kept going backward until he hit the far wall, and slid to the floor. Our head driller quickly got us out of the place.

Although I got to work one month with the crew, before they learned my true age, I cherish that experience. From that one month I learned how close-knit crew members are, and loyal to each other. If one gets in trouble the whole crew stands with you. If someone tries to whip one member of the crew, they had to whip the whole crew. It's hard to put into words the feeling that one gets in knowing fellow crew members will stand with you.

I was called into my big boss' office. He told me they had learned my true age and he had to lay me off. He told me I was a good worker, well like by my fellow crew member, but insurance people would eat the company alive if I wasn't let go. The boss gave me a two week severance pay, and told me he'd gladly give me a letter of recommendation any time

I desired it. It was a really a "down-day" for me. I missed being part of my crew, and I was now out of work.

While trying to figure out what to do about getting work, my high school and college friend, Eugene "Gene" Ross called me. He was on his way to the Texas panhandle to get a job as tractor driver in the wheat harvest, and planned to spend the night with me at my uncle's place, if that was okay. Gene told me the pay was $15.00 per day with free room and board, and they needed more drivers. I had told him I'd been laid off with the oil company. I checked with my uncle and he welcomed Gene to spend the night.

While waiting for Gene to arrive I made some calculations. If what Gene said was true, I could make $360.00 per month. At the oil company job I was making $500.00 per month. By the time Gene arrived the next day I had made up my mind to go with him and try to get a tractor driver's job in the wheat harvest.

Gene never had trouble in finding a girl to get acquainted with. When he and I walked to town that night he met a girl and asked to walk her home. She agreed. Gene didn't know the way back to my uncle's apartment and asked me to follow about a block behind. I didn't like being a chaperon. It was night with a few street lights. I followed Gene and the girl to where I thought they had turned into her house.

While I waited on the dark street, getting angrier minute by minute, a car passed me from behind. Someone yelled out, "Why in the hell don't you go home?" I still had the "oil-worker" spirit. I yelled back at the car, "Why in the hell don't you try and make me?" When the car passed under the streetlight I saw that there were four people in the car. I figured I was in trouble, but, they never came back. It turned out that Gene was further down the street than I thought, and couldn't have helped me in case of a fight.

Next morning my uncle drove Gene and I to Lipscomb, Texas, a few miles west of Shattuck. Gene and I went to the crew boss and applied for the tractor driver's job. We were both hired. I had never driven a tractor before. From visiting my friend Gene on his parent's farm I had heard Gene refer to their John Deere tractor as a "popping Johnny." The tractor I was assigned to was a Case. I got upon the seat and didn't know how it stated, were the gears were and the location of the throttle.

The boss came up to me asking what was the matter? I lied by saying that I was familiar with a "Popping Johnny" but this is a Case. He showed all the controls that I needed. I started the tractor, hooked to a combine and the man that controlled the combine got up on his position on the combine. Our combine had a left cut. By hand signals he directed me on the speed I was to use.

Gene was driving a tractor that pulled a combine with a right cut. When we approached each other I would pull out and make a circle, giving Gene and his combine the cut thru, before continuing our cut. I got pretty good at the timing. Little time was lost in the turnouts. We looked like professionals.

When all the fields in the Lipscomb area were finished, the crew planned to move to Nebraska. I decided to not do that and went back to Shattuck. I got a job working in a creamery making commercial butter. I was put over cleaning test tubes and test equipment. My supervisor was one of those who no matter how well I cleaned his testing devices, they were never clean enough and he'd have me wash them over and over.

When he was giving me a hard time, I was asked by our crew to help unload the churn of butter. The butter was loaded into a holding trough. I would then help one of the guys pack the butter into a plastic lined cardboard box, until it weighed seventy-two pounds. The box was then sealed and stored in a walk-in cooler. Unloading the churn meant getting fresh churned butter on my hands all the way to my elbow, making it difficult to get clean of butter oils.

One day I was told to get a ladder, hot soapy water, a bristle brush, and to scrub the tile where it meets the ceiling. I was up on the rickety ladder scrubbing when the creamy owner's daughter came through the door near where I was working. She was attractive, was wearing a short sleeved blouse and white short-shorts.

At that very moment my ladder broke and I had to quickly grab some overhead pipes. The rest of my cleaning things crashed to the floor. As I called for help, the girl smiled up at me. I got teased about that incident.

The guys teased that the ladder didn't break but it was my seeing this cute girl. After seeing what went into the butter making process for "Land of Lakes" butter, I wouldn't eat butter for several years.

Getting chewed-out daily by my supervisor and the messy-ness of handling butter, I quit and got a plowing job with Orrin Culley. It was now August and he was having all his wheat fields plowed and harrowed for fall planting of winter wheat. Orrin lived in the house above my uncle's basement apartment, he was the landlord.

I, and two of his long-time workers, would meet with Orrin for an early morning breakfast. After breakfast one of the men drove each of us to the field we were to plow that day. I would mount my tractor with its twelve foot wide disc-plow attached and begin plowing. The field was huge. I quickly learned that after the original furrow was cut. The front wheel of the tractor I was driving would stay in that furrow, while cutting a new one, until I used the steering-wheel to turn corners.

The field had lots of jack-rabbits and a part of the field had some stones. While the tractor was going slow through the stone area, I would jump off the tractor and pick up several stones; then run to get back upon the moving tractor. When a jack-rabbit jumped up, I would throw a rock at it. One day Orrin showed up and saw what I was doing. When I saw his car parked near where I would be going by, I stopped by his car. He smiled and said, "I see you're good at plowing." We talked for awhile and I went back to work.

Orrin learned that I would keep plowing until it was so dark I couldn't see the furrow, and then I would quit. He began leaving the pickup with me, telling me to pick up the other two workers, after I stopped for the day. I don't know if this bothered his old farm hands. I hoped not.

Plowing all day can be boring. On a hot August day, if the wind was at your back, dust and wheat stubble chaff would go down my back and feel itchy. If the field was moist in some area, I learned that jumping up and down on the tractor platform I could get through these areas and not get stuck. To better improve the day, I cut out a pinup picture of Betty Grable and taped it to my tractor dashboard. When Orrin joined me, he asked if the picture helped. I smiled and said, "Oh yes!"

One day I was plowing and thought they had forgotten me for lunch. I didn't have the pickup that day. I thought I'd make two more rounds before I'd stop, unhitch the tractor and drive it to where we ate lunch. As I was approaching my last round, Orrin's car pulled in. He called for me to come and go to lunch. I told him I thought I'd been forgotten. He said that it's only 11:30. One can build up an appetite plowing in the hot sun. Orrin's wife had a great lunch for the crew. It was served on an outdoor table, under a shade tree. Cold watermelon sure tasted good on such days.

One day I was instructed to move to another huge field, when I finished the one I was working on. Finishing the field I had been plowing, I used the plow lever to raise the twelve foot disc plows and pulled out onto the country dirt road. Putting the tractor into road gear, I headed for the new field. The tractor was traveling at about twenty miles per hour.

Topping a slight knoll, I saw a small wooden bridge that crossed over a shallow dry wash. I pressed on the tractor brakes and they didn't work. The bridge appeared to be less than twelve-foot wide and I couldn't slow down the tractor before being on the bridge. Since the plow, slightly behind the tractor, slanted about fifteen degrees, I steered the tractor on to the bridge at an angle. When the front-end of the tractor cleared the bridge, I quickly corrected the steering to keep the wheels of the plow on the bridge. It was exciting not losing anything off the bridge.

Shattuck was known for its excellent soft water. It was about 98% pure. I could never get enough of its cold great taste. It's the finest water I've ever had in my lifetime. It was now time to go back to school. I said goodbye to my uncle Bill and aunt Lettye, and thanked Orrin for the work.

I went back home and rode to Stillwater with Frank Ross, cousin of Eugene Ross, my high school friend. We had pre-enrolled and were assigned to Bennett Hall, a new huge dorm that housed 1,100 men. Our room was on the fourth floor, number 424.

The first week in school was howdy week. I learned this when anyone I met on campus, said, "Howdy." I thought what a great way to make new students feel at home. From upstairs windows in Bennett Hall we could see the field-house and football field. In the basement of our building was our cafeteria.

One morning when I went to the cafeteria, half asleep, I was met by a cute coed in A-line skirt, sweater, silk choker scarf, saddle oxfords and ankle socks. She asked me she could carry my tray for me. Now I was wide awake. Turned out she was asked for my vote for her friend, who was running for campus queen. What a great way to get a vote.

My classes were ROTC, Botany, Zoology and Humanities. My plan was to take this light schedule to get familiar with classes at a large school, and then take a heavier load next semester.

The Korean War was underway in the summer of 1950, and I wanted to enlist in the Air Force. My mother and some friends advised me to wait, stating that if the war ended quickly, which they thought, I would have to remain in the Air force for four full years. I went along with the idea.

Frank and I moved into our room. I got a part-time job sweeping and cleaning the gym each morning. It paid fifty-cents per hour. My first class was ROTC. Each class began with the instructor admonishing, "Kill or be killed." If I got any demerits, I had to work them off by cleaning student officer's rifles. I got to be pretty good and fast at field stripping an M-1 Garand rifle. I enjoyed marching —still do.

My second class was botany. It was clear across campus. The first day my ROTC instructor's class went over the allotted time, and I was late for botany. When I arrived late the botany teacher was clearly agitated. Except for a seat near a cute blond, the room was full. The instructor told me in an unkind voice, "Would you please be seated so I can call the roll."

He went on to tell the class he would not tolerate late members, and he would lock the classroom door at five minutes after the class bell rang.

I took the seat next to the blond. The instructor called her last name. I thought he had said, "Moore." My uncle by marriage's last name was Moore, and I whispered if her last name was Moore. She told me it was Mohler. She and I became good friends. Whenever I was late for botany class and the class-room door was locked, I would call Luanne Mohler at the girl's dorm, called Murray Hall. She would tell what was said in class that day, share her notes with me and tell me the next day's assignment.

Luanne and I would go bowling, play tennis and go to movies. She was an amazing girl. She was about 5'2" tall, had a close resemblance to Hollywood actress Doris Day, yet broke horses at her father's ranch, In Tulsa.

I'm 6'2" tall, and have long arms. I thought with this advantage I could easily win playing tennis. She ran me all over the court and easily beat me. I then took her bowling. She picked up an almost impossible split, and got her name mentioned in the campus news paper.

When we went to a movie, we would stop by Brooks Student Store for refreshments. Or, we might stop at Theta Pond, set on a park bench, watch ducks swimming and talk about school or life in general. She was easy to talk to.

One weekend Luanne invited me to her parent's ranch to go horseback riding. I could probably count on one hand the times I had ridden a horse, and I had ridden bareback those times. Luanne saddled our horses. I didn't know how. We mounted up and rode out into her parent's horse pasture. It had a few hilly areas with large oak trees and a large level pasture with a couple of oak trees. Walking our horses, Luanne and I talked about many things. It was a pretty fall day.

As we started back towards the barn, Luanne asked if I'd like to race her. I said I would. She pointed to a single large oak tree far out in the pasture. We urged our horses into a gallop, Luanne in the lead. While galloping, I remembered a western I had read where the main character let out a loud yell that frightened his horse into a run, to get more speed. Closing in on the selected finish race tree, I let out a loud yell. The horse I was riding broke into a run and passed Luanne's horse. Reining in, Luanne with a big smile said, "That's not fair." It would be the only time I won a sporting event with her.

One evening Luanne and I went to a movie. My roommate Frank Ross was broke and wanted to go out for some fun. He decided to go to one of the sorority dances. He went to a sorority that was chaperoned by his married friend. Frank was welcomed at the sorority entry by that friend. Frank said there were several couples in the room, dancing or talking. Frank's friend asked him if there was someone he'd like to meet. He spotted a cute girl and said, "Her", not realizing what would happen.

When Frank's female friend disappeared, Frank began to mingle with the crowd. Suddenly the girl he had pointed out was standing next to him with her coat over her arm, saying, "I'm ready to go."

Frank went into a panic. He only had twenty-five cents on him. He rationalized that Luanne and I usually stopped by Brook's, and that he could borrow some cash from me. He took the girl to Brook's.

Not seeing me he asked if the girl would like some refreshments. Both ordered a coke, a cost of ten cents. Finishing their cokes, they went to the room set aside for couples to dance. There were other couples there, and they were feeding the jukebox. Frank came away from that date, having lots of fun, costing him ten cents.

Frank told me this story when I arrived back at our room from my date with Luanne. He asked why Luanne and I didn't stop by Brook's. I told him we had stopped by theta pond. I asked Frank what he would have done if his date had ordered a meal, him having only a quarter. He said he'd have to work it off by doing dishes for Brook's.

One week, Frank, his high school friend and I decided to go duck hunting on the approaching Saturday. In idol conversation I let Luanne know what I planned to do Saturday. She asked if she could come along. Without clearing it with Frank, whose car we would be using, I told her, "Sure."

I let her know we'd swing by her dorm, early. Frank and his friend decided to leave at 2 AM, to be in the duck blinds before the sun came up. I figured I didn't dare call Murray Hall and ask for Luanne at that hour.

We checked out our shotguns from our dorm's security room and drove to the lake. Frank and his friend took a duck-blind across from mine, on a narrow bend in the lake. The idea of being out this early didn't set well with me. By the time morning arrived, I was tired and sleepy. The warmth of an Indian summer sun compounded sleepiness. Not seeing any ducks and feeling the sun's warmth, I lay down in the tall grass by my blind and went to sleep.

Monday morning, in botany class, I met a very angry Luanne. I tried to explain what had happened and my reluctance to call her dorm that early in the morning. It took a couple of weeks to convince her that I hadn't purposely stood her up, and we were once again good friends.

Frank and I had some good times at college. Only once did he order me out of our room. In my Zoo class lab, I was to dissect a dead cat and make sketches of the cat's internal organs. I thought that by bringing the cat to my room, to finish dissecting the cat, I could get a better grade in class. When Frank entered our room and saw what I was doing, he said, "Out!" I had to take the cat back to the zoo lab.

Frank and I would go to the football field well before the game was to start, to get good seats at the games. We would sit in the sign placard section. It was on the fifty-yard line. The group director would give us a list of what color to hold up, when he called out. After the annual game between O.U. and Oklahoma A & M, Frank and I went to Brook's for a malt, and to see if girls were there to dance with.

The room for dancing was empty. We took a seat in the malt shop and were enjoying our malt when a guy with two girls entered and went to the room for dancing. I think Frank finished his malt in one swallow, and headed for the dance area.

I finished my malt and joined Frank. He was standing along one wall and the extra girl at the far end wall. I asked Frank he was wasn't dancing with her. He said she turned him down. I told Frank, "Well I'll go let her turn me down also." I went to the girl and asked her for a dance. She accepted. When the music ended I escorted her back to where she had been standing, and rejoined Frank. When the next song came up, Frank again asked the girl for a dance. He was refused.

By now the girl knew Frank and I were friends. Again I told Frank she could refuse me also. Again she danced with me. I learned she was an O.U. student. She was pleasant to talk to. I never did learn why she refused to dance with Frank. Frank had a very outgoing personality. The girl's refusal to dance with him, yet dance with me troubled Frank.

A few weeks later he got back at me. We had gone to a dance in town. Frank was good at jitter-bug, I wasn't. When a jitter-bug tune was played, Frank immediately found a cute girl to dance with him. Frank was then cut-in on by a guy. Frank asked me to cut-in on that guy so he could cut-in on me, and finish the dance with the girl. I did as I was asked. Frank didn't cut-in and I had to finish the dance with her. Seeing that I had been suckered-in by Frank, each time I caught Frank's attention I gave him a dirty look. He was laughing the whole time.

One morning I got my towel and shaving gear. I then went to our floor's bathroom to shave and shower. After shaving I went to the shower. The shower wall was concrete blocks, forming a flat U. Two foot of the wall was open at the top to let out steam.

The shower had two shower heads. I had finished my shower and had stepped back near the open top wall to shampoo my hair, when another guy entered the shower. Frank, knowing I was in the shower, got a bucket full of cold water and tossed it over the top of the shower. Since I was against the wall he had tossed the water over, it didn't hit me. It did hit the other guy full. That guy, in the nude, chased Frank down our hallway. Later Frank said if that guy could have caught him, he'd be dead.

One night Frank and I were studying for a test the next day. We heard a lot of shouting and went to our window to see what was going on. A pickup, loaded with girls in back, was shouting to our dorm. After their second pass Frank looked at me, tossed his book in his trash can and said, "Let's go." We never did find out what was going on, and our grade test next day wasn't the greatest.

Frank had an unusual morning pattern. He began his class day with two shots of bourbon. He was an engineer major and was failing all his classes. With the advent of the Korean War, and learning that our draft number had been pulled, we were told by a friend on the draft board that we'd be drafted into the military at the end of our semester.

Frank Ross, Eugene Ross and I decided to join the service. We had all agreed to join the Air force on January 10, 1951. Frank and I packed up our things, to take home, and checked out of school. When we went by to pick up Eugene, he said he decided to enlist in the naval reserves and stay in college. Eugene had been my friend all through high school. His reneging at the last moment didn't set well with me. I thought he was doing so due to fear of possible combat. Later I learned his decision was based upon finishing college, a wise move. He got his doctorate degree in Agriculture.

Years later, while visiting Oklahoma State University, I was pleased to see Frank get his Bachelor's degree in Engineering.

Chapter 10
MY AIR FORCE EXPERIENCES

I was told by the recruiter to catch the train in Tulsa; that it would take me to Lackland Air Force Boot Camp, outside of San Antonio, Texas. I had lost touch with Frank, until months later.

I and several other guys were picked up at the train station by an Air Force bus and driven to Lackland. We were a motley looking group. We were in civilian clothes of many varieties, carrying suitcases. Some were assigned to tents and others to wooden barracks. I was lucky and was assigned to a wooden barracks.

San Antonio was experiencing the coldest winter in twenty years. Four of the new recruits, assigned to tents, caught pneumonia and died. My barracks had central heating. The mixture of guys in my barracks were pretty evenly distributed between north and south. When the weather was raining and cold, our flight leader would let us stay indoors and study our Air Force manual.

First lesson in boot camp was how to make a bed that was approved, by our flight leader, as suitable. Our beds were made of iron with a metal lattice woven network attached by springs to place our mattress on. Each bed had a mattress, two wool blankets, two sheets, a pillow and pillow case.

Our barracks chief instructor demonstrated how we were to make our beds. First our mattress, which was rolled up, was unrolled, our sheets added. The sheets at the foot had to be made with hospital bed corners, same with one wool blanket. The sheets and wool blanket had to be tucked tightly under the mattress. The pillow in its cover was next, and placed at the head of the bed. The second blanket, folded in half was put over the pillow and tucked under the mattress, and pulled tight.

Our instructor then pulled a quarter from his pocket and let it drop. The quarter bounced. He then said that each of our beds must meet the quarter test. All those that didn't pass the test would be required to make their beds over until they passed.

I got my right on the second remake. Some of the guys had to remake their bed several times.

At the foot of each bed was a foot locker. It was a well-built wooden and metal chest that measured about two feet wide by four feet long by three feet deep. It had a shallow top drawer for socks, ties and toiletries. The bottom part was for fatigues and underwear.

I mention these dimensions to give a picture of what it's like to take a nap on the footlocker, of that size. Our beds had to be made first thing in the morning, before shaving and being marched to the mess hall. When we arrived back from the mess, we were not allowed lie down our bed. If we didn't have to practice marching or studying our manual, we could take a nap. Some napped on our cold wooden floor. I napped on top of my footlocker.

About the second day of boot-camp, we were marched over to pick up some of our Air Force clothing. We were issued two pair of fatigue coveralls, underwear, socks, short boots and a

Fatigue cap with bill. A couple of weeks later we were issued our dress blue uniforms, shirts, socks, tie, hat and dress black shoes. We were drilled daily on marching. From being in a band in high school and ROTC in college, close order marching was a snap for me. Some in our flight had trouble with marching, getting constantly chastised by our barracks chief.

In the service one quickly learns to never volunteer. One day while taking a break from marching our barracks chief asked for twelve volunteers. None of us raised our hands. He told us okay and we began marching again. At our next rest break, he asked for a show of hands those that had a complete set of dress blues.

I had one set but needed one more, before I could ship out to a training base. Several were like me. We raised our hand. Our barracks chief told us we had just volunteered. He then told us to fall out, go to our barracks and change into our dress uniform. He said we were to be ushers at the Texas fairground theater, where Eddy Arnold was giving a concert.

We needed no encouragement to hurriedly get dressed and get on board our air force bus. Eddy Arnold's "Cattle Call" song has always been a favorite with me. To see him perform and sing that song was a real thrill. As an usher, we were placed at various posts to direct people to seats. If a cute single girl came to one of our posts, she would be personally escorted to a seat. Others were directed from one airman, as we were called, to another to get to their seats.

One day our barracks chief told us to fall out and police the area. Policing meant to pick up any trash around our barrack's ground. Any cigarette butts had to be picked up, the paper peeled away from the tobacco and placed in our pocket. The tobacco was emptied onto the ground. There was an old saying, "If you see something pick it up, if you can't pick it up, paint it. If you can't pick it up or paint it, and it moves, salute it."

The first thing a unit of marching men must do is to "dress up the unit." Our barracks chief would line up our flight with tall men up front in a column of four. Each man would take his place according to height. The next order was dress front. Each column of men would touch, at arm's length, the man in front of him. Then would come the dress right or dress left order. Dressing meant to use either right or left arm, as ordered, to stretch-out to get a proper distance between the columns.

One day we were called out to march. While our barrack chief called cadence, we arrived at a large building, and were directed to enter. Inside we were ordered to strip down to nature's bathing suit, and hang our clothes on wooden pegs along the wall. Then, single file, we were ushered in one at a time into a small dimly lit room.

Church music was being softly played. On a table with a cross were laid out several pocket size bibles, with a note telling us to take one. We were directed to enter the next room. There stood a double column of medics, four on each side, holding hypodermic needles. As I moved forward, I was given a shot in each arm. At the end of the line was a medic to check for venereal disease. We then got dressed and were marched back to barracks.

By now we had learned to "check the grapevine" to see what was coming up. By this we learned we were to get our haircut next day. The grapevine said what the required length would be. Two in our barracks were barbers from New York. They agreed to cut our hair to the proper length for fifty cents. All but one of us got really sharp "crew cuts." Tex said that no one would cut his hair, which was long and shaggy. When our flight entered the base barbershop those of us who got our crew cuts in our barracks were quickly approved and let go. For Tex, they had him be seated, and he got a haircut. They quickly ran clippers over his head, leaving less than a half inch of hair sticking up in all directions. He learned a good lesson that day.

The day came for us to go to the rifle range. We were given M-1 carbines and a fifteen round clip of ammo. At a given order we were told to fire only 5 rounds to zero-in on our target. After firing the 5 rounds we were told to lay our rifles down and check our targets. The guy on my left was beside me. He said, "Cripps, are you Daniel Boone?" I looked at my target. I had put 4 rounds inside the bulls-eye and the final round was half in and half out of the bulls-eye. That so unnerved me that when I shot for final score, one of my bullets hit the wooden stake holding my target, tearing the target apart. They had to give me a calculated score.

If the weather was cold and rainy, and the barracks chief wasn't present, our barracks would play Civil War. Like overgrown kids we would use brooms as pretend rifles and our finger as a pistol. We'd hide behind footlockers. We were primarily equally divided between north and south.

Our barracks chief, unlike some of the others, was firm but not sarcastic. When our training was over and our aptitude tests completed, we were assigned to a new training base. Before our flight left, we pitched in and bought our barracks chief a nice pocket watch. He bid us all good luck. While waiting for my new assignment, I got a short pass to go into San Antonio. I told a stroll down what is now River Walk. When I visited, it was only a dirt path along the river. Now it's beautiful.

I was flown out to Keesler AFB, at Biloxi, Mississippi.

Chapter 11

When I arrived in Biloxi it was raining. I remember seeing all the stands of young pine trees going to my new quarters. Keesler Field had nice uses of pine trees as part of their landscaping.

I was assigned to squadron number 3385. Our barracks had raised foundations. Inside there was a main isle with bunk beds on each side. I got a lower bunk and a guy from New Orleans had the top bunk. The beds had mosquito netting. I quickly learned it was too hot to use them. Although our barrack's windows and door had screens, mosquitoes got in.

We used to joke about the mosquitoes getting their "flight training" on base. We'd joke that whoever had a top bunk was hit twice. We joked that mosquitoes flew in formation, peeled off and dove to attack the upper bunk, before attacking the lower bunk. I learned how to be cool and comfortable, and not have mosquitoes bother me. I put a small fan in my window. I directed the fan's breeze to hit my body full length. Mosquitoes couldn't buck the head wind.

My first shock at my new base was when our barracks chief woke us the first morning, telling us to get up, sweep and mop the area around our beds, get cleaned up and dress for chow. I looked at my watch. It was 3 AM. I thought the sergeant must be kidding. He wasn't. All the barracks on our street had early morning radio school classes. Classes began at 6 AM and ended at noon. The rest of the day we were free to do as we like.

I learned that to hang around our squadron area, playing pool in our recreation room, listening to music or reading, you might get called to do squadron area clean-up. Several of us would either go into Biloxi or go to a nearby park and take a nap in the shade of large oak trees.

There was a roller-skating rink in town. It was a favorite place for youth of Biloxi. I decided I would try to learn roller-skating. I gave myself two weeks to learn. I would go to the rink each afternoon. After a little over a week, I had fallen so much that my whole body was sore. I had gotten to the point where on the straight-away I could do pretty well. I would get into rhythm with the music being played on a speaker. I never learned to do cross-over on corners. I just used my speed to glide around.

One day I noticed an attractive girl who was a good skater. She made skating look so easy. While I was on the straightaway I had picked up speed. Coasting around the turn, I noticed this girl standing on the sideline. She smiled at me, breaking my skating concentration, and I hit the floor. Trying not to trip her, my legs went "spread-eagle" on each side of her, almost to my crotch. I was so embarrassed. She reached down and helped me back on my feet, then skated off. I never went skating again. I learned that my feet were made for only walking, not for roller-skating or ice skating.

I believed that to wear my uniform, representing my country, my uniform should fit well. I took all my uniforms to an on-base alterations shop and had them tailored to fit well. I disliked seeing those that wore rumpled uniforms that look like they had been slept in.

In Biloxi, I'd attend USO dances, go to the Methodist church on Sundays, and have an occasional lunch. It was relaxing to take off my shoes and walk along a sandy beach, or play beach volleyball.

At one USO dance I was dancing with a girl who was tall and pretty. I asked her name. I don't remember her first name. Her last name was MacArthur. I said, "Like General MacArthur?" Her reply was, "Yes, he's my uncle." That was a big surprise. Here I was a PFC [Private first Class] dancing with the niece of a five star general.

We were marched to chow and back. We usually had a few minutes before our chief had us fall-in on the street and march us to class. A loudspeaker played the Colonel Bogie march. It was a sight to see. Each barrack of about seventy men each were separated into squadrons of marching men, on the way to class.

Barrack chiefs would call cadence. Depending on our arrival at a street where other barracks merged, we occasional marched behind a WAF [Women's Air Force] group. Our barrack chief had some spicy marching songs that he had us call-out, while marching. I'm sure it embarrassed some of the gals. I won't put their lyrics here. Each line of the song ended in Honey Baby Mine.

Some marching lyrics I can mention are: "The Air force coffee they say is mighty fine. It's good for cuts and bruises. It tastes like iodine. Oh I don't like this Air Force life. Gee ma I want to go home." Another: "The Air force biscuits they say are mighty fine. One rolled off the table and killed a pal of mine. Oh I don't like this Air Force life. Gee ma I want to go home."

I learned that my old roommate in college, Frank Ross, was also stationed at Keesler, taking radar school. He still had his car with him. Every weekend we'd go to New Orleans. We'd check into a hotel on St. Charles Street, and then go to a club on Bourbon Street to plan our evening.

I remember the club had a Dixieland band of four black musicians with white hair. They consisted of a trumpet player leader, a trombonist, a clarinet and tuba players. They were great. They didn't use any sheet music. The trumpet player would give the song title, and lead off.

Occasionally the leader would sing part of the song. One song that I remember was "Oh you ugly child." In the song the trumpet player would sing, "Your hair is curly; your teeth are pearly. Oh you ugly child." They would play some of classics of Dixieland: "South Rampart Street parade", "When the saints go marching in", "Muskrat ramble", and many more. I love the music.

One night Frank went on his own way and I decided to take a ride on the USS President, an old paddlewheel steamboat. It would travel a short distance up the Mississippi River and then return. On the main deck of the boat was a dance floor and bandstand. On the second level was a balcony, with tables and chairs, for refreshments. I could look down at the dancers below and enjoy the music. On the top deck were lounge chairs. It was so quiet and peaceful to sit in one of the chairs, watch lights along the shore go by, and feel a cooling breeze.

By the dock I could buy a cup of chicory coffee, which takes getting used to, and some donuts. I found that the only way I could stand the coffee was to mix it and the donut at the same time.

The guy in the bunk above my bed told me of out of the way places in New Orleans, for good food, music and girls to dance with. Frank and I went to one. There was only one door and a short hallway to get to the club area. Tables and chairs were arranged around a large dance floor. The bandstand was at the far end. The room had dim lighting.

When the music began, Frank went to a far table and asked a girl for a dance. While they were heading for the dance floor, I spotted a lone girl at another table and asked her for a dance. While we were dancing and carrying on conversation, I learned she was married and her husband thought she was at church. After the dance I told Frank, "Let's go."

On the outside I told Frank what the girl I danced with had said. I could picture an irate and jealous husband entering the club, by the one entrance, and what he might do.

One night Frank, two friends in his barrack and I went to the Casa Blanco club in Biloxi. It had a large sign that said that anyone who could drink three zombies and walk out was a man. Frank took the challenge. Each zombie consisted of seven types of liquor in a large water glass.

Frank managed to get the three down and walk to his car. Heading for the base he kept telling us to be sure he had his hat on when we went through the checkpoint. Frank drove me to my barracks and let me out. I asked Frank's friends next day how he did getting to their barracks. They told me Frank did a beautiful job at parallel parking, stepped out of the car, folded up and had to be carried inside.

Frank would tell me how great it was to get drunk. My grandfather had told me, "A baby can get drunk, but, it takes a man to drink and stay sober." On one trip to New Orleans, I thought I'd experience Frank's fun. We started back to base and he pulled over to park and sleep in his car's back seat. I was in the front seat, feeling horrible. My stomach was queasy and only the color green came to mind.

When it got daylight, I started the car and went looking for a café to get some coffee. Shocks on Frank's car rear-end were bad. I hit a deep bump in the road and saw Frank bounce up above the seat, in a slow roll. When he hit the rear seat and sat up, he asked, "What in the hell are you doing?" I told him and said, "If you think getting drunk is fun, you're out of your cotton-picking mind." That was the only time in my life that I had too much to drink.

I had problems with Morse Code. Message letters were sent in five letter groups. The total number of groups depended on the message being sent. Learning to copy code, the number of groups per minute begins slowly to increase in speed, over weeks. The beginning was about five groups per minute. To graduate required eighteen groups per minute.

After that hurtle came copying plain-text messages, sent in Morse code. This proved to be a problem to me and almost caused my being "washed-out" of school. It was difficult for me to concentrate on the code, due to trying the read the message at the same time. When typing in letters sent in code, and see that it's telling of a sub off our coast, can be distracting. I and another student were put into two week suspension. If we didn't pass by then we would be shipped out to an Air Police [AP] or cook squadron. On next to the last day, we decided we weren't going to pass and to have fun. Instead of using all our fingers to type the plain text coded messages, we would use only our first finger, pecking style. We didn't have time to read what the message was about. We passed.

The other classes in school didn't bother us that much. After 960 hours of training, I graduated with a grade point average of 3.8, on October 22, 1951. I was selected to become an instructor at the school. I was given a two week furlough and my first stripe. I was now making $70.00 per month.

When I got home I was surprised to be given a 1948 Nash club coupe. It was a graduation gift from my mother and grandfather. After visiting with the family for a few days, I drove to Oklahoma A & M to visit with Luanne. I learned that many of my friends were now in military service.

Going back to Keesler I learned that Frank had shipped out. My now having a car of my own, I would drive to New Orleans, stopping in Gulfport, Mississippi for an Italian spaghetti and meatball lunch. Or I might take a boat ride out to Ship Island, twelve miles out in the gulf from Gulfport. The beach there was white sand; the water a deep blue. There was a hotdog stand that served cokes. On the island were the ruins of an old fort.

My friend from New Orleans told me about an exclusive girl's school in Gulfport. They were daughters of wealthy Central American families. One was allowed to attend dances there and dance with the girls, on campus. I met an attractive girl from Costa Rico. To take her off campus on a date required a written letter from my minister, my local judge and a prominent member in my town, all vouching my good character. I got the required letters a few days before I was to ship out to my new base. I never got to date the Costa Rico girl, off campus.

One day when I returned from teaching, I saw a notice on our orderly room bulletin board. It stated, "Sixteen volunteers needed for flying status." I wanted to volunteer but had promised my mother I'd not do any volunteering. A few days later I was ordered to our squadron's orderly room. I counted sixteen of us. Our master sergeant came out and said, "Congratulations men, you're now on flying status." It was my happiest day.

I noticed on my orders that I was assigned to the 581st Air Resupply wing at Mountain Home, Idaho. I was to report for duty there in two weeks. I made two new friends, Truman Godwin from Lubbock, Texas and Bill Avanzini from Colgate, Oklahoma, who were also heading for Mountain Home, Idaho. We became lifelong friends.

Truman convinced Bill and me that we were now authorized to wear wings over our left breast pocket. We three bought our wings. We agreed to meet and ride to Idaho on the same train.

While home I was asked to be an usher at a wedding. It was a white dinner jacket and black trousers affair. The reception was held in Muskogee. As my escort, I took Jean Vann. Jean Vann is a nice girl and pretty. She was treated unfairly by some in Warner. She was soft spoken and kind.

Jean was two years younger than I. I considered her a good and trustful friend. Unlike some I knew, who enjoyed teasing me in school, she was always kind to me.

In school Jean had invited me to one of her class wiener roasts on Warner Mountain. Boys in her class carried cases of cold cokes. The girls carried the hot dog makings. While everyone was having a good time, I noticed two boys would get a coke and then would disappear, un-noticed by others, into the darkness. Using my scouting skills, noticing the direction they had taken, I slipped away from the crowd, doing a circle of where they disappeared.

By the time they made a couple more trips from the pop cases to where they were hiding their cokes, I located their stash of un-opened cokes. While they made a return trip for more pop, I loaded up their stashed pop and returned them to the pop case. It must have been frustrating to them. I was replacing what they had taken as fast as they took it. They became aware that someone was aware of their scheme, but they didn't know who. They decided it was a losing game and stopped trying to take more cokes.

On the way back to town, I knew the bunch of kids would have to pass a curve down the mountain road. It had a steep upper bank, on their right. In the darkness, I slipped away from the group and took a short-cut to this area. The group, like cackling geese, approached my hiding spot. I gave a loud snarling sound. Someone yelled, "Mountain Lion!" That started a stampede to town. With all the stragglers, I rejoined the group. Jean was never aware that I had pulled that prank.

When I went by to get Jean for the reception, she looked beautiful. Jean wore a strapless light blue formal. Her brunette hair was pilled high on her head. I thought we were the nicest looking couple at the reception. Town people saw Jean in a different light. People in town began treating her with more respect. I was happy to learn that she had married into a well-to-do family. She truly deserved such a life. I'll never forget her. She was a good and true friend.

Before leaving for my new base, I visited college to say goodbye to Luanne. I wore my tailored dress blue uniform and my wings. Luanne had gone home that weekend. Since there was a basketball game going on, I went to the game. While sitting in the bleachers, I was joined by girls I knew in high school and in college. They were commenting on how nice I looked in my uniform. I always had my uniforms and shirts tailored to fit. The girls asked questions about military life and where I was stationed. I told them about my Air Force life, and that I was being relocated to Idaho.

From out of nowhere Eugene joined us. I was still angry about his reneging on Frank and me. The girl's comments on my uniform must have bothered him. He interrupted the girl's conversation by saying, "I have a navy uniform hanging in my closet." I snapped back, "Yes, a damn weekend swabby." Eugene knew I was angry and left. Shortly afterwards I left and drove home. As the years rolled by, I realize that Eugene was wise to have remained in college. He received a doctorate degree in Agriculture and became a college professor, traveling to various parts of the world to help other countries that had agricultural problems.

Chapter 12

I was driven by my mother to Oklahoma City where I met with my friends, Bill Avanzini and Truman Godwin. We boarded the train to our new base in Mountain Home, Idaho. During a short layover in Denver, two MPs [Military Police] questioned if we were authorized to wear wings. Truman showed them our orders and convinced them we were authorized. We weren't all that sure.

Arriving at Mountain Home, Idaho we were picked up by a base bus and driven to the base. The base had been used during WWII, but allowed to run down. Earlier arrivals got the base in shape. Our barracks were long wooden frame buildings. It had forced air heaters at each end. Bunks were all one level, spaced about three feet apart. We got settled in.

Next day I was assigned as radio operator on a C-119, the flying boxcar. I learned that our wing, 581st Air Resupply, was a PSYWAR unit. The wing had twelve B-29s, four C-119s and four SA-16s. The SA-16s were amphibians normally used in air-sea rescue. I didn't like the C-119, and with the aid of my two good friends I switched to SA-16s. Mine, AF1017, was eventually given a coat of black paint, in the Philippines, before going TDY to Korea.

The C-119 got its name for the shape of its cargo compartment. It had two Pratt & Whitney 4360 engines with four bladed props. The normal entry for personnel was through a door in front of the portside [left] engine. To get to the flight deck was a short aluminum stair. On the flight deck were pilot, co-pilot, navigator and radio operator.

The thing I didn't like about the plane was that the navigator and I rode backwards. The plane empty was a rough-rider and the Fairchild manufacturing representative said to never crash-land or ditch. If we wished to survive, we'd need to parachute out. This wasn't the kind of news that I enjoyed. The Representative went on to say that a reward of $5,000 was authorized for anyone who proved either could be done. Only one we heard had collected the reward. He ditched at sea near an island. By the time water had reached his passenger's chest, they slid up on a beach.

Riding backwards, unable to watch the horizon, on a bouncy airplane, looking at your radio instruments giggling up and down, can bring on air sickness. At least it was for me. Since our entire missions are to fly low level, to get under enemy radar, we practiced flying at an altitude of fifty-feet.

While on a flight to southern California, flying at fifty-feet, I heard the co-pilot, on intercom, tell the pilot about some seagulls ahead. I was sending a Morse code message. Suddenly there was a loud bang. I suspected we had hit a bird. My pilot put our plane in a steep climb, to gain altitude. Suddenly there was another loud bang. I glanced at my navigator. His face was as white as a sheet. When we leveled off, I asked him what had happened. He said that each time the starboard [right] engine backfired; making a loud bang, the engine almost came off its mount. We had climbed to gain enough altitude to bail-out, if necessary.

We made it to Norton AFB outside of San Bernardino. While our engine was being fixed, I got permission from my pilot to visit my uncle and aunt at 104 via Las Vegas, Palos Verde, California. I got to be with them for three days before returning, with my crew, to our base in Idaho.

When my crew went on a cross-country flight to Warner-Robins AFB in Georgia; then to Wright-Patterson in Ohio and back to Mountain Home, I was accompanied by my checkout operator Bill Worthington. He was to determine my proficiency as a radio operator. A young lieutenant bummed a ride with us as far as Nebraska. When he entered our plane he didn't fully lock the entry door. When my pilot achieved take-off speed [V2] and began to climb, I started my departure message.

I glanced down the stairs and saw the lieutenant "spread eagle", holding onto the airplane with one hand and the open door with the other, trying to close the door. I quickly pointed out the problem to Bill Worthington. He hurried down the ladder to help the lieutenant. Still doing my message, I looked down. Both the Lieutenant and Bill was "spread eagle."

I told the radio I was in-touch with to stand by, put down my headset and started for the ladder. Before I reached the ladder, I saw they now had the door closed and locked. Bill was visibly shaken and trembled so much that I had to steady his hand so he could light a cigarette. After a few deep drags, Bill said to me, "When we were both "spread eagle", facing that spinning four-bladed prop, that crazy s.o.b. said we should have been wearing parachutes." Continuing, Bill said, "If we had fallen out those prop blades would have made minced meat of us."

While on that trip I tried to send a Morse code message. Some radio kept interrupting my message by sending "You hog, you hog." I told Bill. He listened in, and then took out his high speed radio key, called "the bug." Sending at a speed that I couldn't copy, Bill blasted the obnoxious radio station with several Q-signals. We never heard them again.

When we crossed into mountainous Idaho, it was dark and snow covered the ground. Going over the mountains the air was really rough and I was getting airsick. In the back of C-119s are clam-shell doors for loading and unloading large cargo. Into each clam-shell door is a regular door for those parachuting to exit. I asked Bill to cover radio transmissions. With my backpack parachute, I went to the back of the plane, opened the small door, lay down on the floor and eased the upper part of my body out into space, hanging onto the plane's interior with both hands. The cold fresh air felt great. I felt someone grab my ankles. Looking back it was Bill. When I told him my problem, he let go. When our plane's wheels touched the runway, I emptied my stomach.

Due to air sickness, I think I was about to be grounded. I told my friends, Bill and Truman. They informed me that an SA-16 radio operator was getting his discharge. My friends put in a good word for me and I met with First Lieutenant Stephens, aircraft commander of AF 1017. He chose me as his replacement radio operator and got my release from the C-119. My seat in the SA-16 was in the cockpit, behind the co-pilot. My bank of radios was across a small isle on my left, easy to reach. My Morse code key was mounted on a small table in front of me, attached to the plane's bulkhead.

I liked the feel of the plane. Sitting behind the co-pilot, I had a clear view of the horizon and never became air sick again, even in rough weather. I also learned how to read the plane's instruments, landing and takeoff on water methods, and various functions of the plane. My crew members were friendly and when flying we used first names. We were a united crew be it officers or enlisted men.

It was fun flying at fifty-feet in the SA-16. It felt like being in a race car traveling at 150 MPH. It meant that the pilot and co-pilot had to be very alert and keep a sharp lookout for any obstructions ahead, be it highline wires, windmills, trees or buildings, while flying low over Nevada desert areas or farming land which might have windmills.

On one flight I looked out and saw we were paralleling an interstate highway. Up ahead I could see a large road sign stating "Reno 220 miles." I heard my pilot call our navigator, Captain Rheune Pfeiffer, on intercom, asking our location. Rhenue, who had apparently been looking out his window, quipped, "Hell I don't know. Read the road sign." All got a laugh out of that.

Rhenue was the best navigator I ever worked with. In preparation for what was to come, he had to set a course to be at a certain destination within a five minute target time. Rhenue did it every time.

On one occasion Bill's crew was flying to Tinker Field at Oklahoma City, for a quick stop and return to Mountain Home. I asked permission to ride along with Bill. It was granted. The flight was also to check out Bill's pilot. The checkout pilot rode in the co-pilot's seat. The checkout pilot wanted to see how high an SA-16 could climb to.

It was a cold winter night. When the plane exceeded 21,000 feet the oil lines began to freeze. We were ordered to put on our chest chutes. The plane's flight chief stood by the exit door. The red light came on and we stood ready to jump if the green light came on. The plane was rapidly losing altitude. With the lower altitude the oil lines thawed and the red light was turned off. Needless to say I wasn't happy about the check pilot's experiment.

Upon landing at Tinker Field, Bill and I paid a quick visit to his sister at Oklahoma University, at her sorority. She escorted us to her room on the second floor, calling out to the other girls on that floor, "Men of the floor." A lot of doors were quickly shut.

Weekends Bill, Truman and I would hitchhike to Boise, a distance of about forty miles. Being winter, we would wear our heavy wool blue overcoats, over our uniform, and fortify ourselves with a hot bowl of chili from a café in the small town of Mountain Home. We always managed to get a ride.

On one ride I rode in the front seat; Bill and Truman in back. The road was icy with snow pack. When the driver hit speeds of 105 I tried not to show it. It was a "white knuckle" ride. As we approached Boise the driver said, "Well, I'd best drop flaps." I told Bill and Truman what had happened. We decided to pool our money and buy an old used car, for our trips to Boise.

In Boise we always got a room at the Boise Hotel. We became such weekend customers that when we walked into the hotel the desk clerk, with a big smile, said, "Not you three again", giving us our room key.

Bill and Truman would go ice skating on the city's park pond. From my experience in Biloxi, I sat and watched from the bank. The frozen pond was a favorite place for towns-people. We met Nancy Cochell, two Barbara's and Martha Ah Fong, all nice girls. On our weekend trips we would take the girls to a movie, bowling or on walks about town. I was Nancy's date and later on I dated her cousin, Helen Griggs, from Kuna,

Idaho. We learned that the girls were members of the Church of Jesus Christ of Latter-day Saints—Mormons.

It was my first encounter with those of Mormon faith. Even though I was a member of the Methodist church, I couldn't go along with the Methodist doctrine. The first time I went to church with Nancy in Boise, I thought the service strange. People in the building would stand up and testify about the church or their conversion to the church or family things. I later learned this was their fast and testimony monthly service where any member can stand and bear their testimony, even kids of all ages. Some of the little kids were so small that a stool was used so they could reach the podium and microphone. I was amazed that they had no fear in addressing other church members of about 500 to 1,000. They usually testified of their love for their parents, brothers or sisters. I was greatly impressed.

I caught a bus that ran close to Kuna and hitchhiked from there into Kuna to attend church with Helen and her family. As part of the service a young woman played Malaguena on the piano. I was so taken by the beauty of the song that I almost clapped my hands, in church. After the service I asked the lady the name of the tune and she said, "Malaguena." It's now my most favored tune. It's so uplifting to my spirit. When I played golf, later on in the Philippines, after listening to this song, I played better.

The Mormon families in Boise were kind to my friends and I. Several times we were asked over for dinner. They made us feel at home, which isn't always the case for military personnel.

On one of our trips to Boise in our old 1939 Studebaker that we had purchased, we as usual went to the Boise Hotel. We were shocked when the desk clerk said he had no rooms to rent. It must have shown on our faces. As we turned to leave, the clerk called us back. He said he had one room; that we must promise to go directly to that room, and when we left it to go directly to the elevator. We thought that strange, but agreed. Next day when we checked out he explained why the requirements. He had put us on a floor filled with YWCA young ladies.

Chapter 13

Part of our training was lectures on low-level flight, and escape/evasion techniques. An American pilot who had joined the British RAF, flying mosquito fighter/bombers during WWII, told about flying low-level over Briton country-sides, and its many crisscrossing highline wires. When he was asked by a guy from our wing on how he manage to not hit those almost invisible wires, the ex-RAF pilot explained that in the mosquito the pilot and radar man seats were side-by-side. He said when he heard his radar man gasp he'd pull up sharply and zoom over the highline wires.

On our escape and evasion lectures, I wonder why the usual grapevine didn't pick up on this. One was about a guy who had to bail out over German controlled France. He had stolen civilian clothes and was trying to get back to American lines by rail. He was waiting for a train on the train's platform, with other civilians, when two German soldiers spotted him and started towards him. The guy turned to a young woman next to him, hugged her and told her he was an American. It turned out she was part of the French underground. She quickly helped him to escape, and back to American lines.

In another story the guy was shot down deep inside German. Thinking of no way to escape, he played the role of a deaf and dumb mute, and set up a tobacco shop. He was doing a thriving business when American troops captured the town. They were surprised when this guy came running out of his tobacco shop yelling, "Thank God you finally got here!"

Those in the SA-16 unit would fly to Puget Sound In Washington to practice water landings. We had to keep a sharp lookout for any floating logs. After shooting touch and go water landings, to perfect our skill, we went into the Navy mess hall for lunch. I had put a bowl on my tray, thinking a soup was to be served with the meal. When I reached the end of the line a navy corpsman put a short cake in my bowl and filled the bowl with strawberries. I was shocked. In the Air Force, I would have been given only a large spoonful of strawberries. The navy corpsman thought I was waiting for more and good naturedly said, "Finish that and I'll give you more." I learned that the navy always had good chow.

Our last training flight was a night flight to San Francisco and to the Farallon Islands, and return back to our base, to test our over-water night navigation skills. The ocean at night, with no moon, is very dark. It's difficult to distinguish water from sky, and to find a tiny cluster of islands. For Rhenue it was a snap. Heading back to San Francisco, after circling the Farallon Islands, nothing but blackness was before us. Steve, my pilot, asked me to tune in a San Francisco radio station; that he planned to home-in on it. The station I located was playing music. They were playing the song "Harbor Lights." At that very moment we saw the harbor lights of San Francisco. I'll never forget that moment.

With all crews trained, Colonel Arnold called all air crews together. He told us he was giving all those who wished a two-week leave, before we would ship out overseas. The "grapevine" went wild. Some said we were headed for Korea, others claimed it would be North Africa, and some said Europe.

Truman, Bill and I headed for Oklahoma City in the old Studebaker. Along the way the fuel pump went out, at a station out in the middle of nowhere, in the New Mexican desert. We were lucky that the station had only one fuel pump left for that 1939 Studebaker. That fixed we were off to Oklahoma City. My mother had a lady drive her to Oklahoma City in my 1948 Nash Club Coupe. My mother was afraid she couldn't drive in such a large city. Bill's family met him in Oklahoma City. Truman then drove our old Studebaker back to his home in Lubbock, Texas.

I wanted to drive my own car back to Warner. It was night and the white lines were mesmerizing. I had been following an eighteen wheeler's rear running lights. When I became aware I had passed the truck and didn't remember doing that, I pulled over and let the woman drive.

The two weeks went by quickly. Just before we were to leave, Truman took the Studebaker in for an oil change. The mechanic forgot to put the plug back in the oil pan. The car engine froze up. The engine was totaled destroyed. Truman asked for permission for the three of us to go in on the purchase of a 1943 Chevy. We agreed.

Again we all met in Oklahoma City, bid family goodbye and headed for our base in Idaho. We headed up I-35 to I-70 to I-25 then north to Cheyenne, Wyoming. We took turns driving and sleeping. It was early afternoon when just west of Little America, Wyoming the Chevy's timing gear went out. I stayed with the car while Bill and Truman hitched a ride to Little America to get a tow truck, which hauled us back to Little America.

We told the mechanic in Little America we were service men and low on money. He told us what had to come off to replace the timing gear, and that the new gear wouldn't be delivered until in the morning, a Saturday. We had until Sunday midnight to be back on base or we were AWOL.

The mechanic loaned us some tools and we began removing what had to come off. Bill was working top-side. Truman and I were taking off screws below. At that time I didn't know much about auto repair. As Truman and I were removing the last screws I asked Truman what was in the thing we were taking off. He said oil.

I said, "Oil!"

Oil spilled on me. A spring attached to the pan snapped up and hooked Bill. I was really ticked at Truman and said, "I may be dumb at car repair, but I'd have enough sense to drain the oil pan before removing it."

In 1943 Chevy's the timing gear was a hardened fiber material. The replacement was metal. The mechanic put on the new gear and left the timing to us. Bill and Truman read the book on how to do this. We put the side-panel and oil pan back on, putting in the required quarts of oil. We paid our bill and left.

The oil warning light came on before we reached McFadden, Wyoming. Checking with the dip-stick we learned we were out of oil. A local rancher stopped to help. He towed us to McFadden. A mechanic asked what we had done in Little America. He then asked if we had replaced the oil pan gasket. Learning that we hadn't, he replaced that gasket, put in oil and we were on the road again.

Near Rock Springs, Wyoming the oil indicator light came on, again. Again we pulled off the road. We were out of oil and were towed in by another rancher into Rock Springs. Again the mechanic asked what all we had done. He asked if we had replaced the gasket on the side panel we took off. Again we said no. He replaced it and put in oil. Again we were underway, and worried. We had been towed most of the way through Wyoming and it was late Saturday evening. We had about 230 miles to go before mid-night next day.

Early Sunday morning we pulled into Evanston, Wyoming. Our car engine sounded horrible. We pulled into the local Chevy dealership's parking lot. Truman located the home phone number of the dealership's chief mechanic. Truman called him and explained our dilemma.

Even though it was an early Sunday morning, the mechanic came to help us. He told us the car's push-rods were badly bent. To save us money, he took out each one and straightened them by hand, as best he could. He put all back together, making sure the gaskets didn't leak, and we were again on the road to Mountain Home, Idaho.

We arrived on base at 11:30 PM. It was so dark in our barracks that we couldn't locate our bunks. Not wanting to disturb others in our barracks, we drove back to Mountain Home and got a hotel room for the night, planning to drive back to base by roll-call time.

Being so tired from our trip, we over-slept. When we arrived back on base at about 9 AM, we were marked as AWOL. We showed where we had signed in before mid-night Sunday. That didn't carry any weight. We were put on "detail" work.

Colonel Arnold called the Wing together and notified us that the base was now in lock-down. No phone calls, except for emergencies, in or out of the base were permitted. Emergency phone calls had to be made from his office and be monitored. He told us our wing was being relocated to

Clark Field on Luzon Island in the Philippines. B-29s and C-119s were to fly a direct route, refueling in Hawaii and Guam.

SA-16s, with less cruising range, were to fly the northern route. We would carry additional fuel in drop tanks. Our four SA-16s would refuel in Great Falls, Fort Nelson British Columbia and in Anchorage Alaska. We would spend the night at Elmendorf AFB in Anchorage. Next morning we would fly from Elmendorf non-stop to Shemya, in the Aleutians, to spend the night and refuel. Our last stop for the night and refueling, before Clark Field, was Tokyo.

Before our wing took off for the Philippines, Colonel Arnold had each crew stand by their planes. He went down the row taking pictures. Mine hangs in my office. Our Wing commander, Colonel Arnold, chose to make the journey with our SA-16 unit. He flew with our unit commander, Captain Allen.

Our first stop was at Malmstrom AFB in Great Falls, Montana. While our planes were being refueled, Kyle, flight engineer on another SA-16 brought a large clean empty vegetable can to me. He knew that both he and I had air sickness problems. I never needed it.

Approaching Fort Nelson, British Columbian airport, we entered the traffic pattern. I noticed that at the end of the runway was a canyon. Little did I know how important that would be? Our plane was second into Fort Nelson. Our crew joined the first crew, in the airport waiting room, to watch for our other two planes.

Captain Allen, with Colonel Arnold at the controls, came in next for a landing. The Colonel flared out too soon. The plane's tires hit hard and bounced the plane back into the air. According to my radio operator friend, Harry Maynard, Captain Allen quickly took over the controls and applied full power to the engines. Harry said the plane shook, being close to stalling, but stayed airborne.

Captain Allen brought the plane around and made a good landing. His crew and Colonel Arnold joined us, watching for the last plane in our unit to arrive. A Canadian corporal spotted our incoming plane and called to one of his friends, saying, "Here comes another one of those planes. Let's see what this crazy s.o.b. is going to do." Colonel Arnold just smiled.

While our planes were being refueled, we crewmembers went to the airport's café and ordered lunch. The lady that waited on us had a heavy Scottish brogue. She asked, "'at would ye laddies 'ave?" It was amusing but great hearing the brogue. I remember ordering a cheeseburger, fries and a coke. Since the airport café is civilian owned, each crewmember paid for their own lunch. When I went up to pay for my food, the Scottish lady told me the amount in shilling and six-pence. I held out some dollars and told her to take what she needed.

According to my pilot, our plane was carrying the heaviest load. There were tools packed in our hull. At that time the Fort Nelson airport runway was 5,000 feet long. When my pilot taxied out our plane, he cocked our plane at a forty-five degree angle to the runway, knowing the plane's engine torque would swing us around to line up with the center line of the runway. When our engines reached peak RPM, he let go the brakes. With the end of the runway approaching and airspeed marginal, we lifted off. Immediately after we become airborne, my pilot snapped up our landing gears and lowered our plane's nose to pick up airspeed, utilizing the canyon's depth.

On our way to Elmendorf AFB in Anchorage, Alaska, we flew over heavily mountainous terrain with many small lakes. From our hourly weather reports that I received, and gave to our navigator, we learned that a mountain pass we had intended to fly through was experiencing icing conditions. Steve, my pilot, decided to go around the pass close to Fairbanks. Of the four planes in our unit, we were the last to land at Elmendorf. I remember it was July 22, 1952 and very cold. I told the driver that picked us up, I was only interested in two things—food and sleep.

It seemed that I had hardly gone to sleep when I was awakened by our flight engineer, letting me know it's time to go. I checked my watch to see if it was truly morning—it was. At the mess hall we had breakfast and were given boxed flight lunches for our long flight to Shemya. I'll always remember seeing the tall mountain ahead of us, on takeoff from Elmendorf. I thought, to myself, I'd sure hate to have to land or takeoff from here during a bad snowstorm.

We learned that our plane's interior heating system wasn't working. In the cockpit it wasn't bad. Our radio equipment with tubes and electrical circuitry generated heat. When I looked back into the cabin compartment the flight engineer, ground maintenance chief and our navigator had on their heavy wool overcoats, and were wrapped in wool blankets.

Our box lunches were ham and cheese sandwiches, and a can of beans. I put my can of beans on top of my radio equipment. The heat from the ARC-27 tubes warmed them up. Steve, noticing I was enjoying warm beans, passed back to me his and the co-pilot, John Foster, beans to be heated.

Sending and receiving Morse coded messages over an eight hour period wasn't my idea of pleasure. I would tune in my ground radio contact to a specific tone pitch. I could then catnap. Whenever that tone pitch came on I was wide awake and copying their message. I would then relay to him our position and weather report, given to me by our navigator.

Landing at Shemya, we were escorted first to the chow hall and to our sleeping quarters. All buildings were connected by enclosed passageways. I asked why the tunnels and was told that if I was here in winter, I would know the answer —snow covered all. I couldn't understand how they kept their sanity, living like moles.

Next morning before takeoff, I went out to check my radios and antennas. I tried to get up on top our aircraft to check the antenna and learned the plane was covered in fine ice, making that task impossible. I did check my radios on the inside and learned I could reach my contacts.

The runway here was long and takeoff no problem. Some miles west of Shemya we ran into a radio dead zone. We were in it for better than an hour. When we cleared that area it seemed the whole world was trying to reach us. My wrist became so sore answering all the messages that instead of using my first finger, to tap Morse code, I was using my fist to pound out our messages.

Coming into Tokyo in 1952, I saw signs of the damage done by WWII bombing—there were several ruined buildings. Our unit would spend the night in Tokyo, then next day make a non-stop flight to Clark Field in the Philippines. I couldn't get over how Air Force personnel had it made at the American base in Tokyo. In their mess hall, young and pretty Japanese girls waited on servicemen.

Next morning we radio operators were told to no longer use Morse code, but, go to radio telephone. That was the best news I'd had in a long time. We were given a frequency to adjust our ARC-27s to. I had never used the frequency calculation formula since leaving radio school. I couldn't remember if the x factor went above or below in the equation. I asked Truman. He began giving me a long lecture. I was tired and cross. I told him to forget it —I'd do it my way. My radio worked okay. I had to relay messages for Truman. His set had gone out of operation.

Approaching Luzon, my pilot was fed up with our unit commander's pampering of our wing commander. It was an understanding that our Wing commander, Colonel Arnold, would be the first of our unit to land at our new base. Steve got Rhenue on intercom and asked for a direct shorter route to Clark Field. The plan was to wait until I gave my hourly position report, then swing to the new course. The others wouldn't know our intent for another hour, with our new position report. The race was on. We were the first to land.

Chapter 14

In 1952, Clark Field AFB was a well laid out and up to date base. The base is located on fourteen square miles of land, three miles west of the town of Angeles. The barracks I called home for two years resembled an American motel. It was two stories high, built of stucco with concrete walkways on both levels and pipe railing. There were many louvered-glass windows, about a foot wide with screens, to control ventilation and keep out insects. Inside was a main center isle with rows of bunk beds on each side. Beds were separated by about four feet. At the end of both floors were the bathrooms.

In the Philippines, we had houseboys who kept our barracks clean, made our beds and shined our shoes. They were young Filipino guys. Some guys in our barracks gave our houseboys an uncalled-for bad time. Demanding them re-shine their shoes, or just finding something to complain about.

I've always found it repulsive to me when someone "looks down their nose" at someone of another race or color of skin, or uses crude and vulgar language. I wasn't brought up that way and tried to keep those people at a distance. My grandfather used to say, "Son, if you lie down next to dogs, you'll get up with fleas." It was his way of saying you associate with those of bad character; you'll be looked upon as being the same.

I was always friendly with our houseboys. I wanted to learn Filipino culture and customs. The houseboys wanted to learn about the states, our slang and customs. We'd set and talk while he worked. I had the best shined shoes and made bed in our barracks.

The lawn outside of my barracks was kept close-cut with only a few low-growing shrubs. I learned this was to prevent cobras from hiding there. A Filipino gardener would use a sharp bolo type machete to cut grass. They would squat on their heels and cut the grass in sweeping-like strokes.

I was told by some in our barracks that a cobra came up behind the Filipino, rising to a strike position. Our guys were afraid to yell a warning to the Filipino Gardner; for fear that his sudden movement would cause the cobra to strike. The guys said the cobra would sway back and forth to the gardener's motion with the bolo. The Gardner must have sensed danger. When he made a sweeping cut of the grass, he swung around cutting the cobra in half.

I never saw a cobra at Clark Field. However, when I went to the base theater and took the shortcut back to my barracks, on a dirt path through a weeded area, I ran. I rationalized that by the time a cobra could rise to strike I'd be long gone. I later learned that cobras can't hear. They attack by sight or use their heat sensor tongue to locate prey.

Clark Field had many things we GIs could enjoy. The Silver Wing Club posted a weekly calendar of events. The club was USO operated. They might have a band one night; Maori dancers in their native costumes on another night. Ladies from Angeles were brought on base for chaperoned dances, with music supplied by a local band. Filipinos love American music and their musicians are very talented.

One night a Filipina dance team performed a native dance called tinikling. Two of the team clicks two bamboo poles in a rhythm while others of their team perform a dance similar to skip-the-rope in and out of the clicking bamboo poles. It requires good timing or an injured ankle. Their colorful dresses and effortless graceful movements were thrilling to watch.

On another night, I watched Filipino girls, in beautiful dresses, with high puffed short sleeves, do a dance called pandanggo. It's a dance where each girl cups in both hands a small shallow glass bowl with a lit candle. Lights are dimmed and the girls do a graceful dance to music, while moving the lit candles in many patterns. It was so beautiful. I could never understand how they could do that and not drop a candle.

One night a Maori dance troupe performed their tribal dances, to chants, in colorful traditional native costumes. In olden days the Maori warrior was known for his furious fearless attacks in battle. It's told that our army soldiers were issued .38s at that time; that it wouldn't stop a Maori warrior. The army then came out with the .45 automatic which will knock down a human, wherever hit. Both Maori men and women have facial tattoos. The men's facial tattoos make them look formidable to their enemy.

The Maori troupe did a dance that was called Poi. Before the dance they told us the purpose of the dance and how the Poi balls were made. Poi balls were swung by both men and women. For the men it strengthened them for battle and dexterity; for women it was to strengthen their hands and arms, giving them dexterity for weaving flax. Poi balls, in olden days, were made of flax bags in which a heavy stone was placed. These bags were attached to a woven flax cord about two and a half feet long. These Poi balls were then swung in various patterns to gain strength and dexterity.

The Poi balls the women swung were originally made of cloth rolled up into a tight ball placed in the center of a white or colored piece of fabric and tied. In 1954, tennis balls were used instead of rolled up cloth. This was then attached to a platted cord. If addition weight was needed to gain strength, Poi balls could have added weights of rice or stones inserted.

The troupe I saw had white colored balls attached to a cord of woven black, red and white yarn with a large knot as a hand grip. Swinging the balls in various and different arcs takes skill and dexterity. It's like trying to rub one's head while at the same time patting one's stomach. They were so artistic and graceful in their dances.

Our base had: Kelly Theater, a very up-to-date air-conditioned movie theater, a bowling alley, a beautiful library that blended in among mature mimosa trees, a Post Exchange where we could buy items duty-free, commissary, Base Chapel, Officers and Base General's quarters, large parade ground, an Officer's and an enlisted men clubs, golf course with clubhouse, gym, base operations and flight line with a mounted Japanese Zeke fighter on a pedestal, some snack shops and a skeet range.

My favorite snack shops were Charlie Corn's, ran by a Filipino, and the one at base operations. When I visited Charlie Corn I would have pie and iced tea. He made delicious fruit pies. At base operations I'd have an egg salad sandwich with a coke. When I played golf, which was frequently, I'd have a hot dog, chicken noodle soup and a coke, at the clubhouse.

My first trip outside the base to Angeles was a shock. An eighteen wheeler picked up passengers at prescribed pick up points, on our base. The truck pulled a trailer that was converted into a bus with rows of seats with small windows for ventilation. It would take a load of men to the main gate to our base.

On the outside were parked many colorfully Jeepneys. Jeepneys are WWII jeeps, left behind, that have been converted into mini-taxis'. Filipinos would take out the rear seats of the original jeeps and replace them with a small truck-type bed with wooden benches along outside walls, for passengers. To enter the back passenger area was a wooden platform step. Both front seat and back area were covered. Drivers of these Jeepneys would try to get as many passengers as he could. The most I've seen packed into a Jeepney was thirteen. For ten centavos, roughly a penny in American money, they would drive us about three miles to Angeles.

It was like stepping back in time fifty years, or more. Businesses, mostly bars, lined the major streets. Interspersed among the bars were shops, theater, covered stalls where goods and food products were sold, woven baskets of all sizes sold by venders and a Catholic church. The main street entry for us was along a dirt street with ditches where raw sewage ran. Businesses along this street would use dip cans on broom handles to toss raw liquid fluids onto the dirt street to hold down dust. As temperatures rose, so did the smell.

My favorite places in Angeles were the Esquire and High Hat Clubs. Prostitution wasn't allowed in these clubs. They were safe for ordering meals. One could get a cold coke or San Miguel beer, served by cute hostesses who would sit and talk, or to dance with —a very relaxing atmosphere.

I especially liked the Esquire club's outdoor enclosed patio. It had a round concrete dance floor. Music was piped out to the area by a speaker. The patio had grass and covered wooden seats with small tables for drinks to sit on. At night the area was lit by strings of Christmas lights. Along the concrete walls that kept out traffic noise were colorful hibiscus plants. Other plants made the area a nice place to sit. The hostesses loved to hear about our states. At night the air was so cool and refreshing. It was like being in another world.

Hostesses liked to have pictures taken of them. If I was carrying my Zeiss Contesa camera, they would want me to take their pictures. I learned the best way to diplomatically solve this problem, without wasting a lot of film, was to take the pictures I wanted of Angeles first. With an empty camera, I'd then visit the two clubs and "snap" requested pictures. It satisfied them, their not knowing, and I didn't waste film. I always tried to be polite and use diplomacy with the hostesses.

One night while I was relaxing in the Esquire patio, a girl named Eve asked me if I'd like to hear her play her guitar. My first thought was, "Oh no", but I didn't want to offend her, so I said, "Sure." She played the American song "Jambalaya", written by Hank Williams, in a Spanish fashion. I was surprised. She was good and I complimented her.

One night at the High Hat Club I was enjoying the night air on their upper-story veranda. The High Hat had at one time been an old mansion set back from the street, with a tall mature tree in front. I was talking to a hostess when I felt the ground begin to shake and I heard an approaching siren blowing. Suddenly an American made Sherman tank, given to the Philippine government, came roaring down the street at full speed. I asked what was happening. She told me the tank was trying to cut off some HUKs. HUK was the name given to a communistic Philippine army. Arms for this group were supplied by Russia and China.

Filipino members had been displaced as tenant farmers by the Philippine government, which gave their farms to friends, when this group left to fight their Japanese invaders in WWII. These displaced farmers and ex-army guerrillas turned on their government. HUKs usually attacked only local police and army outposts, leaving the civilian population alone. They would also try to infiltrate our base to steal needed items. Our motor pool and flight line were favorite targets for spare parts and lubricants for the HUK equipment.

When Magsaysay was elected Philippine President, he totally did away with the HUK army. When Magsaysay learned of these ex-farmers and ex-guerrilla grievances, he offered them five acres of their own on Mindanao. They would no longer be tenant farmers but become land owners. The HUK army, except for about five die-hard communist, surrendered.

It's said that a colonel in the HUK army told Magsaysay, when offered the five acres, that he wasn't a farmer. Magsaysay then asked if he would accept being his bodyguard. The colonel accepted. I saw Magsaysay in Angeles one day. He was wearing the typical white Filipino shirt, a see through to a white undershirt—very cool and dressy, cotton trousers, and he was barefooted. He gave a speech and then handed out centavo pieces to the audience. Magsaysay was killed in a plane crash on the island of Cebu.

The roughest time in the Philippines was during the Christmas season. I missed the states. My aunt Lettye and my mother would each send me a fruit cake in a metal Christmas can. I would take one and share with friends in my barracks. The other one I took to Angeles.

I hired a Kalesa and asked the cabbie to slowly walk his horse down the street. I was on the lookout for the most down-spirited and ragged child I could find. The one I found looked so sad, like his world was caving in on him. I had the cabbie stop and I called the surprised boy over. I opened the can and showed him the fruitcake.

I told him I wanted him to take the fruitcake home to his family, no stopping in the alleys. I gave him the fruitcake and said, "Merry Christmas." A big smile came on his face and a very happy child, like being shot from cannon, ran home with the gift. I consider that Christmas my greatest. I felt that some poor family would have a better Christmas, a gift from an unknown American stranger, me. With Truman and Godwin, I took pictures around Angeles of some of rural children.

Children of poor Filipinos suffered greatly. They would beg for coins and could be formable as a group. I used to carry Philippine centavo coins in my pocket. A centavo was about a dime in their currency, and about a penny in ours. If I became surrounded by some of these little street urchins, I would reach in my pockets, get some centavos and toss them away from me. Those little ones would happily run to see how many centavos they could collect. I would make my escape.

One night I was sitting in the club and a young girl of about five approached and asked if I would buy a stick of Wriggle's spearmint gum from her. She was such a cute little one. I gave her an American quarter, approximately worth ten pesos in her money, and told her to keep her gum. She had such a cute smile as she thanked me and left. I'm a real softy when it comes to young kids.

I learned that poor farmers would try to keep their sons at home to help farm their land. I was told that many grown daughters were sent out into the world to fend for themselves, many of which wound up as prostitutes. This made me feel so sad. Later in my life my wife, Dorothy, and I would sponsor a young Filipina girl for twelve years through a children's international organization.

One evening my friend Howard Correll and I went to town to see an American movie —"Ivanhoe." We had just enough money to get us to town and see the movie. While I was watching the movie, Howard passed me a cold San Miguel. I whispered to him, "I thought you were broke. Where did you buy this?" He replied, "I got it from her." He was seated next to a Filipina girl. She had bought both Howard and I the San Miguel's. When the movie ended she went her way and we returned to base.

One day, as I was getting ready to go to Angeles, a radio friend on a C-119 asked if I'd deliver a message to a girl in town that he knew, to tell her he'd be in later. I agreed even though it was at a bar with a reputation. I sat at the table and gave the message I was to give.

Part way through telling the message, a drunken Filipino came to our table. He spoke to the girl in Tagalog. She said no. His temper was on the rise. On base we were told that under such circumstances, its best to ask the girl to dance and move cautiously to an exit door. I did as suggested and asked her to dance. That was what the Filipino wanted, and she had refused him, in Tagalog.

I tried to dance with her towards the door. He stepped in between us, demanding to know how much money I had. I noticed he had a gun in his right front pocket. I decided that if he reached for that gun, I'd give him the haymaker of all haymakers, and get out the door. Another hostess came over and coaxed him back to the table with his friends. I made a hasty exit. I calmed down at the Esquire Club. I was so mad at my friend asking me to go to his girlfriend that I really chewed him out, telling him to never ask me again to go to that place.

My friend Howard Correll told me that one night he had gone to Angeles. He said he drank too much and, along with others, caught a Jeepney back to base. He said Air Police in an armored vehicle stopped their Jeepney short of the main gate, which was blacked-out.

HUKs were shooting at our Air Police, at the main gate. Shots from HUKs in thatched houses outside the gate were answered by a blast from twin mounted fifty caliber machine guns, from our base Air Police.

In the lull between gunfire, an Air Policeman pointed Howard towards the darkened main gate, gave him a shove and yelled "Run!" Howard said he was in a staggering half run and tripped on something. Seeing it was a dead body really sobered him up. He ran so fast through the main gate that he had to be stopped by an Air Policeman, to be put on a bus to the barracks area. Howard said he was so scared he would have run the two miles to his barracks, had he not been stopped.

One night I was asleep in my lower bunk when I heard a blast from an automatic rifle and bullets ricocheting off our barracks. In one quick move I was flat on the floor behind a barracks wall. Air Police, using .45 caliber burp-guns, was shooting at a HUK fleeing down a concrete drainage ditch by our barracks. Bullets from the burp-guns were hitting our barracks. The HUK was killed.

In the beginning aircrew members were not required to do guard duty on our planes, at night. If we weren't scheduled to fly we were free to do as we wish during the day. Members of our ground crews had to pull night guard duty. They complained and aircrew members were also assigned to guard our planes, to keep HUKs from stealing electronic items. We were armed with only .45 automatic pistols, which I wasn't very good at.

One of our Wing guards was posted by the B-29s. He told us he heard a noise that came from inside the plane he was next to. He said he went up the nose ladder and raised the hatch to the cockpit. He was nose to nose with a HUK. He said it so shocked him that he lost his footing on the ladder and fell to the ground. He pulled his pistol and went up the ladder again. As he was easing open the hatch, he heard someone drop to the ground in back. The HUK had quickly crawled through the plane's tunnel to the rear of the plane and jumped to the ground.

With this incident in mind, I was assigned to a guard post on the B-29s. I figured the safest place was to sit down with my back against the B-29's front wheel. By not moving, I blended with the wheel in the darkness. Also by sitting it was easier to see any object that moved by the planes I was guarding. They would be silhouetted against the night sky. While watching I thought I saw movement by the B-29 across from me. Pulling my pistol, I went to investigate. At the spot I had detected motion, I turned on my flashlight. There was a drainage ditch. In the soft dirt were fresh footprints. Whoever they belonged to was gone.

On another guard duty assignment, I was posted by a small shack were oil and lubricants was stored, a favorite target for HUKs. A few feet in front of the shed was a light on a telephone type pole. Corporal of the guard that night was a flight crewmember whose first name is John.

Towards base operations were two other guard posts. John and his jeep driver would make the round of posts, checking on the guards and give them coffee. At night sound carries well. I heard John stop at the two posts before me. As they approached my post I walked out to meet them, under the light.

I was looking at a pistol that John had drawn. It was pointed at me. He gave me a lecture that if he had been an enemy he could have easily shot me. I told him I knew who he was because I had heard him at his two previous stops. His action really made me mad.

On his next run and previous stops, I got in the shadows of some oil drums. When the jeep pulled in under the light, I yelled, "Halt! Dismount and be recognized!" John replied, "You know me. I'm John."

I repeated my order, accented by the sound of my loading a round in my pistol's chamber. John and his driver quickly got out of the jeep. I told them to advance five paces, place their wallets on the ground, then go back to the jeep and place their fingers on its hood. They did as I ordered with John grumbling all the time. I took my time verifying who they were. I then told them they were verified and returned their wallets. The jeep driver was smiling all the time. He knew what had triggered my actions.

I was still angry. I told John, "If you ever pull a gun on me again I'll shoot you." Every time he came around again, he made lots of noise.

Visiting the gym one day I noticed on their bulletin board that a class in fencing, using French foils, was being offered. Growing up I enjoyed watching swashbuckling movies. I signed up for the fencing class. The difference between swords and foils are quite different. With swords, any part of the body is a target. Foils are like elongated ice picks. Only the chest cavity is the target. For sport, the tip of the foil has a small blunt tip. Combatants wear a padded vest and screen mask.

There are six basic moves in fencing and one must never be off-balance. To keep balance, the rear foot is kept at ninety degrees and the forward foot straight towards the opponent. Move only one foot at a time. The six basic moves are to deflect your opponent's blade to pass in front or back of your body, and then use his blade to try and score a hit on him, using the tip of my foil.

In my free time I'd go to the gym, use a string to tie my high school class ring to dangle from overhead at chest high, and practice the basic moves. I would then lunge the point of my foil for the hole in my ring. With my long arms and legs, I could cover a sizable distance towards an opponent. I became good and defeated easily all in my class. The class instructor challenged me. He saw that in my lunge I was slightly off-balance. When I made my lunge, he quickly did two back steps and then attacked me. He won each time.

The B-29 gunners would go to the skeet range to sharpen their gunnery skills. There usually weren't enough going for practice at one time. If I didn't have a flight scheduled, I'd volunteer to go with them to the skeet range. Twelve gauge shotguns and shells, along with boxes of clay pigeons, would be checked out. At the range, we all took turns launching clay pigeons from small metal sheds. There was a high and low shed. When a gunner yelled pull, a clay pigeon was launched. The gunner tried to hit it.

There are several shooting positions on the range. I was good on the clay pigeons launched from the low house —I called it my quail shot. In the other firing positions, the clay pigeon is traveling fast at various degrees from you, requiring fast action and allowing a sufficient lead. Gunners are supposed to face the range, not the house where the pigeon is launched. I was in the high house ready to launch a clay pigeon for a Major. I saw that he had his gun pointed at my high house. He yelled, "Pull!"

I yelled back, "No way, not with your gun pointed at me." When he pointed his gun away from me, I launched the pigeon at his call.

At the base bowling alley it was fun to watch young Filipina girls bowl. They would approach the foul line, let go their ball, walk back and sit down to watch their ball slowly rolling down the alley towards the pins. Many got strikes. I often wondered if the pin-sitter guy had something to do with the strikes.

Chapter 15

Our crew would go on short training flights to Subic Bay or Sangley Point, both U.S navy bases in the Philippines, to practice water landings and takeoffs. At lunch time we'd eat at the navy base. The navy had it made. They had fresh salads, great cheeseburgers and milk. In our Air Force chow halls we were served foods that were de-hydrated. Milk tasted horrible and scrambled eggs were watery. No salads were available. Before I went to the Philippines I wasn't a salad lover. When I returned stateside, I was. When we ate at the navy chow hall I'd get a cheeseburger, green salad and a quart of milk.

Practicing water landings and takeoffs, I would watch closely what my pilot and co-pilot did. When coming in, I noticed my pilot reduced power to the engines, dropped partial flaps and at the proper time flared out our plane to gently land on water. I became so accustomed to this that when we were approaching a water landing I would say to myself, "Now", when I felt the pilot should be flaring out.

Some of the B-29 pilots liked to go with us to get flying time on an amphibian. My pilot would let them try water landings. Many are the ones that in making a water landing, I would be silently saying to myself,

"Now! Now! Now!" to flare out before I felt we might become a submarine. We came up with a jacket patch that matched our thoughts.

On a training flight to Subic Bay with two SA-16s we were to try exchanging a passenger between the two planes, with engines running at idle. I was to be the first guinea-pig. A one-man raft was inflated and a one hundred foot length of rope was attached to it. I stripped to my shorts. My flight engineer, Raymond Pfaff, held onto the rope and placed the raft in the bay. When I stepped into the raft my pilot reversed the idling engines, trying to keep our plane in one spot. Reversing the engines caused me and the raft to be sucked towards the spinning prop. Ray yelled to the pilot, "Forward pitch!"

I was then "shot out" from our plane into the open bay. I began using my hands to paddle to the other plane. I don't know what made me look back at my plane, but, when I did I saw my tow rope coming taunt. I grabbed the sides of my raft and soon had water up to my armpits. Ray quickly took his knife and cut my tow rope, which allowed me to surface again. Cupping my hands I bailed out the water and paddled to the other SA-16.

My radio operator friend, Harry Maynard and his flight engineer Rose helped me inside. Harry's pilot, Captain Allen, told Harry to give the transfer a try. When Harry stepped in my raft, it collapsed. One moment Harry was above water, and then sank beneath. Suddenly Harry popped up again and stepped inside the plane, almost like walking on water. I asked what he was thinking about when he went under. He said, "Sharks!"

I got back into my raft and paddled to my plane. The next time we tried this exercise a six man raft was used. All went well. I rowed, with rope attached, to Harry's plane. A rope from his plane was attached to the other end of my six man raft. Harry and I got in the raft and were pulled back and forth between the two planes.

Flying from Clark Field to Subic Bay required we radio operators to change radio frequencies. Sometimes it was difficult to receive Subic Bay radio. One day Captain Allen couldn't locate his radio operator Harry. Spotting me he directed me to be his acting radio operator. Since Captain Allen was our amphibian unit commander, I couldn't refuse. When it came time to change radio frequencies, I got Subic Bay radio loud and clear. I notified Captain Allen and said I'd now clear with Clark Field radio. He ordered me to not do that; he wanted me to stay on the clear Subic Bay frequency. I did as I was ordered, and wrote all that was said in my radio log book.

When we landed back at Clark Field, we were met by a base colonel and my radio section chief. My section chief, Sam Stromer, asked to see my radio log book. He read it and said I was free to go. I learned that planes all over Luzon were out searching for us, due to not clearing with Clark Field radio. Captain Allen was giving a month of Officer of the Guard Duty for having me not clear radio frequencies. After this incident, I wasn't liked by him.

I was playing golf one day and saw a jeep headed my way. It had my pilot and his driver. He told me to give my clubs to the caddy and get in; that we had a top secret mission. Doing as instructed, I got in the jeep and we were off. On the way to my barracks to pick up my flight gear, I asked what the mission was. He repeated that it was top secret. I was let out at our plane, to checkout my radios. While I was checking my radios, a military truck pulled up and unloaded four hundred pounds of block ice, which my flight engineer strapped down in our passenger compartment.

After filing his flight plan at base operation, we were joined by the rest of the crew. Steve, my pilot, started our plane's engines and we taxied for takeoff. I again asked our mission and told it was top secret. I informed Steve that the minute we become airborne I'm required to give a departure message to ground radio; that it had to contain our destination or every plane of the island would be out looking for us.

Steve then told me our top secret mission. We are to deliver the four hundred pounds of ice to our Base General and the President of the Philippines, on a yacht off of Panay Island. Steve told me to not put that in my log, I was to say we're practicing water landings off Sangley Point at Manila.

Rhenue easily got us to the yacht. In trying to contact the radio operator on the yacht, I learned he didn't have the proper frequency for his radio. I had Steve turn on our plane's running light and used the key on his console so that I could send Morse code.

As we approached the yacht, I sent a message asking if we were okay to land. I received a partial reply as we zoomed by the yacht. I flashed a Q-signal of where I had copied to, and for him to continue from there on our next approach. He started over from the beginning. I was disgusted. When Steve asked what had been said, I told him the problem and that I received enough of the message to know we were clear to land.

The sea was smooth as glass. Steve made a beautiful landing and we taxied to within twenty yards of the yacht and dropped our sea anchor. Two Filipinos in an inflated raft rowed over and took our officers over to the yacht. They returned and shuttled the ice over. Our officers had a cocktail with those on the yacht. Our officers then returned to our plane, our sea anchor was taken in and we were quickly airborne. Steve made a flying pass of the yacht, wig-wagging our wing. We returned to Clark field. Next, we had a secret mission to Zamboang for a meeting for our passenger.

One of my radio operator friends was a black guy whose plane was a B-29. He would tell me how his plane was so much faster than my SA-16, an amphibian. I would come back reminding him that we were located on Luzon, an island, and that one day I'd have to pick him up from the "drink".

A navy PBM went down and all available planes were given areas to search for the downed PBM. Ours was a jungle area. The area had an early morning ground fog, requiring us to fly at just above tree top level to be able to see the jungle floor. My fight engineer, Ray Pfaff, stood by our plane's door, looking out the opened top half of the door. I had opened the small door over the inflatable six-man life raft we always carry, searching the jungle below, on my side.

The ground fog rose. We were flying up what turned out to be a canyon, heading straight for a tall mountain. Steve, my pilot, gave full throttle to our engines and made a steep climbing left turn. This incident got our full attention. If the fog hadn't lifted we would have hit that mountain in less than ten minutes. The PBM was later found. It had crashed into a mountain, killing all on board.

On the way back to Clark Field, I heard my black friend's call to our base. He said his plane had lost one engine, another was leaking oil badly and another was running rough. I used my radio telephone and chuckled. When I walked into our barracks I was confronted by my black friend. He said, "Dat's you. I knows dat's you."

I laughed and said, "Well we came close to having to pick you up." His search area had been over water. I lost track of him when we returned stateside. I hope life has been good for him. He was such a nice guy.

Our wing received word that a tropical cyclone was on a collision course for Clark Field. Our planes were sent to other landing fields not in the cyclone's path. I don't recall where the B-29s or C-119 was sent. Our four SA-16s were sent to Cebu, Island in the Philippines. We landed at their commercial airport. We spent the night at a hotel that overlooked, in the distance, shipping docks. I was fascinated with watching a cargo ship being loaded with copra.

Next morning we were cleared to return to Clark Field, the cyclone had changed course and missed Luzon. All four crews had breakfast in Cebu's air terminal. All windows in the building were opened to allow cool morning air inside.

After our meal all four crews went to their planes. The runway was short and the landing strip was gravel. This caused pilots to request their flight engineers to hook up JATO [Jet assisted take off] bottles, one on each side of our plane. A JATO burn-out time is between 12 to 15 seconds. When they're fired it feels like you've been kicked in the rear.

Being a short runway, my pilot cocked our plane at a forty-five angle to the runway. When our engines reached maximum RPM, he let go the brakes. Torque from our engines caused our plane to line-up with the runway. The swinging around of our plane caused us to begin sliding on the gravel runway. My pilot fired the JATO bottles and we were quickly airborne. The others did the same. I felt sorry for those people waiting in the terminal. All the smoke from our JATO takeoff went in those open windows.

Chapter 16

Our plane and Captain Allen's received a coat of black paint. My friend took a picture of my plane flying in formation for the base parade, before we left for Korea. We received orders assigning us to temporary duty at K-16 airbase outside of Seoul, Korea. Captain Allen's crew, with my fellow radio operator friend Harry Maynard, proceeded to K-16 about two weeks before us.

On our way to Korea, I think we refueled and spent the night at Itazuke Air Base. I just remember it was a wet and cutting cold evening, being so close to the sea. Several of us went into town to a bar. It was the first time I tasted Asahi beer, it had a good taste.

My two friends that were with me decided to look around Itazuke. The bar had a nice barrel stove and was warm. I told them I was staying at the bar and keep warm. They left. Thinking they would return I stayed at the bar and played cards with the hostesses. They cheated outrageously. About midnight I went to the base.

Next morning, we took off early for K-16. We arrived at K-16 in late January or early February in 1953. Korea had experienced the coldest winter in many years. We were housed in tents with our planes parked close by. Our tent had wood floors, wood half walls and wood front door, with canvas for a top. Our tent housed four —two radio operators and two flight engineers. Ground maintenance personnel were housed in tents nearby. Honcho, our houseboy, kept our tent quarters repaired and clean. One day he brought his tiny son with him. We bought the boy a sack of candy. He was such a cute little guy.

In the middle of our tent was a barrel oil heater. Near the front door was a rack with four holes to place our steel helmet in. Our steel helmets were for air raid protection, but, we also used them to give ourselves a "sponge bath", and shave in. We'd heat the water on our barrel heater.

We had a wooden outdoor toilet for body waste and a small square wooden tube in the ground for a urinal. I would drive around to the far side of the base to use base operation's urinal before I'd use ours. Ours was out in the open, close to where Korean women did laundry—no privacy. The urinal at base operations concealed one from the knees up to the shoulder.

When our crew arrived, Harry told me that one night he awoke to see someone's arm reaching inside their tent to unlock the door. Harry woke his flight engineer and told what he saw. Harry took the first watch to protect their tent and his flight engineer, Rose, was to take the second. Rose went to sleep. Harry and Rose woke to find their cameras stolen. From then on, Rose slept with a loaded .45 pistol under his pillow. Our moving in with Harry and Rose made me a little leery. I didn't want to get shot, accidentally.

We were not that far from the front. At night we could see the flashes of big guns to the north. It looked like an electrical storm back home. If we went off base to the small town nearby, we were to carry small arms. In my case, it was a .45 automatic in a shoulder holster. Every shop in town had a sign on its door, "Remove clip from weapon."

When I thought about it I couldn't but think about the old 1930s gangsters, when I zipped down my jacket and pulled my .45 out to remove the clip, and then re-holster it. I could understand being armed. We were so close to the front and infiltrators could be present.

On my crews' missions behind enemy lines, I carefully monitored radio transmissions. On one of our flights we took a man to deserted beach area in North Korea one night. We landed at sea, taxied to the beach, dropped our landing gear and taxied up on the beach. We let him out, taxied back into the sea, raised our gear and left.

On one flight I heard an experienced pilot talk to his wing man. All fighter-planes went by snake names. The experienced pilot said, "Cobra 2 this is Cobra 1, bandit at 10:00 o'clock high." His wing man replied, "Cobra 1 this is Cobra 2. Sir, that's one of ours." There was a slight poise, then, "Cobra 2. Son, that's not one of ours." It became quiet.

On another flight I heard a pilot with a heavy British accent radio his flight, saying, "Heads up chaps! Twelve bandit's at 2 o'clock high. Would four of you take care of that?" Four against twelve! A few days later I spotted a British pilot at our base operations and asked about four going after twelve. He said, "Oh yes old boy, that's the only way to fight. With odds like those anything crossing in front of your guns must be an enemy and you shoot it down."

There's also the story of an Aussie pilot in a P-51 that was attacked by five MIG-15s. The MIG-15 pilots must have figured the Aussie would turn and run. They swooped down like five fingers in a row. Instead of the Aussie running, he gave his P-51 all the power it had, and headed straight at the approaching MIG-15s. Lining up on the MIG-15s, the Aussie began firing his plane's machineguns. Using his rudder pedal, he brought his guns to bear on the MIG-15s, shooting down four and wounding the fifth. When asked why he didn't finish off the wounded fifth MIG-15, he said, "He still had enough power to outrun me back across the Yalu River."

K-16 was a departure base for those going on R & R [Rest & Recuperation] leaves to Japan. If I wasn't scheduled for a flight I would drive to base operations, get a cup of coffee and a dozen donuts and listen to those going on R & R. On one occasion an army guy, seeing my wings, came over and said he'd like to shake my hand. I was surprised and asked why.

He told me that his unit was about to be overhand by a strong Chinese force. He said as fast as he and other machine-gunners could mow down the advancing line, others behind grabbed their dead comrade's rifle and keep coming.

He said that his unit had called for an air strike. He was cussing the air force for not helping them. Suddenly he heard a loud swoosh. He thought it was the Chinese using a big gun, but saw it was an American Saber Jet fighter plane.

The jet dropped napalm on the advancing Chinese. He looked back in the direction the jet had come from and saw another coming. It was so low he thought it was going to hit his trench and he dropped to the ground.

The jet pilot slightly humped his plane over the ridge and dropped his napalm. It destroyed the Chinese unit. He claimed that is why he wanted to shake my hand. The air force had saved him, and I'm air force. He was a nice guy to talk to.

I heard a marine talking about being surrounded at Chosen Reservoir. He said his Major gave an order to do an about face. Some guy in his unit yelled, "Sir, are we retreating?"

The Major yelled back, "Retreat hell! We're advancing in the opposite direction." I felt that's a statement that should be recorded in our history books, alongside John Paul Jones in the Revolutionary War.

On a flight north up the east coast of Korea, we spotted a flight of MIG-15s heading south. My pilot Steve dropped our plane down into a cloud bank, to hide. When he figured the MIGs were gone we popped up above the clouds, and finished our mission.

On another mission we were headed south back to base, following the east coast of Korea. A Navy cruiser spotted us coming and steamed out to intercept us. As the cruiser turned to get ready to give us a broadside with their guns, Steve wig-wagged our wings so the navy guys could see our plane insignias. They let us pass.

We were lucky to have never been shot at while in the air. I asked about possibly having to bailout sometime. Steve said that he planned to ride our plane down, if there wasn't an engine fire getting close to our fuel tanks. I said, "I'm with you."

He learned that I was an Eagle Scout and told me, "If we're shot down, I'm going with you." He let me know he knew about the scout training program.

From previous water landings in the Philippines and in Korea, our props needed replacing. Our crew was sent to Johnson Air Base, outside Tokyo. The crew was short on cash. My pilot Steve vouched for us and got us some advance on our pay. Those of us on flying duty receive extra pay for hazardous duty. We were very grateful to Steve for that help. It meant we would have enough money to shop and sightsee in Tokyo.

Several of us went to the Ginza Mart. In 1953 the mart was rows upon rows of small stalls with Japanese selling items. I remember a silk smoking/lounging jacket caught my eye. As I was studying the jacket a Japanese sales man asked if I liked the jacket. I said I did. He mentioned a price in American dollars. I think it was twelve dollars. I said, "For that? I wouldn't give over six dollars!" He said, "Sold!" I smiled and told him I'd really stepped into that one. He smiled and said, "Here's a lighter to go with it."

Two of my friends and I went to the mote surrounding the Emperor's palace in Tokyo. We weren't allowed to cross the entry bridge and see the Emperor's palace. A Japanese guy used our cameras to take a picture of the three of us standing near the mote. I have color slides of my many adventures in the Far East, Korea and Japan. I have many good memories to reflect on.

We were having difficulty getting props for our plane. To pass the time my flight engineer, Ray Pfaff, and I decided to see what it was like for Japanese citizens in one of their small hotels. We hired an interpreter. We explained our idea to him. He had a cab driver take us to a small hotel. At the hotel he explained to the owner our desire. We were told to remove our shoes and leave them by the entrance. My thoughts were that we'd probably not see our shoes again.

The hotel owner led us to a small room. It had a low table about a foot high. Our interpreter let us know a meal was being served. We sat on a soft pillows. The sliding door to the room opened and a Japanese lady in a kimono bowed to those in the room and brought in our meal. After placing the food on the table she returned to the door and bowed again, then shut the door.

After the meal we were shown our room. There were two pallets laid out on the floor. We were told by our interpreter that we were to get undressed and put on the supplied kimono, then follow the lady to a room for a bath. When we entered the room for a bath, we were told to use a small wooden pail, wood fiber type sponge and soap to wash our self, and then fill the tub to rinse off the soap before getting into the large hot tub. The hotel owner was already soaking in the hot tub.

The hotel owner left and two ladies came in to give us a bath. Both Ray and I made it clear we'd bathe ourselves. The ladies giggled like young school girls at our modesty. Ray had finished his bath first and went over to test the water in the hot tub. He then said he'd pass the hot tub. I chided him for his not going Japanese, and I stepped onto the tub's first step. I jumped back out. My skin from my knees down was a bright red, the water being so hot.

After the bath we put back on our kimonos and went to our room. We were told a lady would be sleeping just outside our room's door in case we needed any beverages or food during the night. Next morning we dressed in our uniform again. When we opened our door, we found our shoes. They had been shinned. We let our host know our thanks and caught a taxi back to the base. It was a great experience.

At Johnson Air Base we were housed in a transit barracks. Before going for a shower, I carefully hide my Zeiss Contesa camera. When I came back from my shower my camera was gone. Someone had watched me hide my camera and then stole it. It made me mad. I went up and down the barracks using language I don't normally use, hoping the guilty individual would give himself away. I then went to the Air Police and turned in my complaint. I never saw that camera again, eventually buying another.

Our unit commander, Captain Allen, thought we were goofing off in Japan and not really trying to get new props. He sent Major Knight to Johnson Air Base as aircraft commander of our plane, bumping my pilot, Steve, to co-pilot position. That didn't set well with our crew. We really liked Steve, and it showed. I once overheard Major Knight say, "Steve you have the most loyal crew I've ever seen." Major Knight put pressure on maintenance; we got our new props and flew back to K-16 in Korea.

One of our first missions upon return was to fly a person, probably CIA, to Yo Do Island. This island is located in the northern part of Korea, near the border with China. The island was controlled by our marines and navy. We landed on the far side of the island and tied up to a floating buoy. Our passenger was picked up by a power boat from a navy destroyer.

The sea was rough. Swells were between six and eight feet high. Steve remained in his co-pilot's seat. I stretched out on one of the cot bunks in our plane. Major Knight climbed up on our plane's wing to get some weak sunlight.

A loud explosion hit the island on our side. An enemy shore battery was trying to hit us. I could hear Major Knight's running footsteps on top our plane. He quickly entered. Ray used his knife to cut us loose from the buoy. I went to my seat by the radios. Steve started our engines while the Major was getting seated. Major Knight then began taxiing our plane, making it a difficult target. When he radioed the destroyer for our passenger, he was told to leave our passenger and leave the area.

Looking at the large sea swells the Major told Steve he was afraid he couldn't get us airborne. Steve said, "Give me the controls."

Steve applied full power to our engines. We gained speed by staying in a trough between swells. Steve then got our plane upon the crest of the swells. Two bounces and we were airborne. Climbing and circling we saw two navy destroyers go around the island and fire their big guns in a broadside at the enemy shore battery. The enemy gun never fired again.

One night I got permission to go on a leaflet dropping mission in a C-47. After takeoff I went forward to chat with that plane's radio operator. When he learned I had asked to go along on the mission he said, "Are you crazy? Anti-aircraft guns are controlled by radar in the area we're to make our drop." I helped the crew shove our leaflets over the drop zone. We were not shot at. I kept one of the leaflets as a souvenir.

While in Korea I received a threaten letter from the IRS. They hadn't received my tax return and they threatened to haul me into court in Denver. I wrote them that I was flying combat missions in Korea, so haul away. Their letter had made me very angry. I never heard from them again. They must have finally received my tax form sent from the Philippines.

Captain Allen's crew, with my fellow operator friend Harry Maynard, returned to the Philippines. My friend Truman and his crew joined us at K-16. Truman would sit for quite a lengthy time in the outhouse working on cross puzzles.

At night a Korean pilot in an old WWI bi-wing plane would fly over our base or that at K14, where our fighter planes were based. He would drop hand-grenades. One blew an outhouse apart. We'd tease Truman that one night "Bed-check Charlie" was going to get him, staying in the outhouse so long.

Koreans would occasionally come on base to empty the outhouses of its body waste. They carried what we called "Honey" buckets. They would use the waste from outhouses to fertilize their cropland. Truman's time in our outhouse earned him the nick-name bucket; the "honey buckets" might get him.

Shortly after Truman's crew arrived, my crew was ordered back to the Philippines. By this time we had flown ten missions behind lines, rewarded the Air Metal, and authorized to wear the Korean War ribbon with one battle star.

Our air crew with all our gear, and our ground crew with all their tools and equipment were loaded on to the Air Force's largest cargo plane at that time—the C-124 globemaster. The C-124 pilot, knowing there were pilots onboard, left his intercom open so the pilots onboard could listen, as he went through his pre-flight check-off list.

That completed, he taxied to our assigned runway and was cleared by tower for takeoff. When he had his engines at full RPM he let off the brakes. When we went past a third of the runway I thought we were sure moving slow. Then came the tower, halfway down the runway and we were still moving slowly. I saw ahead our tents which I knew were two-thirds down the runway. The C-124 pilot had forgotten to turn off the plane's intercom system. We heard him say, "My God! I've misjudged our weight."

All of us in the belly of this goliath went pale. The C-124 pilot caused the plane to bounce and snapped up the plane's landing gears. The C-124 barely cleared the six-foot high base fence. Those of us who had flown out of K-16 knew that ahead was two tall twin smokestacks. We wondered how the C-124 pilot planned to clear them. At the last moment the C-124 pilot did a steep left bank as we zipped between the smoke stacks.

At altitude the pilot realized he was so overloaded he would need to make a refueling stop at Okinawa. His flight engineer told us that only one at a time could get up to use the plane's toilet. The only good bit of information he gave was the bailout procedure. He pointed to a section of the floor between the fuse-lodge's wing areas. He said that in case of bailout, the floor section in that area would be jettisoned; that we would then run and grab the fire pole. When we slid clear of the plane we were to open our parachutes. I liked the idea of sliding down a fireman's pole, with my eyes closed, then pulling my chute's D-ring, when my face was hit by a blast of air. The plane was so heavily loaded that when the pilot eased back his throttles, we descended like an elevator going down. Back at Clark Field, I told my pilot Steve that never again would I ride on a C-124.

Chapter 17

Back at Clark field, with the Korean War winding down, I had a lot of free time. My crew would still keep our skills up by practicing water landings, and getting our flight time in. To get our extra flight pay, we had to fly a certain number of hours each month.

On our last "training flight" to Hong Kong we would land in Hong Kong harbor and taxi-up a ramp to our assigned parking area. These flights were made before Christmas, and we usually had a colonel or two along. They would buy Christmas items for their wife or kids. One bought a new Jaguar for his wife, having it delivered stateside.

My flight engineer bought a beautiful blue star sapphire for $300 and was offered $600 by a Filipino in our base PX. He didn't sell it. I bought a baby-blue cashmere sport coat and a grey-flannel suit, all made in 24 hours. My pilot bought a Rolex oyster-perpetual wrist watch.

We stayed at a top-notch hotel on Kawloon. I went on a rickshaw ride to the shopping district and Mohan's tailors for my clothes. A Chinese girl in a typical Chinese dress, form fitting with high neck and floor length dress slit up to the knee on each side, waited on me. I expected her to talk in a Chinese sing-song brogue. I was surprised when she spoke in perfect British English.

At first I was hesitant about having my clothes tailored there, until they took me into their shipping room and I noticed a box addressed to General Douglas MacArthur. From American magazines I would choose a design I liked and then the type of material. The tailor would take my measurements and tell me to return in four hours for my first fitting. The final fitting would be at nine in the morning, and then pick up at noon.

Killing time until my first fitting, Ray Pfaff and me took a taxi to a nice restaurant. The food was good and the orchestra sounded like Mantovani, a favorite orchestra of mine. I loved the sound of all the string instruments. After dinner Ray and I went to see a movie.

That was a strange experience. When we bought our ticket, we were directed to the second floor of the theater. Since the move was being shown, we were told we'd have to wait for the next showing, and that we could wait in the cocktail lounge area. When we finally got in to see the movie the first thing to appear on the screen was Queen Elizabeth, all stood for the playing of the British National Anthem.

On take-off the next morning, we were told to use the regular commercial runway. When we went to engine run-up area we learned our engines would surge, run away, at the normal 2,100 RPM. If Ray and I didn't get back to Clark field in the Philippines we'd miss our boat back to California. Ray found that our plane's engines would hold at a 1,900 RPM. The decision was made to takeoff.

On takeoff we had to cross two major Hong Kong streets. When the tower cleared us for takeoff, railroad type crossing arms came down to block off cars. As we whizzed past, I wondered if they ever had a car trying to beat the descending cross-arms?

Dark caught us at the flight point of no-return. I was giving my usual radio message when two red lights on our plane's instrument came on. I told my radio contact to standby; that we might be in trouble. He asked if we wanted "Dumbo", a search and rescue amphibian plane. I told him no.

From my seat behind the co-pilot's seat, I had learned the instruments and their location. In the dark, I thought the red lights were the oil indicator lights, meaning a loss of oil. It turned out to be the switch over light for our fuel tanks, located under the oil lights.

Earlier in my stay at Clark Field, through the USO, I took a bus tour to Manila. The tour visited the old walled city of Manila, now referred to as Intramuros. It was built by Spain in the 16th century. The fort that protected the walled city is called Fort Santiago, when Spain occupied the Philippines.

Fort Santiago had a sorted history. The fort was located where Manila Bay and Pasig River met. It was quite a fort in its day. Its walls were eight feet thick and twenty feet high. The fort had dungeons. Cells in the lowest dungeons would fill with water at high tide. Prisoners in those cells would drown. Next day their bodies would be removed and cremated. At the time of my visit, underground passageways and cells were still being found. We were not allowed to see the dungeons. We were told that there was one room where ashes of the deceased were almost full to the ceiling.

The walled city portion, about 160 acres, had several Catholic Church ruins. I was told twelve. They are: Manila Cathedral, San Agustin Church, San Nicolas de Tolentino Church, San Francisco church, Third Venerable

Order Church, Santo Domingo Church, Lourdes Church and San Ignacio church. Our tour guide let us visit several of the ruins and take pictures. Each church ruin had a descriptive marker that gave its name and how it was destroyed. Most were destroyed by an earthquake in June 1863, some by fire, leaving only standing stone walls. I took pictures of all the ruins.

We were then bused to a Catholic Church that had an organ made of bamboo, and it still played. A priest at that church demonstrated how well it still played after about ninety years.

From here we were bused to the White House of the Philippines— Malacanang Palace. We were allowed to visit the lower portion. The upper portion was the home of the President and his family.

One of the rooms held a long table with three massive crystal chandeliers. At each end of that room were floor to ceiling length mirrors. The room had cherry-wood paneling. The lit chandeliers were so beautiful that I wanted a picture. The only way I could get a picture with all three chandeliers was to use the mirror on one wall and take a picture of the reflection. I couldn't use my camera's flash, it would show up in the picture. I set my lens opening as wide as it would go, put my back to a wall so that I could steady my camera and snapped a time delay picture. It came out beautifully, and it was on color film. I still have that color slide.

I then took a picture of the President's patio and the wharf where he docks the presidential yacht on an off-shoot of the Pasig River.

Our tour then went to the campus of the University of the Philippines. The campus grounds are huge. On our way back to Manila, we stopped to watch cadets of the Philippine West Point on parade. It was very colorful.

Perhaps I should touch on Philippine history, at this point. I have great respect for the people. They are talented, usually easy going and friendly. Originally they were Muslims. Then the Spanish conquered the Philippines in the early 16th century, converting a majority to the Catholic faith. Spanish rule was harsh. Spain's reported atrocities in Cuba and the Philippines angered Americans. The mysterious sinking of the American battleship Maine in Havana Harbor, Cuba triggered the Spanish-American war in 1898.

Filipinos fought alongside of Americans in the Philippines, thinking they would become an independent nation. With the defeat of Spain, America took over the Philippines as an American possession. This led to the Philippine-American war in 1901.

Filipino freedom fighters from the village of Balangiga ambushed Company C of the 9th Infantry Regiment on Samar Island in the Philippines, killing 44 and wounding 22, of the unit. Some of these American soldiers had fought in the Boxer Rebellion in China. They were seasoned fighters caught off-guard.

In reprisal, General Jacob Smith ordered that any Filipino male on Samar over ten was to be shot. General Smith was forced to retire. American infantry took down the Balangiga church bells, which had triggered the ambush, as war booty. Two of these bells are presently displayed at Warren Air Force Base, Cheyenne, Wyoming.

The Philippine-American war ended in 1902. It ended the Philippine struggle for independence. The Catholic Church was no longer allowed to be a state religion, as the United States allowed freedom of religion, and English became the primary language. In 1935 the United States allowed limited self-government.

When the Japanese conquered the Philippines, Filipino and American forces fought them, side-by-side, as they did in the Spanish-American War. In 1946 the Philippines were granted their independence. To the Filipino, the bells of Balangiga are their freedom bells, symbolizing their struggle for freedom. It is their liberty bell. Surly American could send back one of the Balangiga bells to the Philippines, leaving the other at Warren Air Force Base. It would establish strong diplomatic ties with the Philippines.

On another USO furnished trip, I went to Baguio in the mountains of the Philippines. To get to Baguio our bus had to go up a steep mountain with many switchbacks. Drop off on the side of the road were awesome. Whether going up that road or down that road I couldn't but help wonder about possible mechanical or brake failure. If either happened and the driver loses control, it was about a two thousand foot drop.

We were housed at Camp John Hay. Due to elevation the night air is cold. Each small barrack had a wood-burning fireplace, and was furnished with wood logs. The camp had lots of pine trees and a nice golf course. I loved to play that course. It made me concentrate on the game. If you had a bad tee-off you could hear your golf ball hitting tree after tree.

On one tee one needed to hit on the sand "green" in one stroke. If I undershot the green my ball would go into a stone drainage ditch. If I overshot the green my ball would land in a forest of pine trees. There was an embankment on the far side of the green that was about three feet high. I would play to either land on the green or hit the bank and bounce back onto the green.

Another of the greens one hopes to hit the green setting on top of a knoll. It's a seven-iron shot. Nothing can be more frustrating than to hit your ball and watch as it rolls back down to you.

On another green you're hitting up a steep hill. Two tiers were made at different levels to keep your ball from rolling back down. It was long yardage uphill, with the green at the top. The object was to get at least to the first tier and from there to the top. Howard Correll and I were playing that tee-off one day. There were two players ahead of us. They were on the second tier. Howard told me to go ahead and tee off, that I couldn't possible hit a golf ball that far, but I did. I had used a two wood with a high tee. We both had to quickly yell "Fore!"

Another green was exciting. The tee-off was on a hill and the green far down below. You hit your ball and watch it go out into space before it begins to drop. To see it hit the green, slashing some sand, is exhilarating.

On the 18th tee, one has to drive over two roads below and then uphill to the green. One day I went out on the course early, due to a tournament being held there later in the day. As usual I had breakfast, a quart of milk and listened to my favorite song, Malaguena. I had found that with this routine I'd shoot a better score.

On the 18th tee this day I managed to drive over the two roads. Walking to where my golf ball lay, I saw a large crowd forming near the green. I used a five iron and laid into it. I heard an audible sound from the on-lookers. When I reached my ball it was on the green, about two feet from the cup. I thought, "Oh Lord, don't let me miss this one"—I'm not a great golfer. I made it for an eagle. With the watchers, I grabbed my golf ball and disappeared. They probably thought I was with the tournament.

The town outside Camp John Hay Base is Baguio. It's a clean a nice looking town. Vendors along the street sold flowers and bananas. Small shops along the way sold many items. Baguio is also the summer capital of the Philippine President. I met Isabel Lim in Baguio. She was a nice young lady and easy to talk to. Her family owned a small bar in town. Isabel was about five feet tall and very pleasant to have as a golfing partner at Camp John Hay. If it was a par four hole, I stopped counting her strokes when they reached twenty.

Isabel told me how it was with the Japanese occupation. It was horrible. She told me that a husband in Baguio was forced to watch his wife and daughter being multiple raped, and then killed. Isabel took me to see some of the ruins from WWII, and a Japanese tank that was now rusty. She and I would sit by a small lake and talk. We were good friends; I considered her my little sister.

One day while Howard Correll, a friend and I were in town, and in a taxi headed for the base, we spotted three young girls about our age. We thought they might be the daughters of some master sergeant, or possibly officer's daughters. Like young fools we leaned out the window and whistled at them.

There was a dance that night at the USO Mile High club, on base. We three decided to go to the club early and shoot a game of pool. When we entered the club, the hostess asked if we'd like to meet some girls. That's a silly question to ask young GIs. We said sure. When we were introduced to the girls, they were the ones we had whistled at in town, and they recognized us.

I danced mainly with Mari Escat. She was the daughter of a wealthy Spanish family in Manila. The other two girls were daughters of a wealthy oilman in Venezuela. The three girls attended UCLA in southern California. I and a navy ensign competed for dances with Mari. It was a pleasant evening.

One night at a bar in Baguio I met a fellow American. We struck up a conversation. I learned he worked for Halliburton and they were building a dam in Baguio. In the conversation I learned they hauled the dam's turbines up the twisting road I'd been on. I asked what the turbines weighted. He told me forty tons. I said, "Up that road!" He smiled and replied that they had trucks with gears so low you'd almost need to drive a stake by the wheels to be sure they were still moving.

On the way back to Clark Field the bus driver would put the bus in compound in its decent on that road, to keep the brakes from overheating.

Chapter 18

The day arrived when I received orders to pack my gear, we were being sent back stateside. It was in the spring of 1954. The Korean War had come to an end; a truce had been signed. My friends, Bill Avanzini and Truman Godwin, rode with me on the bus to Manila, to board USS Morton. Having flown to the Philippines, I was apprehensive about going back by ship.

Arriving in Manila where USS Morton was docked, I got to look at the ship. To me it seemed huge. I estimated the main deck to be at least three stories higher than dock level. I was told the line I was to get into. My two good friends, Bill Avanzini and Truman Godwin were in another line. They had the rank of Staff Sergeant and me the rank of Sergeant.

The line I was in began to move. I shouldered my duffle bag and followed my group to our bunks in the forward hole of the ship. Bunks were in banks of four. My bunk was second up from the floor. Spacing between bunks was slightly large enough that if I lay on my side my shoulders was a few inches from the bunk above me.

Our ship got underway. I was told that I had KP [Kitchen Police] duty. It would be my duty to use a brush to clear any uneaten food from metal trays and run the trays through the clipper [a commercial dishwasher].

Each morning I would put on my fatigue coveralls and go to my assigned KP station to join our clipper room crew. We'd have our meal and then go to our assigned tasks. When meals were over and our work area cleaned, we would go topside and stretch out on hatches. The warm sun and cool ocean breezes felt good.

Before reaching Guam, our ship hit the tail-end of a tropical storm. I was awakened by the up and down thrusts of the ship. On the up thrust I would be thrown upward and hit the bunk above. On down trusts, I would be thrown downward and hit my bed hard. All this motion was making me seasick, but, I still had my KP assignment.

The hole where I slept had two flights of stairs to climb to get to the main deck. Between the stench and slime of others who had thrown up on the stairs and railings, I managed to make the main deck and the ship's rail before I emptied my stomach.

I looked at the ocean. I thought our ship was huge, but ocean waves looked like tall mountains, in comparison. We were like a tiny cork tossed to and fro. Seeing all that motion caused another upheaval. I made my way to the galley, unable to eat but a few bites, then to the clipper room. Between having to clean unsavory metal trays and a large empty aluminum pitcher, which I had used while cleaning trays, I finished my job and went topside. I would lay down on my back inside of an open door well. Rain squalls brought cold fresh air to my position. By closing my eyes so that I couldn't see motion, and the cold air, I made it to my next KP duty.

I think we were in the tropical storm a couple of days. At first I thought I was going to die from being so seasick. By the second day I didn't care if I did. Leaving the storm behind, the rest of the trip to Guam wasn't all that bad. The ocean now had gentle swells; the breeze was cool and the sun warm. I would stretch out on the ship's hatch. I would enjoy this between my KP shifts.

When we docked at Guam, Bill, Truman and I got off ship to see a bit of Guam, while our ship was transferring cargo. Waiting for a stoplight to change, we noticed we still had the "ship roll." Although we were standing on solid ground, our body would sway as though we were still onboard the ship. We laughed because neither of us could stop the motion. We now understood what the navy meant when they spoke of still having "sea legs."

Back onboard the ship, our duties continued all the way to Hawaii. Pulling into Oahu harbor was a beautiful sight. The water was a blue-green and the mountains a lush green color. Hawaiian guys in outrigger canoes paddled out to meet or ship. We'd hold up a coin and then toss it overboard. A Hawaiian would dive and retrieve it, holding it up so we could see.

While cargo was being transferred and new navy recruits came on board, my two friends and I went ashore. We went to a bar next to where our ship was docked. The waitress asked my friends in English what they would like to drink; then asked me in what I thought was Spanish. When she saw the surprise on my face, she asked, "Aren't you Portuguese?" I replied, "Heavens no, I'm American!" She apologized and said, "You're so dark and have blue eyes. I thought you were Portuguese." I let her know the tan came from playing so much golf in the Philippines.

Going back onboard the ship, we enjoyed listening to the Hawaiian recruits play their ukulele, sing and dance to Hawaiian music, entertaining us aboard ship and their friends on the dock. When our ship began pulling away from the dock, the Hawaiians played "Aloha." Hawaiian music is so soothing and beautiful. Their dancers are so graceful. I've always loved their music.

With the new navy recruits onboard, I was informed that I no longer had KP duty. What a relief. Upon getting this good news, I took the fatigues I had been wearing and tossed them overboard. From roughly two weeks at sea, no way to wash them and the tropical storm, they weren't worth trying to salvage.

The two weeks between Hawaii and San Francisco were pleasant. Wearing clean clothes and lounging on deck on one of the hatches, soaking in cool ocean breezes while being warmed by the sun, was a great relief. I finished reading the book "Magnificent Obsession" by Lloyd C. Douglas, a great story and idea.

When the Golden Gate Bridge appeared on the horizon, those onboard our ship began preparing to disembark. Our ship's main deck was flooded by those of us that could hardly wait to get back on American soil again. To always remember this event I took color photos of shipboard activity and our passage under the famous bridge.

On shore, each of us were given our new base assignments, traveling expenses, given two weeks furlough and our pay for the month it took getting to San Francisco. I had wanted to be stationed at Tinker Field in Oklahoma City. To try and outguess the Air Force, I had applied for Warner-Robins Air Base in Georgia, March Field in California and

Mountain Home in Idaho. So, where was I sent? I was sent to Dow AFB in Bangor, Maine. I think it was the farthest place from San Francisco.

I decided to make it a rewarding trip. I flew commercial flight from San Francisco to Los Angeles to visit my Uncle Bill Ellison and his wife Beverley, and my two young cousins, Bruce and Lark. Bruce was about eight and Lark six. My dark tan was a shock to them. My uncle said I was black. My uncle took a picture of me with Bruce and Lark by the beautiful fountain in Malaga Cove.

After a couple of days, I took a commercial flight to Tucson to visit with my college friend, Luanne Mohler. She was a teacher there. I had a two hour layover before going to Oklahoma City. Coming from the Philippines where girls had brown skin, dark eyes and hair, Luanne was a great vision. She was a 5'2", blonde, blue eyes and wore a light blue wool dress. She was a vision of loveliness. Time passed quickly. I owe that lady a lot. She made life on campus pleasant. I hope life has treated her well. She's such a nice person. Saying goodbye to Luanne, I was off to Oklahoma City.

My mother and one of her girlfriends met me in Oklahoma City. My mother brought her friend along because she felt she couldn't drive well enough in a large city. My mother had traded off my Nash Club Coupe for a Nash sedan. That didn't please me. I told my mother that I'd drive the car home, instead of the lady.

It was nighttime. I was tired and became sleepy. The little white spaced center lines would blur. I got behind an eighteen wheeler and was concentrating on its running lights. Somewhere I had passed the truck and didn't remember doing it. That's when I pulled over and let my mother's friend drive.

I traded off my Nash sedan and bought a two year old light blue Pontiac convertible. My aunt Lettye said she wanted me to meet a nice girl who worked in Durnil's with her. I met Jane and began dating her. I took her to a military ball at my old Junior College, Connors State College in Warner, Oklahoma. Several told me that we made a cute couple.

We went on dates about every night while I was home on leave. I became very familiar with 1208 Walnut Street, in Muskogee, Oklahoma. Jane's father, Lou Boyer, was foreman at Brockway Glass Company. He was a nice guy and I enjoyed talking to him, or to go bowling with him. He was a good bowler.

Jane's mother, Gen, was a controlling type of person. She could be pleasant, but, not one to cross. Gen and I got along well. Jane said her mother told her what to wear and what hairstyle was best for her. Jane's father would tell me how Gen would give him just enough money to bowl three games and buy one beer. He would make bets with his bowling partners, to win additional beers. Years later I would learn that Gen's father had been a heavy drinker, thus her restrictions on Lou.

One time when I visited Jane's home, Lou, her father offered me a bowl of homemade chili. He was scolded for that. I thought it was great. I enjoy making that chili even today. It's good but not spicy. Jane's mother used to have a restaurant near Brockway Glass Company in Muskogee, where she served that chili.

When we went on a date, I would ask Jane where she's like to go. She would say, "Wherever you like." This becomes rather frustrating at times. The one time Jane became really angry was when I took her home early. I was really tired that night and had run out of things to do or see. I decided to go home and go to bed early. Next night she let me know that she had been angry. By the time I was to go to my new base in Bangor, we had begun talking about marriage. We decided we'd continue dating others while also considering our relationship; that we'd write letters to each other.

Chapter 19

When I arrived at Dow AFB in Bangor, Maine, I was surprised to learn that my job would be in tech supply, in the aircraft maintenance hangar. Why they would send me, an airborne radio operator, to such a job is beyond me. I still carried my airborne rating and was sent out each month, on various airborne rides, to get my flight time in, so that I could continue receiving my flight pay.

This didn't go well with Master Sergeant Allred, head of aircraft maintenance in the hanger. Even more strange, my boss in tech supply was a civilian named Bill Cody. Bill Cody was a nice guy to work with. After I got to know him better, I called him Wild Bill.

I learned how to find all the parts we had for the shop. Bill would go out our tech supply door and work on something for an airplane he owned. Our tech supply really didn't need two people to run it. The first thing I did ever morning was to neatly organize tech supply and sweep. I would then sit and prop my feet up on the desk, and pull out a pocket book to read.

If a mechanic came to our window, needing a part, I'd get it for him. If I didn't have the part, I'd tell Bill and he would order it. I learned to forge his signature when small parts arrived, so I wouldn't have to take him away from work on his airplane. One day four new engines arrived. Their worth was over a million dollars. I called Bill in to sign for them. He looked over the invoice, handed them back to me and said, "Here, sign these for me. You sign my name as well as I do."

One day while I was relaxing and reading, Master Sergeant Allred came to my checkout window, saw me with my feet propped up on the desk, reading. He angrily said, "If you don't have anything better to do, get a weed-hook and cut grass behind the hanger." I did as he said. I figured he'd be looking out his office window to be sure I did as was ordered.

On my way to a spot outside his widow, I came across some wild strawberries. I picked and ate a few, then went outside Allred's window. I cut away some grass, leaving a small tuff of grass in the middle. I then made like the weed-hook was a golf driver, sized up the tuff of grass and whacked it, yelling, "Fore!" Allred quickly appeared and ordered me back into tech supply, where I picked up where I'd left off in my book.

Since it was still early spring in Maine, I would wear my flight jacket to work, and my car heater on high. I was still cold. The mechanics only wore their work fatigues. They would tease me about being so cold all the time. I'd fire back that they'd be like me if they had spent two years in a tropical Philippines.

In my barracks I made two good friends, Tony and Frank. Tony was an Italian from Queen's burrow in New York. We became such good friends that one day, while he was ahead of me; I called out, and said "Hey wop wait up!" He turned around, ready to fight. I had a big smile on my face. He knew I just teasing. He smiled back and used an expression sometimes used by blacks, saying, "What do you want Honky?" We both had a good laugh.

On a long weekend he agreed to buy the gas if I'd drive us to his home in Queens. He promised a good Italian home-made spaghetti dinner. I didn't need much coaxing, he was always raving about his mother's spaghetti, and I love spaghetti. While in New York I went to a photographer and had a picture portrait done of me in a WWII flight jacket and scarf.

By switching off driving, we made the trip in good time. I met his mother and sister. They were really nice and friendly. His mother couldn't speak English. She brought out the best spaghetti I had ever tasted—I had two big helpings. I then learned it was just the first course of a seven course meal.

I let it be known that I was too full to eat anything else. Tony's mother had a hurt expression on her face. I told Tony to tell his mother that her spaghetti was so good that I had over eaten. That brought a smile to her face. I was glad I hadn't hurt her feelings. Tony's sister showed my flowers she had made out of paper. They looked so real.

Tony bet me five dollars I couldn't drive through Times Square during rush hour. He lost his bet. I personally didn't like New York, but, I had a lot of affection for Tony's mother and sister. They were kind and friendly, and I let them know that. I lost track of Tony when I left the service.

In my barracks was an old guy. He must have been sixty. He had the rank of Tech-Sergeant. He was pretty much the loner. He kept to himself. I and several others in our barracks were curious about him. He had service hash marks on his sleeve that went from his wrist to almost his elbow. Each hash mark meant three years of service. I learned he had even served in the French Foreign Legion. When he put on his uniform to go to town, he would decide which of his many sets of decoration ribbons that he would wear, and there were many.

My friends, Tony and Frank, liked to visit St. John, New Brunswick. Saturday night there was always a dance going on and there were plenty of girls to dance with. Since I was the only one with a car, Tony and Frank paid for the gas for me to drive there. It was about 165 miles and took about three and a half hours to make the drive. We made the trip twice while I was in the Air Force.

The first trip was during spring runoff. We left base after breakfast and entered Maine Route 9, the shortest route to St. John. There were no visible houses until Route 9 joins Route 1, a major highway. The road was flanked on each side with thick stands of young pine trees. I came to a small wooden bridge which covered a brook. The brook had over-flowed and was now also flowing on each side of the bridge.

I took a look and the water looked deep enough to cover my car's exhaust pipe. My friends wanted me to try going on, promising to push me out if my car choked out. I made it to the top of the little bridge before my car choked out. I got it running again and made it through the water on the other side before it again choked out. I got it running again. Several miles ahead there was a curve. The road looked more like a lake than a road. The only way I could tell I was still on the road was by marker posts that ran alongside the road.

When we came to where Route 9 and Route 1 met, there was a highway patrolman parked. He asked where we had come from; that Route 9 had been closed for over an hour. He was amazed that we had made it through all the high water.

In St. John we would rent rooms at a local hotel and go sightseeing and get food. From what I learned, I wouldn't want to be there during winter. I was told it was a bitter and wet cold, bone chilling, due to it being so close to the ocean. I was concerned that my tour of duty in the Air force didn't end until January; that I'd be faced with a brutal Maine winter.

The next time we went to St. John, I was tired and asked Tony to drive for awhile, on our way back to base. This was close to fall. We left St. John's later than usual, night had set in. I told him to be sure and take Route 9, the shortest route to Bangor. I took a short nap. I woke up to see a Route 1 sign go by. We were in trouble.

I told Tony to pull over and I'd drive. We were too far down Route 1 to go back to Route 9. I put "the peddle to the metal." When I went over a railroad track, which had a small dip on the far side, my right tires came off the pavement and I was skidding to my left. A convertible has a heavy undercarriage. When my right tires hit the pavement, I quickly corrected and got back on my side of the highway.

As morning broke, we ran out of gas. I coasted my car to a gas station. He was just opening up. We got some gas, got to base and I quickly changed into my work fatigues. I got to my hanger workplace as roll was being called. I came that close to being AWOL. That was my last trip to St. John.

The Penobscot River flows through Bangor. I enjoyed its beauty and have many pictures. Bangor in the beginning of fall is so beautiful. Leaves on hardwood trees turn a brilliant yellow, red, gold and brown. Against the deep blue of the Penobscot, it's an artist or photographer's paradise.

In summer, two of my barrack friends asked for a ride to a small lake, more like a big pond, to get in some fishing. There was another "lake" further in. I looked at the map and said I'd agree to the "lake" closer to highway 9. When we got there and I parked my car, we went in search of the "lake." The timber was so thick that we made poor time. Finally one of the guys climbed a tree to try and locate the lake. We discovered we had passed the lake. We found a place where a bull moose had knocked down trees on its way to the lake. We followed his trail.

It was a beautiful clear blue lake, surrounded by a mass of trees. While the guys fished, I lay down on a large rock at the lake's edge, enjoying the serenity of the area and the sun. I had dozed off, to be awakened by the growl of a bear which was close-by. I never saw the bear but I was prepared to jump into the lake, if it approached.

I told my friends it was time to go. Since they weren't having any luck fishing, they agreed. When we came out of the forest, my car was about 400 hundred feet away. I was so tired fighting my way out of the forest that I had to mentally command my feet —right foot now left foot —until I reached my car. I then drove to my friends who were also exhausted, and drove back to base.

To get enough flying time in, to get my flight pay, Master Sergeant Allred would let me know when to report to the flight line for a ride. The two that I remember was a flight on a C-45 and a B-25. A C-45 is a small cargo plane similar to that used by Amelia Earhart in her round the world attempt. I wasn't alerted that the two pilots were going to practice stalls, and their recovery. Had I know, I would have probably opted out on the flight.

I was strapped in a passenger seat. When the pilot started nose-up, I'd grab hold of my seat. The plane would begin to shutter, stall and begin to spin downward. The pilots would keep nose down and use opposite rudder to bring the plane out of the spin, and then pull up. Several hours was spent by both pilots practicing this maneuver. I was glad to be back on the ground.

The flight aboard a B-25 was great. The B-25 is the "sport car" among bombers. It's a twin engine plane with plenty of power. It's the only land base bomber to ever take off from an aircraft carrier at sea and bomb Japan in WWII. The pilot on my ride aboard the B-25 was a "hot-rodder". By the time he had taxied down the taxi strip, he was ready to go. The tower cleared him for takeoff. Still on the roll, he swung the nose of the B-25 around to line up with the runway and went full throttle. What an exhilarating feeling.

The flight was to take us from Bangor, Maine to New York, and return. It's referred to as a "round robin" flight. We flew low level, just above tree- level. I sat next to the flight engineer, behind the pilot and co-pilot. I wondered what it was like to sit in the navigator/bombardier seat. I got permission from the pilot to go see. I had to leave my back-pack parachute behind to crawl through the narrow crawl space to the plane's nose.

The nose section of the B-25 has lots of small glass panels. These glass panels came down to chest height on both sides, giving great visibility. In the nose the glass goes down to the floor. Sitting in the navigator/bombardier seat was like being in a single seat race car doing around 300 MPH.

I then began looking at all that glass and the aluminum supporting ribs, remembering I was in the plane's nose without a parachute. That thought and wondering how good a job the riveter did in building the plane began to be of concern to me. I crawled back into the cockpit area and again sat next to the flight engineer, with my chute on.

One evening a couple of guys wanted to get into Bangor. There was a café there that served the greatest cheeseburger. When we reached the base main gate, we were informed that the base was going into a lock-down, due to a hurricane. There were still had high winds, even though the hurricane had been downgraded to a tropical storm. I drove quickly to a distant gate and got out before they had received the lock-down word. The storm hit as I was driving back to Bangor. To keep the car on my side of the highway I had to crab the car into the wind. Youth can make foolish decisions. I was no exception.

In late September Bangor got some snow. I and three other from the base were riding in town in my convertible. The guys suggested we put down the top. I did. We got many stares from town's people, riding with the top down in a snow storm.

Jane let me know she and her parents were planning to visit relatives in Dubois and Clearfield in Pennsylvania, and another in Buffalo, New York. I got a leave and went to meet them. I also decided to see if Jane would marry me. I bought the rings on time payments. I told her the ring she had on had a loose stone and eased it off her finger. I then slipped the engagement ring on her finger while we and her mother watched Niagara Falls.

A family friend in Clearfield took Jane's parents, she and I to a different kind of restaurant, one evening. It didn't have any windows and to get entrance he knocked on a wood door. A small window was slid back and our host gave a password. It was like the old speak-easy of the 1930s. We were then allowed to enter. Inside the lights were dim and a small band played. The food was good. Every time I hear the song "Hernando's Hideaway" I think about that place.

Our host was part of the local Ford/Mercury dealership. In idol conversation he mentioned going to another city to pick up a new Mercury, and that he was finding it hard to find someone to drive the Jaguar back. I immediately volunteered. Jane wasn't pleased with my decision.

The Jag was silver-colored with a hard top. Sitting in it my feet were straight out, not downward as in regular cars. The guy I was going with to pick up the Mercury told me that if I was taking a turn too fast and the tires began to squeal, downshift and boot the car.

At the town where he was picking up the new Mercury, the Mercury's odometer was disconnected. This was to not show any mileage. He gave me the keys to the Jag, told me the name of the town where we would have lunch and to go ahead. I had to almost screw myself into the car and had to push down on the telescoping steering wheel. Once inside I brought the steering wheel back to a good setting for me.

To start the car's engine I turned on the key and then on the left side of the steering wheel pressed the start button. I'll never forget that deep roar of the engine coming to life. I then understood how the Jaguar got its name—the roar.

I left on the return drive. If you don't notice the speed odometer it's hard to tell how fast you're going. Approaching a curve that called for 55 MPH speed, I glanced down at the speed odometer—I was doing eighty as

I entered the curve. Tires began screeching. I quickly down shifted one gear and accelerated. The tires stopped screeching. I came out of the curve at 85 MPH. I was really impressed with how the Jag handled the curve. On a straightaway, where I could there wasn't any side road; I got the Jag up to 105 MPH.

When we stopped for lunch, he wanted to switch cars. I was to drive the new Mercury to the dealership, and he the Jag. He told me to go ahead while he checked the Jag's radiator to see if it needed water, and that he'd catch up. I had other ideas. Not having the speed odometer hooked up, I had no idea what speed I was going. I know that at one place where there was highway ripples, the Mercury "walked" and I slowed down. I arrived at the dealership about five minutes before the guy driving the Jag. On the trip with Jane and her parents, I got to see Lake Erie and the Erie Canal.

Back on base it was business as usual. One Saturday our unit of about seventy guys was called out for marching. There were some sloppy guys in our outfit. After a few maneuvers were called by a lieutenant, my name was called to step out and to join the group already called out. The major group was marched again. I was thinking, "Alright you goof-offs that will teach you to shape-up."

The Lieutenant then let the major unit go and told those in my group to fall-in. I wondered where I had fouled-up. We were lined up into four columns. There were about twenty-one of us. The lieutenant then told us we were picked to be on a special fancy drill team, to perform at parades. Each in our group took turns calling cadence and maneuvers. I came in second place in the group and was given a unit hat as a prize. I knew I was planning for an early discharge, but accepted the prize.

At Dow AFB I was performing a task, Tech Supply clerk, when I should have been assigned to a flight organization. The war in Korea had ended in a truce. I used these two reasons to apply for early discharge, to go back to college. Our unit offered me an addition strip [Staff Sergeant] and a $5,000 bonus to re-enlist. I went for the discharge.

Jane had checked with Oklahoma A & M to find out the last possible date to be able to enroll. It was October 11, 1954. The Air force gave me an Honorable Discharge, with attached DD-214, showing my Air force record, on that day. I had told them I needed out earlier to go to school. Even driving all night from Maine to Oklahoma, I couldn't make it on time.

So on October 11[th,] I headed for home. Since I knew I couldn't make it in time for school, I took the scenic route. I drove through Vermont during the night. The song "Moonlight in Vermont" describes the state well. The moon was full and everything about was visible. My car gave a shadow. In Montreal, French is spoken. I had a difficult time with gassing up, since I don't under French or liters of gas. I drove through Canada all the way to Detroit, and then worked my way south to Warner, Oklahoma.

Chapter 20

MY FIRST MARRIAGE

I was faced with a dilemma. I couldn't get into school until January, no good paying jobs were available in the state and I was getting married. I called my Uncle Bill Ellison in California. He was an instructor at North American Aviation. He told me he could get me hired-on at North American Aviation. Jane and I were married, we packed up our clothes and wedding gifts; the top to my convertible had lumps sticking up here and there, and we began our trip to California.

We left her parent's house in Muskogee late and managed to get only as far as a motel in Henryetta, Oklahoma, before night caught us. I woke up during the night and found Jane looking out our room's window at the darkened parking lot. When I asked what was wrong, she said she missed home. She said she had married me to get away from home, but, now she missed home. She said her older brother had offered her breakfast in bed if she didn't get married. She was homesick. I tried to make the rest of the trip more like a vacation than a honeymoon trip.

Near Winslow, Arizona is a meteor crater. We spotted a road sign that directed us to the sight. Jane would go up to the very edge of a huge drop, in her high heels, worrying me that she might fall. From there we went to see Grand Canyon and take pictures. Like at the Meteor Crater, I had some tense moments. Jane, in high heels, would walk up to the edge of a steep drop into the canyon. I was concerned an unexpected gust of wind might blow her over. The drop was awesome. I don't like heights and would stay well back of the edge.

By this time, I was becoming concerned about getting to California and getting a job. My discharge and travel funds were getting low. We spotted a truly unique motel in Holbrook, Arizona. All the rooms were shaped like teepees. It gave the appearance of an Indian village. It was called the Wigwam motel, and it's still there today.

We arrived at my uncle's house in Palos Verde. We were to stay with him while I got a job and found an apartment. He asked if we'd like some homemade tacos for dinner. We wondered, "What's a taco?" We followed their example in putting one together—it was delicious.

Next morning I went with my uncle Bill to North American Aviation's employment office. I was offered a job as an electrical inspector on the forward section of the F-86D fighter. My pay was $300.00 per month.

The F-86D was an advanced fighter with sophisticated electronics, and the first to use rockets instead of machine-guns. The rocket pod held twenty-four rockets. My job was to see that the aircraft wiring was properly done.

Manufacturing workers would do the wiring and mark off each completed operation on a posted chart. I would then inspect the wire splicing and connections to determine if they met specs. If they met specs I would stamp off their work, with my personal stamp. It was an important job. If the plane were to ever crash and it was determined it was my fault, by my stamp, I would be in deep trouble.

My fellow inspectors helped me to put together a mirror like theirs. A mirror was mounted on a foot-long thin hollow aluminum tube, with a thin solid tube inside that attached to the mirror. By using its attached button to control different angles of the mirror, and a flashlight, I could inspect wiring in tight quarters.

My uncle Bill helped us to find an apartment. It was in Redondo Beach, I think it was on Redondo Beach Boulevard, about three or four blocks from the ocean. It was an old home belonging to Mrs. Venerable. She had converted the upper rooms into two studio apartments. Our apartment had a hide-a-bed couch in the living-room, a small kitchen with a view of the ocean, over the roof-tops and a large bath with small, old white, tile.

I would go to work and learn when I got back to our apartment that Jane was homesick, played records most of the day and cried. Many times I'd go for long walks on Redondo's sandy beach, trying to think things out. When my uncle Bill asked how things were going, I told him.

Without letting me know, he went by our apartment, picked up Jane and took her to North American Aviation employment department. She was employed as a clerk in Engineering. We'd ride to work together each day.

On our first Thanksgiving, we set our small kitchen table in our living-room. I sat up my camera on a tri-pad. Jane dressed up in an evening gown, put on the tear-drop earbobs I had brought back from the Philippines and some of the Joy perfume I had purchased in Hong Kong, for my future bride. I dressed in a white shirt with light grey tie and black trousers. While we were having a turkey dinner, I used a hidden cord to snap our picture.

Things began looking up. Jane found a friend named Patty, at work. I was interested in rock hunting. Jane bought me a geologist rock hammer. The hammer has a square head on one side and a small pick on the other.

One time I planned to go rock hunting in Los Padres National Forest. Jane asked Patty along. The two made a picnic lunch. I found an interesting place and we had lunch. While Jane and Patty talked, I went rock hunting. I found a beautiful outcrop of pure white quartz and broke off a sample. It was a pleasant and relaxing day.

At work I saw in our company news sheet that the Electrical Systems Engineering Department was looking for draftsmen. I filled out a resume and got an interview. The Department Supervisor's name was "Pop" Trousdale. He scanned through my resume. He told me he was looking for someone with more experience and was about to turn me down. He then saw on my resume that I was an Eagle Scout with Bronze Palm. He asked if it's true I was an Eagle Scout. When I said I was, he made an interesting statement. He said, "I've never had an eagle scout fail me. If you want the job, it's yours."

I took the draftsman job, was given a raise and moved up into engineering. Six months later "Pop" promoted me to engineer with another rise. I hadn't let him down. When "Pop" retired, Glenn fielding became my supervisor. He tried to get some of the other engineers to accept doing the electrical system drafting work on the F-86D. None would accept the assignment because of the plane's many "Black boxes." To do the job required tracing circuitry through those black boxes.

Our electrical systems drawings were for field service manuals. If a pilot had trouble while airborne, our field service representative would quickly check our electrical systems drawings to see if the problem could be worked around and the plane land. Glenn was faced with a deadline on the F-86D, and he was a month behind. He asked me if I'd do the systems drawings for the F-86D. I told him I do my best. He promoted me to lead engineer, with a raise in pay, and assigned another engineer and two draftsmen to help me. While I directed the other engineer and draftsmen in their work, I got the schematics of the black boxes and traced out the current flow. I finished the project two weeks ahead of schedule. Glenn then assigned me to work on the F-100 super-saber airplane.

My engineering department was a short distance to where Jane worked. We'd meet at the coffee machine and briefly talk before going back to work. Things were going well for us.

Jane would frequently remark she didn't want to be an old woman of twenty before having a child. A month before company insurance would have paid for a birth, she became pregnant. Since our apartment in Redondo Beach didn't allow children, we went looking for an apartment that would.

We found an upper two bedroom unfurnished apartment at 9410 Airport Boulevard in Westchester, California. It was just across the Los Angeles airport landing strip, a fifteen minute drive to work.

We furnished it on time payments. We loved rustic maple furnishings. The kitchen looked down on our parking space. To leave the front door open in our upstairs apartment, to get fresh outside air, we put a retractable baby barrier. When Jane saw me park, she would put our food on the table.

At night, if Jeff cried, Jane would ask me to give him a bottle. I learned that getting a bottle to the right temperature isn't easy, when sleepy. It meant wrist testing, and heating or cooling. Then there were nights when Jeff was hard to get to sleep. I would gently rock his baby bed and finally get him asleep.

Her doctor was in Hawthorne, a short distance down Pacific Coast Highway. I found out his charges and that of Hawthorne General Hospital. Over the nine months, I paid each their estimated fee, in full.

Suddenly Jane's blood pressure went up and our son Jeffrey Lewis Ellison was delivered by C-Section. This caused the doctor and hospital fees to double. When the hospital called to tell me that mother and baby could go home, they also said they wouldn't be released until I paid their bill in full. I couldn't do that, and they said I couldn't do it on time payments.

I got mad and called my uncle to let him know the hospital had better release Jane and Jeff, or I'd put some of their staff in the hospital. My uncle used to drive ambulances and knew the hospital staff. He went with me to the hospital and got them to take time payments. I took Jane and Jeff home. As previously stated, Jeff would sometimes be difficult to get to sleep.

Osie Ellison, my mother, paid us a visit one year. Primarily the visit was to see her grandson, Jeff. She was a great fan of Lawrence Welk. Uncle Bill and Aunt Beverley took Jane, my mother and I to the Aragon Ballroom to listen to Lawrence Welk and his band. My mother was thrilled. While the band was playing and couples were dancing, Bill and I took my mother to the edge of the bandstand stage, so that my mother could see her fan up close. When Lawrence asked if anyone would care to dance with him, Bill and I lifted my mother upon the bandstand. She got to dance with Lawrence Welk, it made her day. She talked about that for a long time.

My mother was half-aunt to Wamaluke "Jack" Oslin and his wife Connie. They said that since Osie had never been out of the country, they'd take her to a club in Tijuana, Mexico that had a good band. "Jack" was an old WWII navy man and loved to play practical jokes. While Connie distracted my mother's attention at their table, "Jack" placed some liquor bottles in front of her. He said, "Osie!" When she turned around he snapped her picture. She laughed and said, "Don't you ever show that to my preacher, he'd kick me out of church." I've never known my mother to drink.

With Jane no longer working and all the time payments due each month on household furnishings and medical, we were strapped for cash. We'd go to our closest grocery store, in Westchester, and look at roasts. When the butcher came to wait on us, we'd order several pounds of hamburger. Jane made good spaghetti and chili. This looking at roasts then buying hamburger became a routine. On one trip, the kind butcher told us we could purchase a round roast for the same price as we spend on hamburger. We were thrilled to have a roast for dinner, and to make me sandwiches for my lunch at work.

One of my friends at work, Don Baum, always found ways to make additional money. He told me how he worked some nights moving furniture at North American Aviation, where we both worked during the day. I asked if he could help me join the moving crew. I became part of the crew.

I would get off work from my engineering job, go to our apartment for a quick dinner and return to the plant to move department furniture. I would work sometimes until midnight helping move desks and drafting tables to a new locating. Departments at North American were frequently moved to new locations.

One night we had to move a file cabinet. It was very heavy. I think engineers must have loaded much of it with the lead ducks used in drafting work. It took eight of us to carry it down a flight of stairs, we didn't have a dolly. With three on each side and one at the top and another on the bottom, we started down the stairs. Someone lost their grip. It became a chain reaction. How the guy holding the bottom ends managed to let go, and at the same time jump upwards to be clear of the descending file cabinet, I never knew. The rapidly descending file cabinet punched a hole in the concrete, on the lower floor. Working night moving shifts helped me clear off our debts.

In our apartment we made friends with Dick and Gloria Teal. They had a young daughter named Brenda. Dick worked for Hughes during the day and took night classes in electronics at Los Angeles Trade Tech. Both Dick and Gloria were kind and friendly. I also enrolled in electronics at LA Trade-Tech, to get a better understanding of my work at North American.

I enjoyed going to school nights to learn a subject. Night classes were inexpensive and interesting. I took night classes at El Camino College in Income Tax Preparation, Commercial Law and Bookkeeping. I tried to get Jane to choose a class and go with me. She wasn't interested.

I learned that Dick's family was really struggling. Gloria fixed their meals on a hot plate. I mentioned this to my friend, Don Baum. He said his mother had an old stove that was still good and in storage. He got his mother to give the stove to Dick and Gloria. They were really pleased. I was glad to learn that Dick became part of Management at Hughes. He was a good hard working guy, deserving success.

Another couple in our apartment complex was Walt and Nancy. Walt was a security guard at U.C.L.A. I told Walt what had happened with the birth of Jeff. He told me U.C.L.A. had the most up-to-date doctors in the area, working in the college medical school. He said that Jane would get top-notch medical treatment. Due to Walt's suggestion I took Jane to U.C.L.A Medical Center for the birth of our second son, James Hardy Ellison.

Jane and I wanted to have a house of our own. We looked at some model homes in tracts being built along Crenshaw Boulevard in Torrance, California. They were for sale at $13,700 in 1955, FHA. Being FHA, requiring a small down payment, we couldn't afford to buy one.

One day we went to see Knott's Berry Farm's ghost town. We saw a sign about new VA homes being built. We looked at their model homes, found one we liked and applied. With the VA, no down payment was required. We were approved. Our house would be ready in three months. We were excited and happy. Our new address was 5805 Rio Way, Buena Park, California. We were so close to Knott's Berry Farm that we could hear the little train ride engine's whistle.

To drive from our apartment in Westchester to Buena Park meant dealing with lots of traffic. Weekends we'd visit our new home and see how far along they were on its construction. While visiting the construction site, we would go to Knott's Berry Farm to tour its Ghost Town, sit on a bench in a tunnel of wisteria vines and have a cup of coffee and donuts.

One day I noticed in the company news, openings for engineers at their Missile Division in Downey, California. To get the job would cut my driving time from our new house in half. I applied and got the job. My new supervisor was John Atkins. I'd be working on the electrical systems for the Hound Dog Missile. It meant a good raise in salary and no more drafting work. I had my own desk and a draftsman assistant.

When John gave me an assignment, I'd quickly decide an approach to do the task, and get the task underway. John once told me that was the reason he enjoyed my work. He said, "I can't stand it when somebody tries to straddle the fence, unable to come to a conclusion."

John was from Boone, North Carolina. During WWII he was a full colonel, flying P-51s. He retired from the Air force and went to work as a supervisor in Missile Division. He had a heavy southern accent. His favorite expressions was, "You pea-picker" or "I get the picture." Those types of comments caused many to make the mistake that he was dumb. John has two degrees, math and physics, from M.I.T.

One year, before going on vacation, I gave my draftsman a marked up copy of some electrical drawings that needed changes made. I also put an identical set in my locked desk drawer. I instructed him to make the changes. When I returned from vacation, I was called into John's office. He asked me why I hadn't made necessary changes to my drawings; that my draftsman said I hadn't left any changes to be made. I told John I had left the changes, and that I had a duplicate copy of those changes in my desk drawer. He told me to bring them into his office. I showed them to John. His comment was, "I get the picture." I returned to my desk, realizing my draftsman had tried to "knife me" in my back.

I liked working for John. I learned he had a dry-sense of humor. With his southern brogue and sense of humor, his was fun to be around. One day John was at a meeting of supervisors and middle-management. A guy was telling the group of a proposed idea. At the end, John spoke up and told the guy, "That pea-picker won't work."

The guy got angry and fired back, "I have a degree from Harvard and I say it will."

John replied, "I have two degrees from M.I.T. and I say it won't."

With that John went to the blackboard and proved mathematically it wouldn't work. A red faced Harvard grad ended the meeting. John had won the day.

One of the potential problems of the Hound Dog cruise missile, carried aloft under the wing of a B-52 bomber, was explosive bolts. These bolts attached the missile to the bomber. A missile was launched when those in the bomber fired those explosive bolts, by a radio frequency. The concern was that a stray radio signal might cause the bolts to explode, unintentionally, and drop the missile. John went to our manufacturing shop and while tinkering with the problem came up with a solution.

Word got to the navy, who were also having troubles with stray radio frequencies firing their explosive bolt. The navy was planning on some maneuvers off the coast of San Francisco. They called North American asking for John to come on their maneuvers, to see if his idea would work on their equipment.

North American said they'd send a division President. When the navy called John again they said they didn't want a division President, who had no idea of John's device, they wanted John. John in his brogue said, "Well we do work for the Air Force." The navy contacted the Secretary of the

Navy in Washington D. C., who then contacted the Secretary of the Air Force in D.C., who then contacted North American Aviation. John went on the Navy maneuvers.

In our company news, I saw where a department in our company's Autonetics Division needed engineers. A lot of overtime was also being offered. I asked John if he'd mind my trying for the job. He told me to go ahead. I got the job and a pay increase. I went to work under my lead engineer, Phil Fagan. I'd work a dayshift and then return for a night shift, working until midnight, and sometimes until one or two in the morning. It meant nice paychecks and my being tired.

One day my department supervisor came to my desk. He said a guy from my old Missile Division job was in his office asking for a job. My supervisor wanted to know about him. It was the guy who had tried to "knife" me. I told my supervisor I'd rather he ask someone else. He went to his office and turned the guy down for a job. It proved to me that justice will be served.

One night while our little group of four was busy at work and it was so quiet in our partitioned section, someone began low whistling of the song "Rye whiskey." One of group began singing the verses to the song. Suddenly we four burst into a rousing rendition of the song. That stopped when we saw several people peering over the top of our partitioned area. From then on we were referred to as those crazy engineers.

I enjoyed working at Autonetics in Anaheim, California. It was closer to our home in Buena Park. I was bringing in a nice monthly paycheck. I loved working in my yard. I had a cinder-block fence put in to fence off our back yard, so it would be safe for Jeff to play in outside. I also got a cocker-spaniel that we named Sammy. I used lawn edging boards to make a nice area for plants and a lemon tree. I also learned that it was Sammy or the yard. Sammy had to go, if I was to have a nice lawn. I'd plant and he would dig. I tried fencing him behind our garage, but, that became too much work. I gave him to a local farmer where he'd be able to run free.

Jane was now expecting our second son James Hardy Ellison. As previously stated, Walt in our old apartment had told me that the U.C.L.A. medical facility was the most advanced in medicine. I didn't want Jane's blood pressure to get out of control. So, I'd drive her to U.C.L.A. for her monthly exams, a seventy mile trip. They kept her blood pressure down. Jim was born in the U.C.L.A. hospital. On Jim's first Christmas, Jane took a picture of me, Jeff and Jim by the Christmas tree; I was giving Jim his bottle.

When we moved into our new home in Buena Park, we had only one neighbor, Don and Phyllis Owens. Don was good in landscaping and gave me many good ideas, several of which I used. I used flexible edging boards to give an undulating flowerbed design, and planted a lemon tree in the middle of our backyard. In front I put in a split-rail fence. Jane and I would drive to Palos Verde to gather a few wild geraniums to plant in our yard. While working in our front, Jeff would ride his peddle fire-engine truck on the sidewalk. Our tract was competed and many of our neighbors put in beautifully landscaped yards. That summer Jane and I visited my mother, and took Jeff by to visit his great grandfather, Papa Jack in Checotah. On the way back to California, we stopped at Carlsbad, New Mexico to tour the cavern.

With Jim, we now had two boys. We hoped to have a girl but were advised to have no more than three children by C-Section. We applied to California to become foster parents, asking for a little girl to rear. We received a call that they had a new born girl, a preemie. Her parents were Greek. We agreed to take her in. She was only a month old. We named her Debra. I was a fan of the actress Debra Paget. Deb was such a cute baby with lots of dark hair and big dark eyes. The hospital personal had spoiled her by holding her at night.

As with Jeff and Jim, getting up for nightly feeding was still my task. I'd give Deb her bottle and try to get her back to sleep. She would fuss. We had a small bed in her room. I'd lie down on the bed and put Deb crossways on my chest. I'd then pat her back until she went to sleep. Many times Jane would find us that way in the morning—both of us asleep. We bought Jeff a pedal fire engine, Jim a stroller and Deb many nice new outfit. Life was good.

Before Deb joined us, we'd go to Knott's Berry Farm on Sundays. Jane and I got coffee and donuts, donuts for Jeff and a bottle for Jim in his stroller. We'd spend a relaxing day there. Jeff seemed fascinated by the old west settings and staged gunfights by stunt men. We would go to the chapel there. Once seated the lights were dimmed. Slowly, on a picture screen, a door up front opened. A portrait of Jesus appeared with his eyes closed. Lights were again changed. Slowly his eyes would open. This was really neat and had a dramatic effect.

When Jeff was about five and Jim about three, we dressed them up in their Sunday best to go to Knott's Berry Farm. They patiently waited on our front porch steps, on Rio Way.

We received another call from child welfare. They said we had done such a good job with Debbie would we take in a nine year old girl named Charlene. That made her about four years older than our son Jeff. Both Jane's mother and my mother advised us against this.

We were told by Charlene's case worker that Charlene claimed child abuse; mother had died of cancer, and grandparents not wanting to care for her. Charlene's caseworker said that Charlene's present foster parents were treating her like a modern day version of Cinderella, mistreating her. Charlene was then brought over to our house.

We felt sorry for Charlene. It looked like her foster parents had put a bowl on her head and cut her hair; her dress looked like it came from a used clothing store. We took Charlene in and called her Cheri. The first order of business was her trip to the beauty shop for a stylish hair style, then several new dresses and enrollment in a ballet class. Cheri and Debbie shared a room. Jeff and Jim shared another room. We were now a family of four.

Chapter 21

I took a night class in Creative Writing at Fullerton State College. I had always been an avid reader and from the age of twelve wanted to be a writer. Our instructor would give us short, short story assignments to write up. He would read a story to the class and ask the class for comments. The class might rip the story apart, learning later it was written by such famous writers as James Joyce or Earnest Hemmingway.

Between stories written by famous writers, our instructor would read one written by a class member. He didn't read the author but did ask for class comments. One night he read a story that I had written for Hitchcock magazine. The lady next to me, a friend, said, "Anyone who would write such a story has a diabolical mind."

I whispered, "Thanks sport."

She said, "I might have known."

Hitchcock magazine turned down my story. It's now published in my book of short stories, Tim's World. The title of the short story is "The Hunt."

Grammar has always given me trouble in writing — still does. In my writing class my stories would come back with plenty of red marks. To lower the amount of red marks I shortened sentences. One day my instructor called me to his desk. He asked, "Do you know what you're doing?"

I told him I was trying to cut down the number of red marks. He told me that he thought that might be the case. He then surprised me. He said I was writing in the Hemmingway style, and that I had a similar type of interest as Hemmingway, action in face of danger. I went home happy that night.

It looked like I had found a home at Autonetics. Jane and I decided to have a family room added to our house. It was rustic, an off-shoot from our kitchen. We chose a rustic wagon-wheel hanging light fixture. Years later I would revisit the house on Rio Way. Larry took a picture of me standing in front.

While working at Autonetics I became interested in old treasure stories. The stories intrigued me, making me wonder which was fact and fiction. I formed a treasure hunting club. Our club consisted of six. We would take a treasure story we liked and then did the research.

John, a friend of mine who worked in Autonetics manufacturing told me an interesting story. He said his great-grandfather had been with Santa Ana at the Alamo. When Santa Ana ordered the attack, John's great-grandfather deserted and headed for California. Some of Geronimo's warriors lanced him on the desert in Arizona, and left him to die. Some Indian women found him and healed his wounds. He eventually married a chief's daughter and was told of a rich gold mine.

The story was of two German prospectors finding a gold ore outcrop. They captured the tribe's chief and held him hostage so tribe members would work the mine. It was a chimney type of mine; the two Germans would guard the chief while the tribe dug straight down, following the gold ore.

The Indians hatched up a plan. While a bucket of gold ore was hauled to the top in a bucket, they would set some pure ore to one side. When they sent up a bucket almost full of pure gold, the miners thought the Indians had struck a sold vein of gold ore. One went down to check. That was the signal for the Indians to kill both miners. Their bodies were dumped into the mine shaft and the shaft closed off and disguised.

In doing research I verified the mine's existence through the museum of mining ores. John's mine had gold ore mixed in rose quartz, with a trace of black onyx. The museum had such an ore sample. Our gold hunting club went with me to area that matched the description given by John from his great-grandfather, given in my treasure story folder.

I did some panning before trying to get to the mountain I believed the mine to be located. I didn't have any luck. A member of our group did pan a small amount of gold from the stream.

Trekking towards the mountain, I had a "bought" with a ball-cactus and had to turn back. Before I did, I took a picture of that mountain. It showed what looked like where slag had been dumped off the top, which should have been.

I've written up this treasure story and several others that I have verified that exist. They are located in my three-ring binder titled Mines and Lost Treasures.

I saw in the company news that engineers were needed in our new Division in Tulsa, Oklahoma. I sent off my resume. I got a call from John Atkins, my old boss at Missile Division. He asked why I would ever want to go to Tulsa. I told him that Oklahoma was my home state. He then asked what it would take to get me there. I thought John had seen my resume and was kidding me. I replied, "You know me John. All I can get." I got a surprise. He said, "Alright I'm cutting the paperwork."

 I asked, "Are you serious?"

He said, "Yep, I'm now a manager in our new division."

While the paperwork was coming through, Jane and I had to go to court to get approval to allow Debbie and Cheri to go out of state to Oklahoma, and put our house on the market. We moved to Broken Arrow, Oklahoma in 1963.

A realtor in Broken Arrow found us a home at 310 West Commercial. It was on the outskirts of Broken Arrow. It had two and half acres. The house had three bedrooms, bath, and dining-room, living-room with fireplace, kitchen and large enclosed rear porch.

The back part of our lot had a thick growth of trees, and at the very back was a stream, mostly dry during the summer months. Our stream had a deeper pool of water that remained during the summer. One early morning Jane came face to face with a wolf getting a drink. The wolf went one way and Jane the other.

Under the trees I built a small brick lined fire pit. We'd occasionally take the kids back there and roast wieners and marshmallows. The kids seemed to enjoy being in the "forest", when they could see the lights in our house in the distance.

Between the house and the trees were a small pasture, and an old shed barn. Cheri was interested in horses. Not knowing that much about horses I bought a buckskin colt, too young to ride. When Cheri would head for the shed to put out feed for the horse, Tony would run at her and scare her. When I went into the pasture, Tony ran at me. I stood my ground and Tony ran around me. He was playing a game.

I bought a used Ford pickup to be able to haul hay and feed for the horse. Both it and the horse gave me problems. It seemed that I always had to repair the truck, and the horse kept getting out. I put in an electric fence, but, Tony learned to charge the fence and break the wire. Jane would call me at work telling me to come home, that Tony was loose and in our neighbor's yards. Between these frequent horse calls and truck repairs, I decided this kind of life was not for me and sold off both.

One Christmas Eve Jane and I gave Debbie a big surprise. There was a knock at our front door. I asked Debbie to see who was at the door. When she opened the door, there stood Santa Claus. She had a shocked look on her face. Santa had come to personally talk to her. Jane and I had hired the Santa. He came in and had a nice chat with Debbie, asking what she wanted for Christmas. Debbie was a happy little girl.

At work I was assigned to design a complex junction box piece of equipment. It was to be located next to the Apollo spacecraft. It had to be explosive and radio frequency proofed. Twenty other checkout console's wiring went through my unit.

I was assigned an assistant engineer and two draftsmen, due the constant changes being made by other consoles. I would complain to my supervisor that the other consoles need to freeze their design so I could finish my design. Those designers of the other consoles would complain to me that they only changed a few wires. I would answer, yes and the other twenty of you.

I came up with the idea to mechanize the wiring information. I was sent with the idea to my manager, John Atkins. He saw the merit of the system and told me to take it to our data processing group to put in action. When I explained my idea to the supervisor in data processing, he became agitated.

My idea was for data processing to extract from engineering drawings all wiring and what they were attached to, and the indicated signal on that wire. Data processing called a week later and its supervisor said he couldn't make perfume out of garbage. When I told him I thought he could, he slammed down the phone. I went to John Atkins. He said, "I get the picture." A couple of hours later I got a call from the data processing supervisor — he was the "milk of human kindness."

A program was written and everything was going great, liked by the other console design and test engineers, and manufacturing. With the engineer wiring now printed in data processing, changes could be made quickly. By resorting of the list, manufacturing had a complete list of what wires went into each pin of a plug or piece of equipment, making it easier for them in building a console. The list could then be resorted for testing, showing what signal was on the wire.

Our main customer, the Air Force, called our mother company in El Segundo, asking, "How is it that you have such a lousy wire data system and your division in Tulsa such a good one?" I was put on the next flight to our El Segundo plant to put my Mechanized Wire Data System into our corporation's Standards and Operation Manuel [SOP].

John Atkins, my manager, took me out of engineering and promoted me to Senior Management Analyst, with instructions on finding better more efficient ways of operation for our Tulsa Division. I had a secretary to write up my request letters to American companies. I'd set up a meeting with one of their field representatives.

The response from Burroughs Corporation was the best. Their random access computer would take the parts list from engineering, for a unit being built. Notices of that list would go to purchasing, manufacturing, quality control and manufacturing stockroom. When individual parts are ordered the computer is updated. If a part is behind in being ordered, it had best be not an oversight, it would show up in top management's by-weekly report.

With the information sent to manufacturing, they could quickly began making assembly plans and alert their stockroom of incoming parts. Quality control was alerted as to what equipment was coming in, so they could properly test it to see if they met our quality standards.

This Management Information System allowed middle and top management officers to quickly determine how departments were functioning, current costs of each unit under construction and cost if the unit is cancelled in mid-production.

I presented the Burroughs plan to John Atkins. Since Burroughs had their own computers and Tulsa Division used only IBM computers, I suggested Tulsa division buy the Management Information System program from Burroughs and have our Data Processing group convert to IBM language. I estimated this would cost a million and a quarter dollars. John took my idea to top management.

When the word got around through the company "grapevine", Supervisors began to worry. They realized it would reveal how well they were doing their job. They tried keeping everything "Status Quo." Top management wanted the system and assigned the Data Processing Director the task. He appointed his sailing buddy to be supervisor over the project, a position that John wanted me to have. The Director won his choice.

About three months later, management was called to a meeting by the new supervisor to describe the new Management Information System's progress. John took me to the meeting. I was shocked. The guy who got my job was "re-inventing the wheel." It was the basic Burroughs system that I had proposed we buy and modify. My proposal would have been up and running, in the time he had reached the present basic level one, and he had already spent a million dollars. When the guy finished his presentation, John spoke up.

In a voice that could be heard by all in the room, John said, "Joe that's the same system you proposed three months ago, one that we could have purchased three months ago for the same amount already spent on this basic step." I thought to myself, "John you've just made me a marked man for Data Processing and supervisors who didn't want my system implemented." That's what happened. That year I received twenty-one company awards for company improvement suggestions. When our Apollo contract ended, I was sent back to Autonetics in Anaheim.

Knowing that I would probably be sent back to California at the end of the Apollo contract, and wanting to remain in Oklahoma, I tried to start some kind of business in my spare time. I took Mellinger's International Trade course. I made my own letterhead, a large script E with a small T and C in the curves of the E, inside a box. The company name was The Ellison Company, 310 West Commercial Street, Broken Arrow, Oklahoma. I would type and sign my letters as J. H. Ellison, President.

While visiting Jane's parents, now living in Freehold, New Jersey in the 1960s, I drove the family to the New York World's fairgrounds. I was very impressed with the GM exhibit, and their futuristic ideas. It showed model cars moving on roadways, controlled like airplanes. It showed a machine going through forested areas cutting down trees and laying a roadway at the same time.

Later, we went to the Kutztown fair in Pennsylvania. I think I and the family enjoyed this more than the World's Fair. The fair gets into the folklore of Pennsylvania Dutch. Their apple pan doughty tasted great, but oh so rich. If the receipt normally called for a quarter cube of butter they added the whole stick. They demonstrated how young couples would court by holding onto a long stirring stick. The kids had fun climbing onto a huge manager of straw and jumping off onto a huge pile of straw. I was impressed by Pennsylvania. Near Kutztown is the town of Lancaster, known for its producing Revolutionary War rifles.

While in Freehold, New Jersey I got to visit the Monmouth battle grounds. It was a major victory for George Washington and his troops. I saw the well, which Molly Pitcher brought water from, to give the troops, swabbing their cannons while the troops took time to get a drink.

Dealing with the business I was trying to start, Jane's father asked how I could sign a letter as President, and asked if it bothered me? I told him that companies I'm writing to don't know that I'm a one person company. If I remember correctly, Jane's father, Lou, didn't finish high school, but, he came up with many good innovations and design changes to increase production of glass molding operations. I kept telling him he should patent his ideas. He would reply that he hadn't finished school. He was smart in many ways but lacked confidence when it came to patents. He settled for bonuses by increased production.

My home address appeared to be a business address. I let foreign Consulate Generals know that I was looking for gift store items. They would send me the names and addresses of companies in their country that produced possible item that might be of interest to me. I would look over the list and write companies of interest. Some of these companies sent me samples. I received a beautiful carving set from Japan. Italy sent pictures of many beautiful glassware items and leather goods. Peru sent pictures of their gold coins. All had a cost list attached, and that they would drop ship.

I began importing human hair women's wigs from Hong Kong. They arrived not styled. I called them my Wimberley wigs. I wanted Jane to give wig parties and sell wigs to women attending, like a Tupper-ware party. I would get examples styled by a beautician, for the women to try on. Jane said she was no salesperson, and left it to me.

I got the word around and began having wig parties. I had a blonde, brunette, auburn and black wig styled. The beautician that styled them for me gave me a discount. I'd offer the host of the party a discount. I took the wigs to parties on Styrofoam heads. I received the wigs at a cost to me of $16.00. I sold them for $32.00.

Most of the time husbands were gone. I'd place the wigs on the host's dining-room table and go sit in her living-room. The women would try on wig after wig, giggling like school girls. After about an hour or so, I'd tell them its decision time. I'd make my sales and go home.

On one occasion the husband stayed home. He had a somber look on his face. I thought, "No sales here tonight." His wife, a brunette, would come in wearing first one color wig after the other, to show to her husband, and asked if it looked nice. He'd give an uh huh and she would go get another wig. When I called for decision time the hostess asked her husband which one she should buy. He said, "All of them! It's like seeing a different woman each time." I made my most sales that night. I saw the lady in a store a few days later. She was wearing the blond wig. I quipped, "Do blondes have more fun?" With a big smile she replied, "You better believe!"

I got a call from a wholesaler of women wigs. She had heard about my wigs and asked me to show them to her. She carefully studied the nape and attachment of human hair. She then asked what price I was selling them for. I said, "Before I tell you, what would you sell them for." She studied my wigs again and said she would market them at $72.00. She was shocked to learn I was asking $32.00. She told me if I'd sell only to her, she would buy in bulk.

At this time, in the middle sixties, LBJ was President and had a Democratic congress. Because of china's involvement in the Viet Nam War, congress passed a bill that any goods coming from Hong Kong had to have a Comprehensive Certificate of Origin that the goods didn't come from communist China. They approved this method after a six months moratorium. My imported wig business was destroyed. I finally did get my certifications, but, too late.

I then concentrated on trying to find good gift articles. I signed an agreement to lease a store in a proposed new shopping center, when it was built. It was on the southern edge of downtown Broken Arrow. Businesses in downtown Broken Arrow went to the City Planning

Department saying the new shopping center would destroy downtown business. It was causing a lot of contention.

A local attorney called and asked me to serve on the Planning Department. I accepted. Even though I was hoping the shopping center would go through, I agreed with the businesses argument. The attorney and I learned that the Planning Department chairman, supporting the shopping center, had some ownership in the project. The shopping center and my lease were rejected. Even though I had a lease, I voted against the project. It was the honest thing to do. My gift shop went "out the window."

I was back to square one. I was working for the Tulsa Division during the day and trying to put together a business of my own at night and weekends. On top of that I tried to not ignore my family. I got Jeff and Jim into Cub Scouts and Little League. Shortly after becoming cub scouts, the Cubmaster resigned. Upon learning that I was an Eagle Scout with bronze palm, I was asked to be Cubmaster. I always believe scouting is a great program for boys. I became Cubmaster and Jane as Den Mother. I learned it was difficult to get adult volunteer helpers, all claimed they were too busy.

One recruiting meeting I asked a guy if he would be the cub's transportation chairman. I got the usual I'm too busy. It was the same with the other fathers. I asked the guy if I could match him business for business and still be Cubmaster, would he volunteer for transportation chairman. He agreed.

I told him I worked in aerospace, was an importer, and was on the city planning commission. I then told him I was on the Methodist church finance committee. He said, "Okay you win. Where do I sign." After that we had plenty of volunteers.

It was fun working with the boys, watching them progress in scouting and giving out their earned awards. Our scout committee would meet in our dining-room. For one regional Cub Scout fair our committee came up with a clever idea—an African safari.

Den Mothers had their kids cut out small pictures of African animals that stood around two inches tall, then glue them to poster-board paper, and then glue that to a half-inch square piece of balsa-wood. One of our husband volunteers built a two by four shooting gallery frame, for the tiny animals, and helped den Mothers decorate our booth.

We found some toy rifles that, when cocked, shot a small cork stopper. If they shot one of the animals off the rack they were given a small inexpensive prize, about two cents cost to us. Our booth was kept busy during the whole fair. We had kids lined up three abreast with long lines behind, to "go on an African safari."

Broken Arrow has a Rooster Day parade every year. Kids could dress up in costumes and walk in the parade. The kid with the best costume won a $25 gift certificate. I would try to come up with costume ideas for our kids to be in the parade. Jim was the only one of our kids to win the big prize.

I found a discarded refrigerator box and cut it to look like a big shoe. I took brown cord to look like shoe laces. On the sides I hung some of the girls dolls. Jim wore one of my unset wigs. His theme was nursery rhymes "The old woman in the shoe who had so many kids she didn't know what to do."

Even though I had a somewhat hectic schedule, I'd still get in some quail hunting in the fall. I went to the old abandon coal mining area east of Broken Arrow. I would take Jeff and Jim along. It was tricky shooting. Quail would take to wing, flying low, and then quickly go over the slag hills left by mining.

Several Sundays we would drive to visit my mother and aunt Lettye. We'd have fried chicken and visit. Both spoiled the kids, Lettye most of all. While the kids were being spoiled, and Jane talking to Lettye, my mother and mother Emily, I got the opportunity to talk with my uncle by marriage Bill Moore. He was a "tough as a boot" Irishman. He was used to being a boss over men, and had many interesting stories to tell about his youth.

One story that I can remember was when he, as a kid, was allowed to drive his mother in their buggy. They met another lady, approaching in her buggy. Uncle Bill was concentrating on driving his team and didn't politely doff his hat to the lady, in passing. Uncle Bill said his mother boxed his ears so hard, for not showing the courtesy that he fell out of their buggy.

Another story he told about was the time he hitched a pet young bull to his mother's buggy, planning to go for a ride. When he used a buggy-whip to get the bull to move, the bull realized something was attached to him. The bull went wild, destroying the buggy. Uncle Bill's punishment was left up to his father. His father, an oilman, laughed about the incident, saying he'd buy a new buggy.

I enjoyed listening to his stories of what life and customs were like in his time. In his days a good woman was given respect. Men failing in that were looked down on. We enjoyed each other's company.

At one time he had a thriving water well drilling company. He lost that business when his brother Luther, while drinking, destroyed a lot of his trucks. Luther went on to be successful working for oil companies in India and Indonesia.

I was in Muskogee when Luther and his wife had returned for a visit from India. We all sat around listening to his adventures. Luther told that while living in India his oldest son came into the living-room, where Luther and his wife were, paused a moment before casually getting a machete off its hook, and killed a cobra that was close to the couch Luther and his wife was sitting on.

Luther's pay was good so they had a native cook, housekeeper and nanny for the kids, both in India and Indonesia. Theirs was a luxurious lifestyle.

In visiting family in Muskogee, they had their four boys with them. The youngest one was making as lot of noise, he was about four. Luther would stop talking to us to scold his young son. The boy would look with a puzzled expression, and then go back to making noise. Luther told his older son to tell his little brother if he didn't stop the noise he'd get a spanking. The older boy in a India dialect conveyed the message to his little brother. The little one understood and became quiet. He couldn't understand English, yet.

Chapter 22

At work I became a friend of Gaylord. He worked in manufacturing at the Tulsa Division. He "moonlighted" evenings and weekends for a fast food Mexican place. I would visit with him at times; he would treat me to a plate of enchiladas and refried beans.

In 1966, just before Jane gave birth to our daughter Elizabeth Jane Ellison, Tulsa had a huge oil exhibition. For the exhibition Tulsa built a ground level building about a football field in length. At the entrance to the building was a huge statue of an oilman worker wearing a steel helmet, with sleeves rolled up? Oilmen from all over the world would be attending and exhibiting their products.

Gaylord told me we could get on as ushers, during evenings and Saturdays; that the pay was good. With looming hospital bills, I decided to go with Gaylord and apply for the job. We were hired. I got the chance to look at the exhibits, while helping people find certain exhibits.

One day I heard a lady behind me ask if I could help her. I turned around and faced who I thought was Elizabeth Taylor. She was asking directions to the Lear Jet exhibit. I became so flustered in trying to give directions, to what I thought was one of my favorite actresses', that I had to finally say, come with me.

On the way to the exhibit I said who I thought she was. She smiled and said others had made that same mistake about who she was. She then told me her name. I left her at the Lear Jet exhibit. I got many questions about her from fellow ushers. I was shocked to read in the newspaper, a few weeks later, that she had died in Dallas.

When I got rid of the horse and truck, I bought a used VW bug with sliding cloth sunroof. That way Jane or I had a second car. Going to the oil show, I'd drive the VW. When the show closed at the end of two weeks, exhibitors got rid of some items. I chose a tall potted indoor plant.

To get it home that night became a challenge. The only way I could get it in my VW was through the top. I managed to get it placed onto the passenger seat. Several inches of the plant stuck out of the top of my VW. The plant was so thick with leaves that I could barely see out the passenger window. I had to search, by feel, for the gear shift. Needless to say people, in passing, looked to see who was driving. I could hardly be seen.

One day Gaylord came upstairs to my desk to get my opinion on an outside project. I was surprised to learn from him that the guy who got my Management Information System project was also building apartments for married college students in Weatherford, Oklahoma. When I asked how the guy could do that kind of a project that far from Tulsa, Gaylord said he was a pilot and rented a plane. Gaylord suggested we build apartments for married college students. I told him I'd think about it.

A few days later I decided to see if there was a market for such. I wrote several letters to colleges in the region. Several didn't indicate a need, but, the one from Kansas University in Lawrence, Kansas did. They said they had a need of over one hundred. I drove to Lawrence on a Saturday

With that letter in hand, I went to an architect who had won an award for a high school design, his name was Bill. I told him of my idea, showed him the letter from Kansas and asked if he was interested. He said his business was in a slow period and he could take some time to come up with a design, if I could find a financial backer.

By looking through Tulsa contractors, I came across Ralph. He was a builder of several shopping centers. I got an appointment with him at his office. In his office I noticed a picture of him, rifle in hand, standing next to a dead Kodiak bear. I had read the book "How to win friends and influence people" by Dale Carnage. In the book Carnage said that every person has something they are proud of on display; it was up to a person to discover that object or thing. Once discovered you can then get a good conversation going. That conversation makes you a friend.

Although Ralph knew what I was coming to see him about, he enjoyed telling me about his hunt for the bear. He and his guide had tracked the bear for hours. They came upon the bear among a stand of young pine trees, about the size of a muscular man's arm. The guide said the bear was too close to shoot. A Kodiak bear can cover quite a distance before dying, even when shot in the heart. Ralph said he shot the bear in its hump to eliminate its mobility. The bear, when hit and going down, splintered a young pine tree with a swing of its paw.

After listening to Ralph's story and my asking questions, we became friends. He considered our project and how he'd make a profit building the project, and he would have part ownership. It was win-win for him. He told me to go head and set up a meeting with Bill and Gaylord, and let him know.

I sat up the meeting two weeks from Saturday. In that time Bill made a great color artist conception drawing of the proposed apartments. The apartment buildings were octagonal. Each apartment was pie shaped. The living-room and single bedroom was up front. The kitchen and bath was in back near the apartment building's center repair core. The center core allowed easy access for plumbing and electrical repairs, if needed. Each apartment building had eighteen apartments. The design was of six buildings with green zones in between. By this design each apartment building could be built individually, removing the possibility of over-building. It was a great idea.

At the meeting, Bill went through the plans. I had gone to Lawrence, Kansas and found some acreage for sale near the campus. When Bill finished his presentation, He said that he should be President of our new company. This didn't set well with Ralph, I could tell. Ralph said, "Alright. Joe will be vice-president, Gaylord in charge of rentals and promotions; as for me call me chief janitor."

Everything appeared to be a go. Then Ralph ran into a problem with the city over one of his shopping malls. They put new regulations on him, a big costly problem to correct and he pulled out of our project. He acknowledged it was a good project, one of the best he had seen.

I went searching for another backer. I found a company in New York that indicated an interest. They wanted to see the plans and layout. Bill decided he'd rent a Cessna 170 and we'd fly the plans to New York. He took along a couple from Pryor, Oklahoma to share expenses. While in New York, a friend of Bill got us tickets to two great Broadway Plays, *Hello Dolly* and *Barefoot in the Park*. *Hello Dolly* had Carol Channing. *Barefoot in the Park* had Robert Redford and Jane Fonda. To read about that experience, go to my book of short stories *Tim's World* and read the short story called *Pilot's Error*.

The day arrived that I dreaded. Our Apollo contract had wound down. I was given the choice of being laid-off in Tulsa or return to Autonetics in California. I stalled as long as I could. I put out my resume to various local companies. Since Oklahoma is considered an oil state, with several oil companies, and I was in aerospace, I was turned down.

It seems that bad news comes in bunches. I learned from my mother's postal clerk that my mother had to take frequent rest breaks, lying down on a cot in back. In 1969, I drove my mother to see a doctor in Muskogee.

In questioning her about postal operations, she would answer quickly and accurately. Then as though an after-thought, as though he had forgotten, he asked her who our nation's President was. She snapped back Harry S. Truman. Her so positive response made it hard for the doctor and me to keep from laughing. The present President was Lyndon Johnson. Truman was two Presidents in the past. The doctor and I learned that my mother had Alzheimer's disease. It was in the early stages and my mother wanted to try to work until she was seventy.

In 1969, I left Jane and the kids in Oklahoma, planning to keep sending resumes from California to other nearby states, hoping I could find work. We really hated to have to sell and move. I left our ford station wagon with Jane and drove the VW bug to California. Put-putting along, big cars would zoom past me. Later these same cars would again pass me. I realized they had probably stopped each time to get gas, where I didn't have to. That made me proud of that little bug.

In California I found a motel that gave a discount for renting by the week. They had a machine that dispensed a can of hot soup for a quarter. That became my evening meals. For breakfast it was coffee and a roll at work. Lunch was at a fast food place. On special days, my work buddy Kris and I would have lunch at the Silver Saddle restaurant. It was self-serve, all you eat, on that day. Where Kris could put all that food was a mystery me. He would load up his plate to where even an olive wouldn't fit on top, and then order strawberry shortcake for desert.

Kris learned that I was washing my shirts and underwear in my motel room sink and living off canned soup, sending Jane all my paycheck over and above my expenses in California. My weekly expenses being motel rent, food and gasoline for the car.

Kris and his wife Myrna loaned me a hot plate and a small pan, so I could have hard boiled eggs.

I looked in the help wanted newspaper ads and got a night job working for a pizza parlor nearby. I was tender of the beer bar and "buzzed" tables. The job meant that I could get a free hot meal each night I worked.

They had great spaghetti and green salads, as well as pizzas. I made good friends with several of the workers, especially a young Italian maker of pizzas. He spoke broken English and several others treated him badly. One night he saw me trying to make my own pepperoni pizza. I had used the brush to put the sauce on the bread, had added a few pepperonis and was sprinkling on some cheese. He said, "No! No! Lots of cheese ah." He then took handfuls of cheese and put it on my pizza. He was a great guy.

As beer bar tender, I learned what various customers usually ordered. One older couple would order a pitcher of beer, saying, "With little foam." When I saw them coming I had a pitcher of beer waiting, little foam. The band leader would order a special bottle of beer, during breaks. When the band took a break and the band leader headed my way, I had his special bottle open and ready. One lady tipped me a dollar to taste her pizza. She thought it didn't taste right. I told her it must have been the combination taste of beer and pizza. She thanked me and gave the tip.

My motel room was at the end of the air-conditioning run and got very cold at night. I came down with a bad cold with fever. I called the pizza place to let the owner know I was too sick to come to work. He fired me. I told him I'd be in on Friday to pick up my check.

When I went in, I sat at the bar while he went to write up my check. Some of my old customers came up and asked why I wasn't tending bar. I told them I had been fired. As the pizza parlor owner approached with my check, one of my old customers spoke up loud enough to be heard by the owner, saying, "You're the best bar tender this place ever had. I'll miss you."

I wasn't too pleased when Jane asked for additional funds to join a bowling league in Broken Arrow. From my room I'd type up resumes tailored towards the job I was applying for, and mail them to various companies.

At work, I was assigned to work on standards and procedures. I shared a cubical with another guy, who wasn't friendly. It was a relief when I was called upon to go meet with those that had an idea for the company to investigate and consider.

I looked at a patent that one scientist had come up with. It used small VW engines in series to power what was now a big diesel truck engine, with poor gas mileage, pulling a trailer. The idea would mean a lower cost for trucking, but, not practical at the time.

He also had a patent on what he called the "kneeling camel." For big rigs hauling trailers, they normally back up to an unloading dock. If an unloading dock isn't available, it takes more time using a ramp to unload. His idea was using a hydraulic system to lower the trailer to the ground. Once unloaded the trailer, by hydraulics, would return to its regular height. It's a clever idea but not practical at the time.

I then had a meeting with four PhDs on an idea that really excited me. Their proposal was an American Transcontinental Canal. The proposal called for using existing dry river beds, dry washes and existing water ways to cross from Brownsville, Texas to below San Clemente, California. They had the route mapped out. By this route less digging was required. The canal was to be 1,000 feet wide, to handle big ships crossing from the Gulf of Mexico to the Pacific Ocean, a shorter route than the Panama Canal.

If I remember correctly, the proposed route would follow the Pecos River to around Roswell, New Mexico, then cut across to the Gila River and on to an area near San Clemente, California. The total distance would be around 1,500 miles. This really shook up the Corp of Engineers. In their mind it meant digging a huge canal 1,500 miles. They didn't consider the existing waterways and dry river beds.

True, these waterways would need some expansion. To go over mountain ranges, they proposed what they called a "Ripple" system, instead of expensive locks. When water is squeezed closer together it will rise. Thus the canal would be narrower when going over mountain ranges.

The canal is to be started at both ends, using GPS guidance to meet up. Old mothballed LTS ships from WWII would be converted into floating dormitories to house canal workers. Workers would be trained in using fast drying cement. The canal would make available jobs for thousands of workers with many skills.

Once built the canal would open up millions of acres of desert to agriculture. A 1,000 foot wide channel would aid in controlling illegal immigration from the south. Passage fees levied against ships using the canal would pay back construction costs. Presently close to 15,000 ships use the Panama Canal yearly and China has the concession that controls both ends of this canal. If they ever decided to close the Panama Canal to our ships it would cause a lot of havoc. Think how many more nations would use a shorter route? It's a good idea that should be considered.

The guy I had to work with became intolerable to be around. Kris went to his boss and got me on in his department as a Logistical Engineer. I was assigned the Guidance System on the Minuteman ICBM Missile. I was to determine the expertise of the Air Force personnel and equipment needed to enter the missile silo and repair the missile's guidance unit, if needed. This unit was usually removed and taken back into the shop to be repaired. Another unit was installed in its place. I had to determine how long this took. That would determine how long the missile would be down. It was interesting work and I liked the group.

In the winter of 1969, I could stall the company no longer in moving my family back to California. It was a sad day for me and my family. We'd have to give up a home we loved so much. I flew back to Oklahoma and contacted a moving van to pick up our household goods. I rented a small trailer for some of our personal things. It was in the dead of winter. The moving van called the weather station and learned that Flagstaff, Arizona was having twelve-foot snow drifts. The driver told me about this, saying he was going south to El Paso, Texas and then Interstate 10 to California. I decided to follow the same route.

In Oklahoma an ice storm had hit. A person was a real gambler, if he drove more than 5 MPH. We had car trouble midway through Texas, to add to our misery. We were already depressed about having to leave Oklahoma.

By the time we reached El Paso the weather was warm and pleasant. We spent a miserable night at a motel in Lordsburg, New Mexico. They were having a dust storm. I tried to help my family by positive comments about the warm weather and all the greenery in winter. We stopped at a rest area in Arizona that had teepee type covers over tables. I thought it would be a fun experience for the kids.

Autonetics put us up for a month at the Apollo motel in Downey, California. We had a unit with a small kitchen. The place had a swimming pool. Property behind the pool's bordering cinderblock wall had an avocado tree, whose branches overhung the motel property fence. Our kids picked those avocados and we'd have them at a meal. Each workday I'd drive to Autonetics Division in Anaheim.

With our motel time running out, I talked with my uncle about properties for sale, to see if I could work out a deal on one, while our home in Broken Arrow was being sold. My uncle told me of a house at 24220 Park Street in Walteria, a part of southern Torrance. He said he'd use his commission for selling me that house, as my down-payment. We quickly accepted his generous offer and moved into the house. It meant a long drive for me and several close calls on the freeway system, but, we had a home. We had our first Christmas there in 1969.

The house on Park Street was a two story townhouse on a 25 x 100 foot lot. It had a Spanish design and was attractive. Walteria was a nice neighborhood. A major grocery store was across Pacific Coast highway accessed by stop lights. Cheri would attend South High. Jeff, Jim and Debbie Walteria grade school.

One day at work I got a call from my old El Segundo boss, Glenn fielding. He was now a scientist on the new F-107 contract proposal. He asked me to join a group of fourteen working on the plane's wiring system. I would head up the group and be promoted to supervisor. I quickly accepted the offer, and its pay increase. Now I would have only a short drive to work. When Rockwell didn't get the contract, it was awarded to Republic's F-105 Thunder-chief; it meant I was out of a job. Others in my group had more seniority than my fourteen years.

I studied and got my real estate salesman license, and went to work for my uncle at Provincial Realty on Hawthorn Boulevard in Walteria. Jane learned that her father had leukemia. She, with Elizabeth, flew back east. She was there when he passed away.

When Rockwell didn't get the F-107 contract, they learned that the F-105's flying abilities was to be shown to the Secretary of Defense at Wright-Patterson AFB in Ohio. One of Rockwell's Field Service representatives managed to get a seat behind the Secretary. The F-105 flew low over the field, fired after-burners and climbed quickly to its peak altitude before stall speed was reached. Our company's F-107 dropped its landing gears, bounced its tires on the runway a couple of times, fired after-burners and did barrel rolls out of sight. The surprised Secretary asked, "What was that?"

Our Rep tapped him on the shoulder and said, "That's the plane you didn't buy."

I liked real estate, seeing what people had done to improve the values of their homes. I learned that trying to be a salesman and being called to go grocery shopping can be frustrating. My uncle and boss would tell me to get Jane to walk the two blocks to the store, but, I never did.

When Jane's father died, her mother moved to Hamilton, Montana to be near Jane's brother, Robert. Jane took the kids and went to visit her mother. One day missionaries from the Church of Jesus Christ of Latter-Day Saints came by. They asked if I'd like to know about their church. I bluntly told them that if what they taught couldn't be proven, they were wasting their time. They told me fair enough.

Although we had several bibles in our house, none had been read. The missionaries would teach a lesson that had bible quotes and ask me to read the scripture from my bible. They would then leave a missionary tract, with the bible references, for me to study for myself. I was determined to prove them wrong. I took one of our bibles and would read several chapters of scriptures in front and behind the quoted scripture; to be sure it wasn't taken out of context.

The more I read the more excited I became. I had grown up listening to preachers give sermons. They would mention some scriptures, none of which completed a clear picture, to me, of god's plans. Minister's teachings were like a large jigsaw puzzle where pieces fit here and there, but no clear picture showed. I became so frustrated with all this, when we lived in Broken Arrow; I told Jane I was considering forming my own church.

The LDS missionaries in their third lesson taught the Plan of Salvation lesson, again having me read the bible for me to see for myself. I remember telling them, "I'll be! It all fits!" After all those years of wanting to know God's plan for me, but never getting it from preachers, I now had a clear picture of the truth. I began reading the bible with a deep desire to learn more. I became a bible scholar. I decided I wanted to join the Church of Jesus Christ of Latter-Day Saints. I could hardly wait to share the good news with Jane and the kids.

My family returned and I excitedly told the good news. I got a shock. Jane wanted nothing to do with the LDS church and told me not to tell our kids anything about what I believed. For awhile Jane wouldn't let the LDS missionaries into our house. When she did let them in, she would take the kids upstairs, so they couldn't hear.

On the next trip to Montana, I went along. I had never been in that part of the country. It was absolutely beautiful. The streams were clear, mountains all around and sparse population. Jane and her mother encouraged me to try and get a job in the area. I applied for a position as an insurance agent for Prudential. It had a small trainer's salary for the first quarter. They said they would let me know, since I would also need some moving money.

Back in California things were not going well with the kids. A bully in the Walteria School was trying to pick a fight with Jeff, chasing him home almost daily. Cheri was signing my name to notes to go off campus and was almost failing in her grades. We forgave her. Jane baked Cheri a small individual cake and I bought her an orchid. I took these to south High and left it with a councilor to give to Cheri.

I had been chosen to be scoutmaster of the local troop. I was later "drummed out" and became a member of the Order of the Arrow, a prestigious award. I have always loved scouting. One night at a troop meeting, I got a call from Jane to come home immediately, that Cheri said some boys had poured something down her throat.

I got home and quickly rushed Cheri to the hospital. While Cheri and I were on our way to the hospital, Jane called the police and told what had happened. They met us at the hospital. The hospital pumped Cheri's stomach. The police came out to where I waited in the waiting room, telling me that Cheri and her girlfriend had gotten into the girl's father's liquor cabinet.

Cheri graduated from South High. About that time I heard from Prudential. They had accepted me and told me to come to work in Missoula. With all that was going on in Walteria, I quickly accepted the job. We spent one last Christmas at our home on Park Street in Walteria.

It was decided Cheri would go with me to Montana to get a job, we'd both stay with Jane's mother while I was trying to see if I could sell insurance, then if all went well the family would move to Hamilton.

I got a speeding ticket in Utah, requiring me to go before a judge. I told him I was going to a new job and agreed to pay the fine out of my first check. This delay caused Cheri and me to have to stay in a motel in Nephi, Utah. I made sure the room had two double beds. I was so tired that I went to sleep immediately when my head hit the pillow. I didn't know when Cheri went to sleep.

We had been traveling I-15 from California but took highway 43 at Dewey, Montana to cut over to highway 93 and on to Hamilton. We went through the small ranching town of Wisdom. Ranches in this area are huge. Next day we arrived at Jane's mother's place.

I began my work with Prudential and Cheri got a job as waitress in a Chinese Café in Hamilton. I would drive to work at Prudential, driving forty-four miles to and from Missoula each day. I was taught how to analyze customer's policies, write policies and balance my books.

The idea was to see if customers had enough insurance to cover their last expenses, home free of debt, income for wife and money to cover kid's education. I would spend the day calling people to get an appointment to go over their insurance needs at night. When the family arrived, I didn't like being away from them at night.

I did well in insurance, but I didn't like it. With the approach of fall, it was time to go pick up Jane and the kids before winter set in. In October 1970, I rented the largest U-Haul truck they had in Hamilton. I learned it was cheaper to rent the truck in Montana and drive down to California, than catch a bus and rent a truck in California. The U-haul place in Montana also attached a fourteen-foot trailer to the truck, telling me if I didn't need it, leave it in California.

Retracing the route that Cheri and I had driven, I arrived in Salt Lake when it was dark and raining. I was in the center lane heading south. I noticed several police cars with flashing lights ahead of me on the shoulder. When I glanced to see what had happened, the truck, trailer and I ran out of paved highway. The drop off from the concrete highway to a new roadbed being prepared was about eight inches. There had been no warning signs or barriers. It bounced me around a bit. I put the truck in compound and eased back upon the concrete highway, a lane to my right.

Arriving in Walteria, I was happy to learn that Jane had set up my being baptized into the Church of Jesus Christ of Latter-Day Saints. Many refer to the church as LDS or by its nickname, Mormon. So, on October 13, 1970, I was baptized. She and the kids were there to view the event.

Joining the LDS church caused a big change for good in my life. I would spend a great deal of time studying the bible, trying to understand Heavenly Father's plan. I wanted to share what I was learning with Jane and the kids. I was surprised when she told me I wasn't to teach our kids anything from the Bible that indicated what I believed. To do so would end our marriage.

Since I had become more scholarly in my in-depth study of the Holy Bible, this caused a hardship for me. I was excited with what I was learning, and I wanted to share what I had learned through my study. However, I promised Jane I wouldn't try to teach the kids what I had learned.

Our neighbor Don Carter and his wife Judy offered to help us pack our things in the U-Haul. Don at one time had worked for a moving company. With their help we soon had both truck and trailer fully loaded. We left our VW with Don and Judy, asking that they not drive it. I said I'd return for it. Writing this I wonder why Jane didn't drive the VW to Montana, following me in the truck. Jane and Elizabeth went by bus to Montana.

Jeff, Jim, Debbie and I rode in the cab of the truck. I think it was south of Pocatello, Idaho that I pulled off the highway and found a place where we could spend the night. The boys had their sleeping bags and slept outside on the ground. Deb and I slept in the truck's cab. It was a miserable night for all. The boys didn't use a ground cloth and the morning dew soaked their sleeping bags. It got so cold in the cab that Deb and I got very little sleep.

With an early morning start, we reached highway 43 heading towards Wisdom. It was a warm Indian summer day and I dozed off. The warmth of the sun and lack of sleep the night before took its toll on me. Highway 43 is a gravel road.

When the truck headed into the ditch, the kids screamed and I became wide awake. Split second thoughts told me I couldn't correct and get back on the highway, so I steered the truck into the ditch and back up on the far side. All of us in the truck cab were bouncing around.

A highway patrolman pulled up and came over to check on us. Both truck and trailer was upright. He asked what happened. I told him a white lie. I said the trailer had slipped on the gravel causing me to lose control. He told me he was amazed that I hadn't turned over. He radioed Wisdom and a tow truck came to help. With the tow truck's power winch and my putting our truck in compound, we were back upon the highway.

The rest of the way to Hamilton, I worried how much of our furniture had been broken. We had a French Provincial Hammond organ with spindly legs. I could just see those legs broken. When everything was unpacked and put into storage, only a desk we had refinished for the boys had a small scratch. I had to take the truck and attached trailer to a shop that used a torch to bend the trailer hitch down so that the trailer could be disconnected.

After a few days we found a house to rent. The previous tenants had left it a total mess; there was even human waste on the some of the walls.

255

Our whole family and Jane's mother pitched in to scrub and clean. We made some of the basement into bedrooms for the boys.

Later we got the chance to rent a nice place on 4th Street. It was large and roomy. Deb and Liz shared a room, Cheri made an enclosed porch her bedroom, Jane and I had a large master bedroom. The boys had separate bedrooms in a nicely finished basement. The house had a good heating system and kept the whole house warm in the winter. Later, Cheri moved to an apartment of her own.

Sundays were always a full day for me. I would spend three hours at my church and then two hours, with Jane and the kids, at the Methodist Church. I finally quit going with Jane to her church. I was well versed in bible scripture and could quickly tell when her preacher wasn't quoting a scripture correctly. So, I stopped going to her church. I tried to get Jane and the kids to go to church with me. She did let Debbie and Liz go once with me to an LDS service. I became very active in my church. I was ordained a Deacon on December 20, 1970 in Hamilton, Montana.

One summer two of Jane's uncles, both Methodist ministers, paid a visit to Jane's mother. During the visit, all in the family decided to take a hike up Blodgett Canyon, a beautiful place. During the hike I found both the uncles my companion. We traded scriptures. Eventually I found myself alone.

At our house on 4th Street, we told the owner that if he ever decided to sell, we would like to buy it. He said that he would let us know. On cold winter mornings, I would delay going to work and drive Liz to her kinder garden class. Jane would say she could bundle Liz up and Liz could walk to school, but I preferred to drive her to school. I'd leave work in Missoula early to drive her home. Liz was the baby of the family and I spoiled her. If

I sat down to watch TV, Liz would climb up on my lap and snuggle down in my arms. If I was stretched out on my stomach on the floor, Liz would get on my back and dangle her arms over my shoulders, watching TV. Things were going good.

On some weekends Jane and her mother would ask me to drive them to Missoula, in her Mother's Toyota, to shop. I was then asked to get them home so they wouldn't miss the next program of "As the World Turns." I, tongue in check, called it "As the World Churns."

One winter Jim borrowed my shotgun to go duck hunting. He broke through the ice on the edge of the river. I got a call from him asking to be picked up. When I picked him up, he was walking towards town. He was wet and cold. I got him home and got him in warm dry clothing. Jane made him some hot chocolate. He was one cold kid. What amused me was that here he was bone chilling cold, but, more worried about my gun getting wet. He informed me that he made sure my gun didn't get wet? I've always felt close to Jim, we were hunters.

In the early 1970s, I got a call from my aunt Lettye that my mother was in the Muskogee hospital, and that she thought my mother wouldn't make it. My mother had been retired from the post office and was living with Lettye. Lettye had a car and earned a small living. I thought with my mother's retirement income that she and Lettye would do quite well being together. That was not to be. Leaving the kids to be looked after by Jane's brother and his wife, Jane, her mother and I left for Muskogee in our Ford station wagon.

Arriving at Muskogee General Hospital, my mother couldn't walk very far without being winded. I asked what medicines she was taking. I was informed that for her nerves, she was being given 100 mg of Valium and

100 mg Thorazine. I learned that combination of drugs would be enough to put down a race horse, much less a human. Then, I learned she was allowed all the coffee she wanted. I got very angry at her doctor. I told him that he was giving medications to calm her down and coffee, with all that caffeine, to stir her up, that I wanted her released from the hospital, now.

He cancelled his and the hospital fees and released her. We took my mother to her sister's house to rest a few days, before taking her with us to Montana. In the process we missed Cheri's, our foster daughter's wedding. My mother finally gained enough strength to make the trip to Montana. I made the back of our station-wagon into a bed for my mother and Jane's. My mother stayed with Jane's mother. At this time Alzheimer's hadn't taken its toll. My mother just had trouble remembering some current things.

At work I was doing well. With the indication from Bill, my boss, that he was grooming me to take over his job as Staff Manager, when he moved to Seattle. I began doing training of new agents; helping them to balance books. This took away from my production time. My rationale was that before the next quarter ended I'd be the Staff manager, with a salary and enough production to make it to the following quarter.

One Saturday morning, while I was balancing out books, Bill's wife dropped in. Bill was on a short errand. When I asked her if she was looking forward to moving to Seattle, she gave me a shock. She let me know that they would never move to Seattle. About this time, our landlord told us he had sold the house we were renting to a friend; that we must move in thirty days. We'd have to put our things in storage again and move in with Jane's mother until we could find something to rent.

I realized that unless I could sell some large policies soon, we couldn't make it on my income the next quarter, and Jane didn't want to get a temporary job. I made several calls to businessmen. I got an appointment with Fred Kunselman.

When I met with him he told me of a metal forming company he was putting together and he felt he needed additional insurance. He said he had two partners. I asked what would be done with the company in case one died. He hadn't thought about that. I then asked, "Would one of the widows own that part of the company?" He hadn't thought about that either. I presented him a plan that would use insurance money to buy-out the widows.

I asked, "When would the company come into existence?" He let me know that when his company was funded, he would buy the insurance I had recommended. They were three $300,000 dollar whole life policies. They would have made up what I had lost this quarter, while helping my staff manager.

In conversation he let me know about his invention of a machine that with hydraulics could bend metal without work hardening it, solving a difficult problem in metal working. He showed me some lab test of metals formed by his machine. I asked how he planned to build the machines, and how he would market them. He said he'd build one machine at a time and sell it, then start on another. I let him know about my engineering background, telling him that his approach was not a good idea.

I had gone over the machine's plans that he showed me. I told him how to build it on an assembly line, and that since his machine was one of a kind he should lease them out, giving him a steady cash flow. He asked if I would join his company as an advisor with some stock shares and a salary. The offer was good. I was faced with a dilemma. I couldn't sell the policies I needed to have a decent quarter earnings until his company came into being.

When I got back to the office, Bill asked what had happened. Since he had put me in a financial mess, I didn't tell all that happened, and the offer made to me by Fred. For once I would "straddle the fence." So that I'd still get some income from Prudential, I said I'd be working closely with Fred to get his company funded, and my large insurance policies for the company funded. That seemed to satisfy Bill, and my being away from the office.

Fred let me know that a mine owner in Laramie, Wyoming had agreed to put up dory bars, valued at one million and a half dollars, for a share in Fred's company. Fred asked if I would go with him to Laramie; he had a private pilot flying up in a Beechcraft A-tail aircraft. I had double reasons to go with Fred. If Fred could get his company underway, I would have a good job and income, and I would have the sale of two large insurance policies. Fred said his company would be located in Rhinelander, Wisconsin.

Fred drove me to the Billings, Montana airport to met Chet in the Beechcraft. It being winter, I listened in on Chet and Fred discussing weather conditions between Billings and Laramie. When I heard there was a storm front and Fred still wanting to try for Laramie, I was concerned. Chet indicated he would try to fly between two mountain ranges. He could tell I wasn't too happy with Fred's decision.

It was dark when we left Billings. We began our flight in a valley with high mountains on each side. Chet informed us he had IFA [Instrument flight Authorization] approved license. It began to snow. When I couldn't see the wing tips of our small plane, I could remain quiet no longer. I told Chet and Fred if they we foolish enough to fly in this between two mountain ranges, put me on the ground. Chet smiled and told me he had already changed course; that we were headed back to Billings. He had no more than said that and I saw the lights of Billings.

The storm front moved through that night and next morning the sun was out clear and bright. Since Fred had implied he was considering buying a plane, Chet had Fred fly us to Laramie. Again I wasn't too happy that Fred didn't have a license, and we had a strong cross-wind at the Laramie airport. Chet talked Fred down. It was a rough landing—Fred didn't control well.

Bob, the mine owner, met us at the airport. I went with the three to talk to a possible person who would take the dory bars as collateral for the loan. Chet and I waited in the receptions room. Discussions in the office got heated between Bob and the guy with the money. The guy with the money was demanding more collateral and a piece of Bob's mine.

Suddenly I heard the guy tell Bob that he'd better accept his offer or he'd call Louie in Chicago. Bob fired back to the guy that if Louie came, he'd send him back in a box and come after him—the money guy. We were dealing with an organized crime member. I could hardly wait to get out of there.

That avenue closed, I brought up that Banks in Oklahoma have loaned on speculative oil drilling, and maybe they would take the dory bars as security for a loan. Fred agreed to give it a try. He sent Chet and I with half of the heavy dory bars to Muskogee, Oklahoma's Hatbox Field. I called my aunt in Muskogee and asked her to pick me up at Hatbox, and drive me to my vacant mother's home in Warner. She agreed. Chet went back to

Laramie to pick up Fred and the rest of the dory bars, and join me in Warner.

With a million and a half dollars of dory bars stashed in my mother's house, I called some banks. I got appointments with the two major banks in Muskogee —Citizens and First National. My mother had a long and good standing with Citizens. Both banks said they were not interested, even if we had pure gold and silver bars.

Fred used his credit card and made several calls. He tied up a mine near Homestake Pass outside of Butte, Montana. He received an assay that showed the mine had platinum oxides. Another of his calls was to a guy in Santa Fe, New Mexico, who claimed he could extract out the precious metals from the dory bars. Fred and Chet flew to Santa Fe with the first load of dory bars. Chet then returned for me and the rest of the bars.

After Chet took off from Muskogee's Hatbox Field he told me he was tired from the back and forth flights, and needed a nap. He knew of my flying interest and asked if I'd take over flying and get us to Santa Fe. I told him I would. Having flown as a radio operator in the plane's cockpit, I knew the plane's instruments. Chet gave me the heading and at what altitude to fly, then went to sleep.

Heading west I had to occasionally ease back on the plane's yoke to keep the proper altitude. It was interesting to note that the land below seemed flat when it actually was rising. Later I learned that we had flown from 600 foot elevation to 7000 foot elevation. I woke Chet up to make our landing in Santa Fe.

We were met by Fred and the guy who claimed he could extract the precious metals from the dory bars. I don't recall his name. The best way to identify him is "crook." I soon learned that there are many shady characters, when dealing with precious metals.

Fred had rented three separate rooms for us at the La Fonda hotel, in the heart of Santa Fe. It is located at the end of the old Spanish trail. For the next few days we kept pressuring the "crook" for information on how he was doing. He would stall us by saying it'll take a few more days.

Fred and Chet decided to go to Salt Lake City on the business of tying up the mining property outside of Butte, Montana. I was to stay behind and keep pressure on the "crook." I would call him three times a day, always getting the not yet story.

To kill time I visited the Catholic Church with a mystery. The church had been built in the 1800s. A choir loft had been built in, but without stairs. The story is that a carpenter appeared one day, carrying his small wooden box of tools. He said he could build the stairs. He built a spiral staircase that supported itself, without any set of plans, and then disappeared without getting paid. I saw that staircase. It's beautiful.

On another other day I spent time at the old Governor's Presidio. It's the place where governor Lew Wallace, in the late 1800s, finished his famous book *Ben Hur* by candle light, for fear that Billy the Kid might try to kill him. During the day, Pueblo Indians would spread their beautiful wool woven blankets on the porch of the Presidio. They would then place their hand designed jewelry of turquoise and silver on it for sale to tourist.

One day I was sitting in the lobby of the La Fonda, studying people. It always was interesting, to me, to study people and how they act, tying to guess their occupations in life. Men began bringing in large lights on stands. I got up from my chair and went to the back of the room, to see what was going to happen. A guy that came with the camera crew

263

identified himself to us as being a Director. He said he was setting up a scene for the movie *Ginger in the Morning;* when he gave the signal, all in the room must remain quiet.

While the crew was setting up for the shoot, I asked the guy next to me if he had any idea how the crew and cast were paid. Was it by the month, by time or contract? He told me and asked if lived in Santa Fe. I told him the purpose of my visit to Santa Fe. I then asked the same question to him. He told me he was the producer of the movie.

We were briefly joined by Susan Oliver, the supporting star of the movie. When she leaned I had flown in on a Beechcraft A-Tail airplane, she asked if she could get some flying time on it—she had flown several other types of planes. I told she would have to ask Chet when he got back. I promised to let her know.

After Monte Markham's scene was shot in the lobby of the La Fonda, the next scene was in the dining-room. The scene has Susan Oliver and Sissy Spacek sitting at a table talking. The director was using a small spoon as he talked about what he wanted to get out of this shoot. He put the spoon down and the scene was shot. He realized that his putting the spoon down before the shoot meant there would be two small spoons on the table. He ordered a retake. All of this was going on in 1972 and 1973.

I got tired of waiting for the "crook" to produce results. I called Fred and told him I was heading back home. He took care of my hotel bills and had my airline ticket waiting at the ticket counter. I got back to Hamilton, Montana and learned that our landlord had sold the house we were renting to one of his friends. We were given our notice to vacate. We had to move in with Jane's mother.

Fred called me and asked if I'd go with him as an advisor to a one day meeting with some top businessmen and lawyers in Salt Lake. Again hoping I'd get something for all my efforts, I agreed to go. He said he'd drive us down. We met in an attorney's office, in SLC. There were six of us in the room. Most of us were dressed in dark suits, except for a guy in western-wear and cowboy boots. He was asked why he was there. He said he was representing a countess who owned the Hatpin ranch near Wisdom. I later learned the ranch had 219,000 acres. One of the other in the meeting was the President of Tuma Corporation in California. Fred showed them the black sands he had brought along, and an assay report.

Those in the room were skeptical and about to turn down the offer to be part of the project that Fred offered. They wouldn't accept that in the container holding the black sand was platinum ore oxides, locked up in the sands. I got them to issue Fred a letter of intent—if he could produce the precious ores, they agree to buy so many tons. When Fred and I were walking back to his car, he waved the paper saying, "I'm richer than Howard Hughes." I informed him he had nothing but a piece of paper, until he supplied the precious refined ores.

About a week after Fred and I returned to Montana I got a call from Fred. He asked if I would come to the mine and help him with the work. Fred had used his letter of intent to rent a shaker-table to separate out the black sands from raw materials. He was storing the black sand in fifty-gallon drums in a bonded warehouse in Butte. I agreed to help.

I arrived at the mine to find Fred, and the "cowboy" at the meeting in Salt Lake, busy at work. We would be staying in a two-story cabin on the site. Fred had rented a gasoline power generator to give us lights and run the shaker table. Fred's wife was also on site. Food was prepared on a wood-burning stove. When I arrived dinner was being prepared. Fred asked me to take a bucket to the spring and get some water. When I got back with it, he lifted a metal plate on the stove and poured in the water. I wondered why he was putting out the fire. It was then that I learned the stove had a separate tank to heat water.

The "cowboy" and I had a room upstairs. Walking caused that floor to oscillate. I didn't trust the floor and moved my bed next to a supporting wall. Every time Fred went into Butte, it seemed he brought back some piece of equipment. I advised against this, but he wouldn't listen. Since the material being mined was in a small pocket, I figured it was alluvial material, which must come from a vein somewhere up above.

I advised Fred to do some core sample drilling and use an atomic absorption specter photometer to try and find the source. A friend of mine in Muskogee uses this instrument, and had told me about it. Fred was separating out plenty of black sand on the shaker-table and ignored my advice. He was getting his operation deeper and deeper in debt, and became paranoid. When he purchased an automatic pistol and began sleeping with it under his pillow, I decided it was time for me to leave. A few weeks later Fred, and the "cowboy", left. Fred was being pursued by bill collectors.

I needed some kind of work to provide for my family. My aunt Lettye said she could use me to hang the drapes she was selling. She said the guy she was presently paying made good money, charging by the bracket. She offered me the job. Since our furniture was in storage, I rented a fourteen foot trailer, to take our personal items of clothing and some toys for the kids, and hooked it behind my Ford station-wagon. Jane, my mother, the kids and I headed for Oklahoma.

Before leaving for Oklahoma, I received a call from the owner of the mine by Homestake Pass. That was how I learned that Fred had abandoned the project and left the state. The mine owner said he trusted me. He wanted to know if he had a platinum mine, as Fred had said, or not. I told him I have a friend in Muskogee who could answer that question, but, I'd needed ore samples. On our way to Oklahoma, I went by the mine owner's house in Butte, Montana, to get the samples. I took samples of raw material and of the black sands that Fred had been putting in a bonded warehouse.

It was the dead of winter. I had watched the weather report to try and catch a high front going through the area—a high front meant clear weather. With the beginning of the high weather front, we headed for Billings, Montana. My plan was to go down I-90 to I-25, and on in to Denver before a low front came through.

Outside of Billings, the left tire on the trailer blew out. I had to hitch-hike back to Billings, get approval from U-Haul for a new tire, and then be driven back to our car and the guy mount it. This caused quite a delay.

A new weather front moved in as we left Chugwater, Wyoming. We ran into a ground blizzard. It was snowing hard and being blown by the wind. I could barely see past the front of our car, requiring travel at about 5 MPH. When I tried to go up a small hill, my tires spun. Getting out of our car, a trucker, who had been following behind us, offered to help me put my chains on, using his big eighteen-wheeler truck with flashing lights to protect our rear in the dark. I took the windward side of our car to put on chains. Before I could get them secured, snow was flowing over me.

The trucker told me to follow him; that he would knock holes through the snow drifts that were now building up. I followed him all the way to Cheyenne. As a courtesy for his help, I bought him his dinner.

I was determined to get far enough south to not be caught in another storm. We left Cheyenne and headed south to Denver. Along the way, I removed the chains so we could travel faster. The warmer air felt good.

When we arrived at my aunt's house in Muskogee, my mother wanted to stay in her home. Jane and the two girls, Debbie and Elizabeth, wanted to stay in Muskogee and enroll in school there. Although I preferred my mother's house in Warner, I stayed with Jane and the two girls. Jim said he'd stay at my mother's house, fix meals, look after his grandmother and enroll in Warner schools.

My largest drapery hanging job with my aunt was a new nursing home under construction. It took me until almost midnight to get all room drapes installed. She then had a few individual drapes for me to install.

I checked with Bob, my friend who was testing the material I had given him from the mine owner in Butte. He told me that the black sand samples were worthless, but, the raw sample indicated a noble metal. I asked if it was platinum. He told me it was in the spectrum of platinum. To be sure of the mineral, he sent the sample to a highly respected lab in Ohio.

A few days later Bob called to tell me the Ohio lab came back negative on platinum oxides; that the noble material was Columbite and Niobium. I said that meant the mine is worthless. He told me not so, that this mineral is used for coating the rotors on jet engines; that the only source has been from South America. To have this material in Montana would be as valuable as platinum. I thanked Bob and told him I'd let the mine owner know. Bob then told me of his idea to produce feldspathic glass sand from sands in the Arkansas River.

Bob told me that this type of sand was used in the glass industry, who presently buys it from foreign sources. He told me about the process for making it locally, the equipment needed and the cost. I let him know that I was interested and would see what I could do.

When my aunt's jobs ended, I got a job assisting Otis Eversole in real estate appraising. I took to appraising like a duck to water, and the pay was good. Otis would send me out in his company VW to record and measure all improvements of a property. I would then take pictures of the improvements and go to the county courthouse records to copy recent sales of similar properties in the area.

Back at the office I began studying Otis' previous appraisals, and learned how to use the Appraiser's handbook of values, to come up with an estimated value. I would tell Otis what I thought the value might be. When he finished his appraisal, he would let me know what value he came up with.

One day he came to my small office and told me I was the best appraiser he had ever known; that I should get my license as an Independent Fee Appraiser. Coming from Otis, who was considered the best condemnation appraiser in eastern Oklahoma, I was really pleased. I did pass the exam and became a licensed appraiser. It would change my life forever.

Some of the job assignments for Otis were a ranch that the Federal Government was taking a narrow strip of land from the owner, by condemnation, to build a high powered transmission line through. Otis came to my office with the picture I had taken of the guy's barn. The picture showed an old wind-sock. Otis had called the ranch owner and asked about the wind-sock. The rancher told Otis that years ago he used to fly from the ranch, but no longer. Otis told me that wind-sock was worth its weight in gold. When Otis went to court on this project, he took me with him. During his testimony at the trail he told the government's attorney, "You took this man landing field away." The rancher won a good settlement.

On another assignment was in Macintosh County, south of Checotah. Oklahoma State highway department was taking a small sliver of land from in front of a business that was on the south side of a major highway's corner. The owner of the land was offered $100 for that piece of land. Studying land sales in the area, and the effects the widening of the highway meant on the business being affected, I came up with an appraised value of the land being taken as $4,300. The main expense came from having to move the business back a few feet. If the highway department had moved the road a few feet north it would have saved money.

I think the two most interesting appraisal assignments was a ranch property near Bartlesville and the Cherokee historical buildings in Tahlequah. The Federal government was taking several acres of ranch land for a reservoir, near Bartlesville. What made this appraisal interesting was putting a value on a pumping oil well and a railroad spur track to the property. The property also had a nice ranch house and several outbuildings. I came up with a value of $1.7 million. Later Otis said the rancher settled out of court for $1.4 million.

I was interested in the appraisal for the Cherokee Nation in Tahlequah because my Grandmother Ellison's mother is Cherokee, so we decedents think. In studying historical data I learned how the town got its name. There were three chiefs involved in the Trail of Tears forced movement to Oklahoma of the Cherokee nation. Two of the chiefs arrived early and signed a treaty with the Federal government, saying "Tahlequah", in Cherokee it meant "Two's enough." This angered the chief arriving late. When the Civil War began, the late arriving chief went with the south; the other two with the north.

On my last appraisal, I collected data for Otis. He rented a pilot and plane for this one. Otis gave me a detailed map of the Arkansas River, showing alluvial land made by the river. The appraisal was for the Cherokee nation. My assignment was to photograph the alluvial land from Muskogee to the Arkansas state line.

The plane used was a Piper super cub. When we approached the sites I was to photograph, I would lower my window, lean out and have the pilot crab-fly the plane. By this means I got a clear picture of the site without the plane's wing struts showing. Otis complemented me on the photos, and being good at taking pictures. He also let me know that he was now caught up and wouldn't need me. I was now out of work again.

Seeing nothing left, I called my uncle Bill at Provincial Realty. He said I could come back to work for him. He said I could stay at his house, and he'd pay me a base salary against a draw. The salary would give me a steady income and Bill would get paid back through my sales.

I drove the family back to Hamilton, Montana. My mother stayed with Lettye. Jane and the kids stayed with Jane's mother. Jane told me at the airport in Missoula to make lots of money, so she could buy a house in Hamilton. As the plane sped down the runway, I had an uneasy feeling it'd be the last time I saw them.

Chapter 23

My Uncle Bill and Aunt Beverley met me at the airport in Los Angeles. It was a pleasant drive to their home at #2 Fig Tree, Portuguese Bend. It was one of the nicest homes I had seen. It was a single story ranch style, two bedrooms with large family-room home. By Bill and Beverley's bedroom was next to a private Jacuzzi. There was a great view of the ocean. A telescope allowed one to see the ships heading in and out of Los Angeles harbor. The house had a small orchard and gazebo. The lawn and landscaping was taken care of by a gardener. Bill and Beverley's home was a picture of tranquility. The only problem it was near a slide area, but not in it at that time.

I started out sleeping on their huge couch in their family-room. Later I was moved to my cousin Lark's room. Mornings, Beverley fixed breakfast and left for work. Bill and I did the dishes and then drove to work in his Cadillac Coupe Deville. I worked hard at listing and selling real estate. Weekends I'd hold open house, a good way to pickup people looking for a nice house.

Bill had a Rolls Royce that he would drive to work. Beverley had a Chevy corvette Sting-ray that she drove to work. Bill then made it possible for me to buy the Cad, by bank financing, saying I needed to have a nice car to show expensive Palos Verde and Rolling Hill properties. He also rented me one of his studio apartments on Hawthorne Boulevard. From the sales and listings I got, I was able to make my payments, buy food and send money to Jane. I quickly learned that I could burn up a lot of gasoline and time with people who had Champaign tastes but only a beer budget.

I would get calls from Jane pressing for more money to buy a home, to get out of her mother's home. They were not friendly calls. I was sending what I could, above what it took to meet my bills in California. The secretary at Provincial Realty, Dorothy, would let me know Jane was on the line. I didn't know until much later that the office was aware of these calls due to a temporary change in my personality. I was told I'd go from a happy outgoing person to a depressed introvert type of personality.

I discussed these things with my uncle Bill. My older son Jeff had joined the Navy. My next oldest son, Jim, was planning to join the Navy. That would leave only our foster daughter Debbie and Liz at home. Bill said that since Jane was staying with her mother, she should get a job and get her mother to watch over the two girls. To make matters worse I sent a large box of Christmas gifts, worth over three hundred dollars, for Jane and my family, by bus, at Christmas time, and it never arrived, and I had forgotten to insure it. Christmas 1974 was a disaster.

When I called Liz to wish her a happy birthday in 1975, Jane came on the line and asked for a divorce. She said she was going to a local attorney next week. Although Jane had mentioned divorce before, she sounded sincere this time. I tried to picture how that might affect our kids, since it would be in the local papers. I wondered if she had met someone else who was more compatible. I took a few days to consider Jane and my differences of interests. I could see that we didn't work all that well as a team. I couldn't expect any temporary help from her getting a job, until I got back up on my feet, again. I finally decided on going to a local attorney in Torrance, California, and filling for divorce. I told my attorney I'd leave everything that I owned in Montana to Jane, it was all that I had accumulated over the years. Such things as our Ford station-wagon, Hammond organ, my mother's roll top desk, my father's coin collection and his scout .22, and stamps my mother had given. I was to be allowed to have Liz visit me during the summer and would pay child support. Jane agreed to the terms, but Liz only visited me one summer, for a short time.

It was a sad time for me. I moped around the office. My help at this time came through my church. The harder I worked at church duties the less time I had to consider what was happening in my life.

I found that Dorothy and I were kindred spirits; we were similar in our interests. She was kind and always ready to help me. I began dating her. Her husband had divorced her; she and her kids were going through difficult times. He had been a big controller and had been unfaithful to her. However, he applied for the divorce. I enjoyed her kids; they were a brave bunch in spite of their hardships. I greatly admired their spunk.

Susan, a very pretty girl of sixteen, was spunky and outgoing, as well as her brothers Larry and Ron. She babysat kids, some on cruises in their parent's sail boats, and worked as a waitress. She was good in art and drama. Dan, the quiet one, and his youngest brother Ron would rake golf balls out of water traps on the golf course and sell them to golfers. Later Dan went to work for Radio shack. Larry raised a garden in their tiny back yard to help their finances. The family received no support from their father.

Before going to work for Provincial Realty as a secretary, Dorothy had worked as a sales and alteration clerk for a women's apparel shop; designed and made dresses for women. She also worked for a local ballet group, designing and making their costumes.

The kids would visit their mother at Provincial Realty. They were so friendly and outgoing. Dorothy and her kids were fun to be around.

With the wide range of our interest, in so many similar things, Dorothy and I found we enjoyed each other's company. It was relaxing to be around her. She, like her kids, was full of energy. During lunch breaks at Provincial, she and I would have lunch at Dos Amigos, a small Mexican restaurant among a series of shopping strip stores. Or, I might order a sandwich, a single order of potato salad and some half-pints of milk.

We'd park near the ocean to eat. We'd talk about movies, plays, music, ballet and what it'd be like to travel, both in the states and foreign. She would tell me about her life in Arkansas, Connecticut and California. I would tell her about Oklahoma and my adventures in the Air Force.

Dorothy was born in Little Rock, Arkansas February 25, 1933. Her father Gibson Emery Thibault was superintendent of schools in Pottsville, Arkansas. He had a Bachelor of Arts degree from College of the Ozarks in Clarksville, Arkansas. He majored in English and minored in History. Dorothy and I traced the Thibault ancestry back to Paris, France [PAF].

Her mother was Olive Doris Stevens from Orange, Connecticut. Olive's father was a prominent architect in Orange. Olive's mother was a Treat whose great-great-great grandfather was Governor Robert Treat of Connecticut, in the 1600s. Dorothy and I have traced the Treat line back to the 1400s in England.

Gibson Thibault and Olive Stevens met at a religious retreat at Bowling Green, Kentucky. They were married in Baton Rouge, Louisiana. They settled down in Pottsville, Arkansas, a few blocks from the school where Gibson was Superintendent.

Gibson was an Eagle Scout with all three palms, and the scoutmaster of the local troop. He would take his troop on trips to Petite Jean Mountain, and took Dorothy with him a few times.

Dorothy told me that when she was about three or four her mother had put her down for a nap, and lay down with her. When her mother went to sleep, Dorothy got up, tied her mother's shoe laces together and ran to the school where her dad was teaching. Her mother woke when Dorothy shut the front door, and was in hot pursuit. Dorothy burst into her father's class room, calling out, "Daddy, Daddy save me! Mommy's after me." This caused a lot of laughs from the students.

Gibson gave up his job as superintendent to join Olive in Connecticut. Her father had a serious operation, needing her to take care of him. Gibson then became an associate professor at Yale, teaching English Literature.

Dorothy loved living in Connecticut. They lived in Olive's father's large two-story house on several acres. Dorothy was given a Welch pony named Kris. She would ride him around the farm, or take neighbor kids for a ride in a cart that was her mother's, when she was a child or slay-ride in the winter. Her friends included Calvin Coolidge's, past President, grand daughter and a daughter of Weatherby rifle inventor.

Dorothy had a special area in the barn hay-loft that was used for practicing ballet, when she wasn't swinging from one side of the barn hay-loft to the other. When her father learned this he had a stack of hay placed below in case she fell, knowing she would swing over the open ground floor when he wasn't around.

Both Dorothy and I are avid readers, and enjoyed sharing stories we had read. We both enjoyed music. She enjoys classical music and ballet. She once played and taught piano. The music I enjoy ranges from country/western to light classics. Dorothy has learned to love and enjoy my range of music.

Among her many memoirs are: The famous Russian ballet dancer, Rudolf Nureyev, in1972, spotted Dorothy among a group of his waiting fans, came over and kissed her hand. She received noted   credits as wardrobe designer for Beach Cities Peninsula Ballet Company's Sleeping Beauty ballet in March 1966. In 1942, when she was 9, had her drawing as a young artist shown at the Seventh Annual Exhibition held at the American Museum of Natural History in New York. I enjoyed listening to her tell of these things. She eventually showed me the clippings of these things.

I would tell her about my growing up in Warner, a town of three hundred in 1930s; my adventures in scouting; Air Force experiences and my kids. She would ask me many questions. Both of us enjoyed each other's experiences in life. After lunch I'd go back to work full of her zest for life and facing the challenges in life.

Dorothy would ask lots of questions about the Philippines. She told me she had never been to another country. So, I took her and the kids and drove to Tijuana, Mexico. The only thing I can remember about the trip was Dan wanting a huge clay piggy bank, which I gave in and bought for him. Dorothy and her kids could now say they had been to a foreign country.

Around Christmas in 1975, Dorothy was laid off by my uncle. She got a job with Tarkington Realty in the plaza of Palos Verde. She became Hilda's secretary and would also write up real estate ads for Hilda.

One of our favorite places was a restaurant called 488 keys. The owner had been an engineer and built from scratch an organ. He had used an oscilloscope to get the different sound waves from many instruments, and then built all into this one of a kind organ. The guy who played this organ was great.

I once asked him if he could play Malaguena. He said, "Ah, a Pasa Dobla." He then played Malaguena, my favorite uplifting song. First using the piano keyboard of the organ, and then switching the melody to the foot pedals. He was a real master of this organ. This organ is now located on Catalina Island's grand ballroom.

Seeing the movie Dr. Zhivago, I began calling Dorothy, Laura. Dorothy's middle name is Lorraine. It is rumored that her middle name comes from the French Duke of Lorraine, rumored to be a relative. I morphed Lorraine to Laura.

Being around Dorothy and hearing how she had met her challenges in life renewed my interest in Bob's feldspathic sand project. After several calls, I learned Bob had left his job in Muskogee and was now in med school at Loma Linda, California. I was given his phone number and address.

When I called I told Bob I was ready to see what I can do with his project. I asked if I could bring Dorothy with me, that she could take notes. We sat up a meeting. Dorothy had taken some shorthand lessons and came out with her own morphed version. At the meeting Bob gave the name of each piece of equipment, how it was used and its cost. I then drove Dorothy to her home and went to my apartment to begin writing up what I thought I'd need to do.

After work at Provincial the next day, Dorothy and I stayed after work to put together a proposal for the sand project. From the verbal description Bob had given, Dorothy came up with an artist sketch of how it would look. She showed an office building up front with the processing plant building in back. In back of the processing plant were two huge tall storage tanks. In front of the office building she drew in a tree line street. It was absolutely beautiful.

Between her notes taken at the meeting with Bob and my familiarity with corporate operations, and several nights perfecting the proposal, we had come out with a good proposal. Dorothy typed up the proposal and I got a sharp looking display folder. The proposal looked very professional.

From recent real estate sales, I had some money to work with. I told my uncle what I was interested in and that I was going to take some time to go to Oklahoma to see if I could put the sand project through. He wasn't too happy with my decision.

I asked Dorothy to fix me some things to munch on while I was driving. I had a cooler for pop. I planned to drive straight through, sleeping in the cad, to my mother's house in Warner. I learned a valuable lesson on that trip, don't eat raw green peppers and drink pop. By the time I reached Gallup, New Mexico, I thought I was having a heart attack. I checked into the ER. They said it wasn't a heart attack but insisted I stay overnight for observation. I left the next day. I called Dorothy and let her know what had happened, and that I was okay. She was very concerned.

At my mother's house, I made several calls, first of which was to my mother who was staying with Lettye. Those business calls that I talked to suggested I'd have a better chance if the project was a corporation, then go through Small Business Administration [SBA].

I called Bob and it was agreed that the new Corporation would have Bob as the President and me as VP. I contacted an attorney who drew up the corporation papers. Our corporation was called Advanced Mineral Processing, and we were authorized to sell two million shares of preferred stock at one dollar each.

I met with a stock broker in Tulsa and showed him the proposal Dorothy and I had put together. After looking it over, he took me to a meeting with a large law firm in Tulsa. They looked it over. With the help of the stock broker, they redid my proposal into a very professional package required by SBA.

With the new proposal in hand, I drove to Stillwater, Oklahoma to meet with SBA. I arrived in Stillwater during SBA's lunch hour. I went to a local Mexican fast food place for my lunch. I was standing in line to place my order and the guy in front of me in the line asked if I was attending college in Stillwater. I told him I had in the past but I was here on business. He asked what it was about. I told him politely I wasn't at liberty to tell him. He asked if I was here alone. I told him yes. He said, "Why don't we have lunch together?"

We got our lunch and went to a booth. I had barely sat down when the guy said, "I should have warned you that I'm a Baptist theologian."

I told him, "I'm a Mormon."

I could hardly contain myself from laughing at the expression on his face. He conceded that Mormons were nice individuals but he couldn't go along with their beliefs. He then quoted a scripture, book and verse from the bible to back up his statement. I countered it with book and verse from the bible. He was surprised to learn I knew so much about the bible, and some bible quotes he wasn't familiar with. He could hardly wait to leave and check out what I said, to see if I had quoted the scripture correctly—I had. At the end of our meal we said a friendly goodbye and went our way.

SBA looked over my proposal. They approved the proposal to the amount of $800,000, saying that I'd have to come up with the $200,000 upfront money before they would approve their loan. I wondered where I could get that amount. I had just so much time left before I'd have to return to California to sell more real estate.

Seeing that it was going to take some time, I called Jane to see if she'd let Jim and Liz spend a week with me in Oklahoma. She agreed and I bought airline tickets for them.

I took the kids on a float trip on the Illinois River. When I needed to go to Tulsa to keep pressure on the sand project, Jim liked to go with me and drive the Cad. Liz preferred to stay with Lettye and my mother, who spoiled her.

It became apparent that the sand project was in a hold pattern for the $200,000 dollars up-front money. Flora fax said they would put up that amount if we gave them ninety percent of our stock. We were not about to do that. I had tied up the necessary land and sand we'd need, and I had written letters from companies that agreed to purchase more of the material than we could produce. Kerr Glass Company would have been our biggest buyer. Their lab had tested a sample of our product and liked it.

Knowing I was going to drive back to California, Jim wanted to go with me. Liz was ten and would fly back to Missoula. I made arrangements with

Jane to meet Liz at the airport, and asked the airlines to look after her during the trip.

The last night before Liz was to fly home, we stayed at my mother's home. It was to be a very eventful night. I slept in my mother's back bedroom. Lettye, my mother and Liz slept in the front bedroom. Jim slept on the couch in the living room. Lettye told me that she and Liz slept on a pallet on the floor, letting my mother have the bed in their room.

During the night a thief slipped into the house though an unlocked window in the living-room. We never heard him enter. He was very brazen. He took Jim's boots and big knife. He then helped himself to donuts and milk, setting across from Jim. He saw me turn on the light by my bed, to check my watch. I didn't want Liz to miss her plane in Tulsa, 62 miles from Warner. When I woke again to check my watch, it was gone. I got up to go check the wall clock in the kitchen. The front door of our house was wide open.

I woke up everybody and called the police. Jim and I drove around in the Cad to see if we could spot anyone on foot at three in the morning. We told the police what was missing and gave a good description of the items. We stayed awake until it was time to drive Liz to the airport in Tulsa.

When we went through Muskogee, on our way back to Warner to pack and leave for California, we stopped and checked with the sheriff's department in Muskogee. They said that though our quick awareness and call, they caught the thief walking on the railroad tracks on the west edge Warner. We received back our stolen goods. The sheriff said the thief had first raided our neighbor's house across the street, helping himself to biscuits and gravy from a leftover meal.

Jane married Bill in October 1976. Dorothy and I were married in November 1976. Both of us have experienced a great life with our new spouses. I've always thought that Jane is a nice person. We just had too great a difference in our interests. I was glad to hear that Bill and she had similar interests, and that they were happy. Dorothy and I have shared a great and rewarding life together.

I was ordained an Elder April 10, 1977 in the Rolling Hills ward. I was called as a teacher and then as a member of the Sunday-School presidency. I was finally getting to do what I had always wanted to do, to teach scripture. From non-members we're called by the nickname of Mormon. This is derived from our belief that the Book of Mormon is a second witness that Jesus is the Christ. It's the history of the tribe of Joseph, mentioned in Ezekiel 37:16.

Some evangelicals say we're not a Christian faith. My reply to that is how can you say that when the name of our church identifies us as the Church of Jesus Christ. The latter-day part is to indicate we're followers of Jesus Christ in this day and time. If one would only take the time to study how the ancient church was set up, they will see that our church is built on the same foundation as the original church—See Ephesians 2:20.

After our marriage, I gave up my apartment and joined Dorothy in her home. I was doing well in real estate sales. Both Dorothy and I were working. One sale I'll never forget. I had been showing a Jewish lady several Palo Verde houses. She always kept me going back to one particular house. I tried and tried to get her to make an offer, but she would decline.

Finally I asked why she wanted to revisit this house; what was the problem. She said she couldn't stand the stone planter in the living-room.

I told her that if she made an offer, and it was accepted, I told her I would personally see the planter removed. She made the offer and it was accepted.

On closing day, I went with her to their new home. She said, "You promised to remove that planter."

I had already discovered the planter was more of a decoration thing. The original owners had put down heavy duty plastic to protect the wood floor, and built the small cemented stone planter on top.

I let the lady know I had promised to remove the planter. I went to the planter, broke it apart in three large pieces and carried them outside. She was shocked. She had thought they went through the floor to a concrete foundation.

I went out of real estate sales into appraising when I lost $7,500 in commissions on the same day, the day before my three sales were to close. I had wasted a lot of my time and gas. In appraising I would get paid upon finishing my appraisal.

I went to work for Southwest Savings and Loan in Inglewood, California. It wasn't all that great for working conditions or pay; we three appraisers had a table top in a large hallway. I quickly improved my appraising skills. While at Southwest I put out discreet feelers to other companies. I got a call from Union Federal Savings and Loan. The offer was good, and it included a company car. I was assigned to their Gardena branch, closer to home that at Southwest.

My fellow appraiser there was Ray Gattis. He was a great guy. He'd say, "I'm a red headed Texican." He introduced me to freelance appraisal work on evenings after work and weekends. Some of his favorite expressions when leaving to do an appraisal were, "I'm off like a herd of turtles" and "I think I'll make like a tree and leave." Or, when a waitress asked if he'd like a refill of tea or coffee, he tell her, "Yes, up to the pay line." He has passed away, and I miss his great sense of humor.

Both Ray and I, as senior appraisers, covered a wide area. Our area was from Del Mar in the south to Oxnard in the north, and from the beach cities on the west to the mountains in the east. I learned that if I didn't leave the Oxnard area by 3:30 PM I wouldn't get home until almost 8, traffic on the freeways was bumper to bumper.

I'm grateful to Union Federal and to Taylor Dark, Chief Appraiser, who allowed me to get experience in several types of appraisals. Union Federal allowed me to take several classes in such appraising skills as computer, housing tracks, strip malls, apartment and condo complexes.

Taylor Dark once said to me, "Damn but you come on strong." With that he assigned me to do a small housing tract. My appraisal priced each house as selling for $82,000. The builder said I was crazy; that he was planning to sell them for $65,000. Knowing it would take him three months to build each house, I told the builder I would buy five. Others in the office that heard the conversation called out, "I'll take five!" I and the other office appraisers agreed to buy out the whole tract. The builder told us that we were all wrong and he would prove it by using my appraisal value. The tract sold out in two weeks. He came back to the office and thanked me.

Taylor sent me to appraise a four unit condo in San Clemente that was under construction. After my usual research I can in with a value of $225,000 each. Taylor said no way that the condos were worth that. We went to re-look at the units and the comparables I used. He was surprised when he came up with the same value as I.

Doing an appraisal gives one an insight into the home owner's personality. In one home I appraised in Rolling Hills there was a bar in the foyer. It became the only common ground for the home. To the left were the bedrooms and baths, all done in light baby-blue. To the right were heavily Mexican motif family-room and a billiard room. It was easy to tell that the wife decorated one half and her husband the other half, the bar was neutral ground.

From a class I had attended while working for Union Federal, I became the office computer appraisal authority. I would use the computer to analyze sales, come up with a value and attach the computer analysis to an appraisal form.

We got a call from my aunt Lettye that she couldn't take care of my mother any longer. When Lettye was out on a drapery job, my mother would go for walk and get lost. Dorothy and I talked it over and had Lettye put my mother on a plane to Los Angeles.

When she arrived, my uncle Bill told Dorothy and me about a great assisted living unit on the west side of Palos Verde; it had an ocean view. We cleared my mother's agreement to be a resident. We put a reef on her door to help her find her furnished apartment. We got a call a few days later that we had to remove my mother because she kept entering other's apartments, being lost.

Dorothy volunteered to take care of my mother in our home. It meant less income for Dorothy to quit her job at Tarkington Realty. We finally decided that we could use some of my mother's retirement income to make up the difference.

The decision meant that Susan would give up her room to my mother. Susan and her brother Dan would sleep in our living-room.

Cheri and Rod visited Dorothy and me one summer. They spent the night with us and then went to Disneyland. The following fall Dorothy and I took a vacation to see where we'd like to retire. We went to places in Idaho. Dorothy's father, working for the railroad, had traveled to Lewiston, Idaho. He had told Dorothy that he liked Lewiston.

We didn't care for Lewiston. We headed to Montana by way of Lolo Pass. It was a beautiful drive. The evergreen forests had brightly colored Aspens showing in batches here and there. From Missoula we drove to visit my daughters Liz and Debbie in Hamilton. We took them out for a pizza. Going back to Missoula, the drive to Helena was full of colorful trees changing to fall colors, and clear running streams. Dorothy had me stop several times so she could take pictures.

Cheri and Rod asked us to spend the night with them. We got to meet their two daughters, Sarah and Patty. Sarah became my shadow. Cheri encouraged me to apply as an appraiser at Home Federal, where she worked, that they were looking for an appraiser. Both Dorothy and I loved the beauty of the northwest, and its less congestion lifestyle. We decided we'd like to live there.

Following Cheri's suggestion, I applied to Home Federal for their appraisal job. Their Chairman, John Schroeder, visited a friend in Southern California and asked me to meet with him. We had a good discussion. I offered to show him how to do appraisal research using a computer, but he declined. We found that both of us were history buffs. The interview went well. He told me he'd like for me to visit Home Federal and have an in-depth interview with its VP.

A few weeks later I got a call to bring my wife and visit Helena for the interview. Dorothy was taking care of my mother and couldn't go. She decided to send Susan with me, to be her eyes. Susan and Dorothy had similar interests. Our plane to Helena made a stop in Butte. I don't think Susan saw my concern on landing. Any time I'm in an airplane that has to land in a valley between two mountains, I'm concerned.

We were met at the Helena airport by Joe B., Home Federal V-P and taken to our room in what is now Guest-House motel and suites on Eleventh Street. Our room had two queen-size beds. That evening Joe B. took Susan and me to dinner at the Black Angus restaurant, on the top floor of our motel. I told Joe why I had brought my daughter instead of my wife. He was quite impressed with Susan.

Next day I had a long interview with Home Federal management and loan officers. Susan spent the day looking over Helena. On returning to our home in California, Susan gave a report to her mother about the gift shops, art shops and what Helena looked like. This sounded good to Dorothy. I was given the job and went to Helena by myself to begin work, and to look for a house to buy.

Cheri seemed pleased that I was going to work where she worked. She asked that I stay with Rod and her, and put me downstairs in one of her daughter's rooms. At work she'd introduce me to others as her father. In front of others he'd greet me and kiss me on the cheek. She'd call my office to see if I'd take a break with her which I would do. One father's day she gave me a card. Above her name she said, "You were a strict father. Thank you."

I located a nice empty spilt-lever home for Dorothy, the kids and I, about eight miles south of Helena. It was a brick house in Clancy's Gruber Estates. It was a mountainous setting on 2.19 acres, half of which was timbered. The house had 1200 square feet on each floor. The living-room and family-room was 12 feet by 27 feet with fireplaces and large picture windows on both front and side. Sitting on a couch in either of these rooms gives one the feeling they were sitting outside. It had three bedrooms, a nice sized kitchen and a bath on each floor. The laundry room was downstairs.

Dorothy and I had a large master bedroom with two individual closets. Dan's room was across from the master bedroom on the main floor. Susan had her own bedroom, Ron and Larry had a room with bunk beds, my mother's room was across from Ron and Larry. Those on the lower floor had a walk-out door to the yard, from the family-room.

This house has many fond memories. We lived there twenty-one years. We bought the house in 1979 from a local doctor who had built a new home above ours, on our road's switchback. Our street was dirt and a dead end. There was only five houses past our place. It was so quiet at night, and in the day. It was a great relief from all the traffic and noise of California.

Dorothy and the kids were still in California, when I found the house. I told her all about the house and sent pictures to her. She told me to go ahead and make an offer. I was reluctant to do this without her being there to go through the house. She again told me to go ahead, which I did. We got the house.

We were quite the spectacle when we moved. Our furniture was moved by a moving-van. My mother, Dorothy and I drove up in the Cad with three family pet cats. Dan and Susan drove up in Susan's VW with Dan's dog, Koyak—an Alaskan mal-mute, dripping saliva down Susan's neck. The VW's speedometer had quite working so we became the pace car.

We spent the night in a motel in Nephi, Utah.

Dan, Susan and Koyak were in one room, the rest of us in another room with three cats trying to get loose. During the night my mother stepped on one of the cat's tails, causing a commotion. I don't think any of us slept well that night. Larry had stayed in California to finish his senior year in high school. Ron, at the time, was staying with Rod and Cheri in Helena.

All of us fell in love with our new home, especially Susan who now had her on private room. The kids would have friends out. Ron had enrolled in Helena High. One of his friends was Troy smith, son of Tucker Smith, nationally known western artist. Tucker smith and his wife invited Ron, Dorothy and I to their house for dinner one evening. Tucker showed us how he made his paintings so realistic. He would take color slides of interesting subjects and, using bushes and oils, combine them into a painting, using a viewer to study the slides. We own three of his numbered paintings: *Shallow Water, Skidding Logs and Barn Cat.* Dorothy and I enjoyed being around the Smith's. They were down-to-earth friendly people.

On one occasion there must have been better than twenty kids at our house. Some were sitting on our L-shaped couch talking; others around the piano playing and singing. But the two that got my attention were playing a game of chess in the middle of our living-room floor, completely oblivious to all goings-on in the room.

On other occasions we had church members out for a hootenanny. One couple brought a guitar and we'd sit around and sing. I love the song *Preacher and the Bear.* The couple with the guitar played and sang that song.

On another occasion, a member of the Hatch family came by. I asked him to play and sing the *Happy Auctioneer's song.* He was really great.

After graduating from South High School, Susan went to college at Ricks College in Idaho. She didn't like the cold and had come back to California, in time for the move. She would then attend BYU until she got married to Dan Park, a graduate from Montana State in Bozeman. He was now a licensed architect.

Ron and Dan finished Votech in Helena. Before family members went their way in life and college, I took all of us to Glacier National Park. We had rooms on the top floor at Many Glacier hotel. At night we could hear the wind howling like a banshee around the eves of our building.

Boating, dining and sight-seeing was enjoyed by all. To be able for them to say they'd been in another country we crossed into Canada and visited the Prince of Wales hotel, getting souvenirs and taking pictures. We also took pictures of Mountain
Sheep that roamed near the Prince of Wales hotel. Dan and Ron had brought along their inflatable one man rafts. They floated down the stream leaving Many Glaciers area.

We then drove the famous Going-to-the-sun road, stopping several times to take pictures of magnificent breath-taking scenery. Leaving the park we stopped so the kids could take pictures of a huge Bull Moose grazing on water plants. I was concerned that they'd get too close. It was an enjoyable trip before they all left for college.

Dan left for California and went to work with Hughes. Larry and Ron went to BYU and got their Bachelor's degrees. Ron went to work for Novell in Provo, Utah, traveling to Germany, Japan and Columbia for the company. He speaks fluent Spanish and had served a mission in Argentina.

Larry went to work in Provo for a computer software company; then, over a period of time, bought six houses in Provo, renting rooms to college students. That is his sole business now. Larry has learned to play six different musical instruments: piano, accordion, flute, cello, violin and harpsichord. Both Larry and Ron are clever at repairing things.

On a snowy winter Dan Park had his brothers and Susan's brothers build a large message of straw on the mountain-side. That night with a signal from Dad's headlights, they lit the straw. It said, "Marry me Sue." Susan accepted. The brothers got the fire put out and left, passing a fire truck heading for the sight of the sign.

We modified our house by adding a sliding glass door off our dining area and added a large deck. While having a meal we could observe our deck and the timbered hillside that was our back yard. Our three cats loved to roam the land; it must have been a form of paradise to them. We'd leave food and water out for them. We learned that other "guests" enjoyed the food and water we left out.

Dorothy and I would sit and watch as a mother skunk and her kits enjoyed the cat food. A mother raccoon and her little ones would also visit. One really harsh winter a doe and her yearling came on our deck to eat cat food. We made a slight movement and they bolted.

The yearling was so weak from starvation that it collapsed on our deck. Dorothy took some bread out and fed it to the yearling. It gained enough strength to get up and run after its mother. This was the beginning of a friendship between Dorothy and the deer.

The deer seemed to realize that Dorothy was a friend and not a threat. She would take a loaf of bread outside and tear off pieces to feed the deer. At first it was just the doe and her yearling. Then more deer appeared. They would gather around Dorothy and gently nudge her arm to receive a piece of bread. We began buying sacks of what was called cob, from a feed store in Helena. It was a mixture of ground-up corn cobs with a little molasses added. The deer loved it. To my chagrin, I realized they liked flowers that I had put out.

Dorothy, being an artist, would sit on our lawn with the deer ganged around her and sketch them. I put a sheet of these sketches in her memoir binder. One doe gave birth to her fawn in our front yard, near our water-well pipe. While the mother doe was away the tiny fawn would lie very still. When she returned the fawn was very active and would nurse.

When Dorothy wanted the deer to come to her, she would go out on our lawn and whistle. Like overgrown dogs they would come running from the forest area of our yard and gather around her. One was a three prong buck. People on our street would stop to watch the inner action between Dorothy and the deer.

One day Dorothy forgot to close our sliding glass door. A young doe came in and was enjoying some of our dachshund's food, located just inside our kitchen. Penny, our dachshund, came around the corner from our living-room and ran barking towards the deer. The deer bolted out the door and into the forest.

Everything at work was going well. Home Federal supplied me a gas guzzling Chevy Suburban. I would be called upon to carry loads of things for the company. John Schroeder realized I, like him, was a history buff. He would call my office and ask me to help him take some things to the company's office in Bozeman, a 90 mile trip each way. John was Chairman of the Board at Home Federal. He and I would talk history during the trip.

John had pictures of early Helena. These were finally put into book form. John wrote about Helena in the late 1800s and early 1900s, using his old pictures so readers could get an idea of earlier times. He gave me a copy of that book, which I still have.

I really enjoyed John's company and that of his friend "Shorty." Both were in their eighties. I had been with Home Federal only a year when John died, a fall in his bathtub. "Shorty", an avid cyclist who at his age would go for several hundred miles on his bike, was killed by being hit by a car in Helena. I was greatly saddened not being able to listen to these old-timers talk of early Helena.

Dorothy and I were called upon to baby sit Cheri's daughters, Sarah and Patty, on occasions. My mother enjoyed their company in our family room. We really enjoyed taking them to see plays at the Little Theater in Helena, or to the Helena Civic Center for ballet or some event. This ended when I told Cheri of an incident that I thought had put Sarah at risk.

Not too long after this incident, Home Federal changed to a new banking system and use of computers. I was called into the VP's office and told that Cheri wasn't able to adapt to the new system. The VP, Jim S., told me he was going to let Cheri go, but hoped I'd stay on. He gave me strict instructions to not tell Cheri before he talked to her. I honored his request. Cheri has always assumed I got her fired. I tried several times to tell her that it wasn't due to me that she was fired. She wouldn't listen. I bear her no hard feelings and wish the best for her in life. I don't believe in vendettas. We no longer talk to each other, and that is best.

We would also baby sit Nancy and Kim Marshall's three kids. They ranged in age from Nathan, Nyleen and Noreen. Every time we baby sat the three; Nyleen, about four years old, would always ask to watch the movie *Wizard of Oz.* I would put the movie on our TV in the family-room and then go to our master bedroom to stretch out on the bed and watch TV. I would soon see Nyleen's little black hair going around the foot of the bed. She would climb up on the bed beside me, being sure she duplicated the way I was lying, and watch TV with me.

We got a call one night that Nyleen was missing. Kim and Nancy had taken their kids with them to a radio ham operator meeting on the mountain above their home. When Nancy had to leave for work, Nyleen was left with a babysitter. It was later learned that Nyleen had been abducted. Local sheriffs and FBI were brought in on the case. Nyleen's picture was shown on TV.

The man who abducted her called from Wisconsin to tantalize her parents. The FBI traced the call but missed capturing the guy by a few minutes. To this day Nyleen has never been located. On top of all this Nancy was murdered in Mexico City. She and her husband were planning to move there from Japan. Kim was a technician for installing radio telephone systems. All this was a great shock to Dorothy and I. Kim and Nancy were like family.

Not long after Cheri was fired, Home Federal decided they would let me go. Most of the banks in Helena were eliminating their staff appraisers, also. I became an independent appraiser and worked out of my home. I would do my appraisal field work, come home and write it up in pencil. Dorothy would then type it up for me to sign and deliver.

I went to an appraiser's convention in Denver and learned how to use a computer to type up my appraisals on pre-printed tractor forms. While in Denver I took a tour trip of the Air Force academy in Colorado Springs. I was very impressed and proud of the young cadets I saw.

From pre-printed tractor forms I went to an appraisal program that used laser printed forms. This freed up more time for Dorothy. With the advance of my mother's Alzheimer's, requiring more help from Dorothy, my mother couldn't recognize anyone else but Dorothy. Dorothy said that since she had lost her mother, she looked upon my mother as her own.

On July 31, 1986 my mother had a massive stroke in our home. She lived for eleven days in a coma at St. Peter's hospital in Helena. She died at about 10 PM on a Sunday. As a family we had gone by the hospital and I gave my mother a priesthood blessing, freeing her to rejoin her husband, my father, if that was her wish. Each of these eleven days is recorded in my *Book of Remembrance.*

Our Daughter, who had been living in Alaska, brought the kids to visit us in 1989. I gave Ben and Josh a hug. Veronica was about three years old. I picked her up and kissed her on the cheek. In very correct English, she said, "Don't do that." It has been a joke between she and I ever since.

Chapter 24

I found that appraising properties in Helena was interesting and challenging. Helena is the capital city of Montana with a history that needs brief mentioning here, so one can understand how appraisal work is difficult. Helena came into being with the finding of gold in the gulch by four Georgians on July 14, 1864. One of the four Georgians was John Cowan. I find it interesting that my great-great-great grandmother Abigail Cowen was born in Green, Georgia in 1795. Is there a connection? Cowen is a Scottish wording; Cowan is an Irish wording. Both coming from Georgia was an interesting find.

John Cowan and his partners had gone to Montana in search of gold. Finding none in their search around the territory, at that time, they were on their way back to Georgia. They saw the gulch with its tiny stream. They decided to try it for gold. This they said would be their Last Chance. They struck it rich. Others coming into the area also struck it rich. The city of Helena was born.

Helena, pronounced Hel-i-na, has several old mansions in what is referred to as the mansion district, on the western section of Helena. They have interesting historical facts. When I appraised these old mansions, I would go to Helena's Historical Society to learn all I could about the house and include some of these facts in my appraisal.

During the mid to late 1800s, Helena had more millionaires per capita than any other city in the world. It's reported that Helena had fifty millionaires around 1888, with a population of around 3,600. Much of this wealth came from gold mining. Some came from ranching —miners loved to have steaks. The wealthy ones enjoyed building mansions out of brick. They also enjoyed culture. As with many mining towns, outlaws and robbers robbed and killed people. This was finally brought to an end by a vigilante group, led by prominent city members.

A good book to read on this is Historic Helena. It also has many old photographs. Originally gold ore was shipped by heavy-duty wagons pulled a twenty-mule team or oxen. The ore was hauled to Fort Benton and loaded onto steamboats, to be processed by refineries downstream. These shipments were protected by U.S Calvary troops. The Calvary was also used to protect citizens along the route, since it passed through part of the Blackfoot lands.

When Charles Broadwater arrived, he brought in the railroad and his hotel. According to Historic Helena, "The largest shipment of gold bullion, by train, from Helena was on July 4, 1883. One million pounds was placed in 36 new boxcars on the first run of Northern Pacific to leave Helena."

To better get a feel for that time. In the mining town of Bannack, Montana, the first capital of Montana, a sheriff named Henry Plummer was elected. It turned out that he was the head of an outlaw group. He was the first to hang on gallows he had built to "hang thieves", by a group of vigilantes. Plummer had distinctive color eyes. When he robbed the son of a judge, and let him go, the son, by Plumbers eyes, recognized Plummer as the man behind the mask, and told his father.

At the time of the battle on the Little Big Horn, in Eastern Montana, where General Custer's 7th Calvary was wiped out by Sioux and Cheyenne warriors, led by Chief Sitting Bull and Chief Crazy Horse, Helena was a thriving city. Helena was called the *Queen of the Rockies*. It had banks, Ming Theater, a brewery, a railroad, a school and several churches.

A railroad magnate named Charles Broadwater opened his fabled Hotel Broadwater and natatorium, home of the world's first indoor heated swimming pool. It was heated by hot spring water. At the time I appraised property in Helena this was all taken down due to the earthquake damage in 1935. I have a color picture of what it looked like when people came from miles around to stay there.

To this day a decorative tiny stream flows through the downtown walking mall of Helena. When a local bank did some remodeling, gold was found. Thus, Helena's Last Chance Gulch Street and walking mall is paved over gold placer ore.

The Montana Club, the oldest men's social club in the northwest, is located in the heart of downtown Helena. It was originally built as a club for millionaires and wealthy cattlemen to be able to get together for meals and socializing. One floor was a ballroom. Above it were quarters where some could stay. The club was visited by Mark Twain and Teddy Roosevelt.

I was fortunate to get to appraise the home that was once owned by Thomas Cruse. He found the Drum Lummon gold mine in nearby Marysville, which was extraordinarily rich. Marysville is now a ghost town with only a few residents. Several of the old buildings have collapsed. It's an interesting place to visit. I did an appraisal on a couple of homes in the area, getting a chance to look over the ruins of the town and Drum Lummon mine.

In doing research for the appraisal, I learned that he contributed heavily to the construction of Saint Helena Cathedral. It's a beautiful gothic structure patterned after the beautiful Votive cathedral in Vienna, Austria. It has beautiful stained glass windows. The cathedral is well worth seeing. The cathedral has two tall spirals, each holding a cross at the top. Story has it that a few pilots had gotten drunk and made a bet that no one could fly between those two crosses. One took the bet and flew his plane between the crosses. He had only inches of clearance.

Word has it that Cruse once tried to get a bank loan to develop his mining claim. They turned him down. In the panic of 1873, banks were going through a financial depression. Cruse had struck it rich and had millions on deposit. The banks asked him for a loan. He told them, "I won't give you a damn dime."

I appraised a piece of commercial land on 11th street in Helena for the Cruse Corporation. I determined the highest and best use was a restaurant. KFC now stands there.

I got to appraise the Conrad Kohr's mansion. Kohr's made his fortune in supplying beef to mining camps. He owned many butcher shops. He found that miners paid well for good beef and sausages. He sold both wholesale and retail to the mining camps. At one time he had fifty thousand head of cattle grazing over 10 million acres, spread out over four states and two Canadian provinces. He would ship 10,000 head annually to the Chicago stock yards. Before settling down in Helena, he owned a ranch near Dear Lodge, Montana. He purchased his home on

Dearborn Avenue in Helena in 1899. He was called the "Montana Cattle King."

Conrad Kohrs was also a friend of President Teddy Roosevelt. When I appraised Kohr's old mansion in Helena I noticed something different. Most of the old mansions had bathrooms on only the main floor. Many of the old mansions had three stories, a difficult task to measure from the ground level. In Kohr's house there was a bath on the second floor. I learned this bath had been added for Roosevelt's planned visit.

The Kohrs lived well and loved to travel. They paid visits to their German homeland, traveled up the Nile in Egypt, shopped in New York and Chicago. Kohrs' wife had seasonal tickets to New York City Metropolitan Opera and once spent a year in German so their children could benefit from the culture.

I learned many historical things while appraising these old homes, many who had 5,000 plus square feet, and carriage houses. One of the prettiest old mansions, that I appraised, is the old Tatum home. Its design is old English tutor.

One house I appraised, I noticed some interesting photographs. I asked the lady about them. I learned that during the silent movie era she played the organ music for the movie scenes. I don't remember the lady's name, but, her husband had been the only Republican elected sheriff in Helena. I also appraised their ranch house north of Wolf Creek on highway 434. It sat back off the highway about a mile or so, with beautiful cliffs behind. It was like a picture out of a Zane Grey novel. It was such a beautiful setting that I took Dorothy with me, taking lots of pictures.

My most unique appraisal in Helena was a distillery. When I was called about doing this appraisal, I told the requester that I had no experience in appraising a distillery. The attorney handling the case of this distillery, which had gone under, said he had heard of my reputation of honesty and preferred that I do the appraisal, if I would accept the challenge. I came up with a pretty high fee, thinking he would decline. He accepted my fee.

The building was vacant of workers. On the second floor was a number of stainless steel vats. One was marked Gin, Bourbon, another Rye and another Brandy. I had to look up the cost of the vats and other equipment, cost to build building and take off depreciation. It took me several weeks to finally come up with a value. I was thanked for my appraisal and was paid.

I got a call from an attorney in Arizona asking that I do an appraisal for him near Great Falls. I told him the distance I'd have to travel and the mileage cost I'd have to charge. I recommended it would be less expensive if he got an appraiser out of Great Falls. He wanted only me. Arriving at the house it was in poor condition. I could tell by water stains on windows that the house leaked. The upper floor oscillated when I walked on it. It was too far gone to try and repair, cost wise. When I got back to Helena I called the attorney and asked if he really wanted me to complete the appraisal. He asked how badly the condition of the house was, and what my recommendation was. I told him that my recommendation was two sticks of dynamite and run. He paid me a nice fee.

I enjoyed getting to appraiser Gary Cooper's ranch house and individual cabins for his visitors. Gary Cooper is one of my favorite actors. The property is near Craig, at the Dearborn exit off I-15. His ranch is a short walk to the Missouri River. It has a peaceful setting. I could visualize

Gary using this place as a getaway from the Hollywood hustle. Gary was born in Helena. His parent's old home is on Eleventh Street in Helena.

In doing an appraisal, an appraiser needs to have three of the most current sales, adjusting the subject to these sales. On some appraisals in the Townsend area of Montana, I had to go miles to find sales that I could reasonably use for comparison. Doing an appraisal for a firm in Pittsburg, Pennsylvania, and having to use distant sales, they asked why I used sales so far from the subject. I explained this way, "Montana is the 4th largest state in the union and has a population of 800,000." Their reply was, "Oh my God!"

Some other notable people who called Helena home: Stephen Ambrose—author and historian. I appraised the house he bought; Liz Claiborne fashion designer; Russell B. Harrison son of President Benjamin Harrison; Casey Fritz-Simmons—tight end with the Detroit Lions; Norman Holter—biophysicist and inventor of the Holter monitor; L. Ron Hubbard—founder of Scientology; Myrna Loy famous actress; Leo Seltzer, creator of Roller Derby, to mention a few.

I joined the Helena Chapter of Independent Fee appraisers and served a term of President of the chapter.

Helena is very unique. It's the home of Kessler brewery. Some of the sights in the Helena area are a boat trip through the Gates of The Mountains. On the Missouri River, one approaches what appears to be a solid rock wall. As one continues the rock wall appears to open, like a huge gate. In the narrow channel one usually sees Mountain Goats that come down the sheer mountain sides to drink.

There are several Yogo sapphires mines near Helena where one can buy a bucket of high grade material for five dollars, to try and screen out beautiful sapphires. One person found a $1,200 blue sapphire gemstone in his bucket of material. Dorothy's cousin from England found some nice pale green sapphires.

In 1952 the Archie Bray Foundation was founded. Its internationally know as a ceramics center. My wife Dorothy took lessons there, learning how to work clay for sculpturing. Helena is a good vacation site.

Chapter 25

Our home was located in the foothills of the Elkhorn Mountains north of Clancy, a bedroom community of Helena. Clancy consists of a small grocery store, bar, school, churches and post office. From our elevated position we looked across the valley at Sheep Mountain. The drive to Helena is eight miles on I-15. Traffic was very light. My uncle in California was telling of his traffic problems and the construction of a twelve-lane freeway being built. I told him we have traffic problems in Montana, I saw five cars in the last eight miles. He told me to shut up. We loved to joke back and forth.

My wife, Dorothy, took emergency response training from the Sheriff's office in Boulder, Montana, our county seat. If she was paged, it was a mad race to give aid. On a few calls, I drove her to the scene. It was exciting to get on the interstate, turn on my flashers and "put the pedal to the metal."

On one case a man had driven to a remote area and shot himself. He was dead. On another case an alcoholic had drank too much and had died.

Dorothy had taken the course in medical emergency help to be able to help me if I had medical problems. I had heart acceleration problems.

I became involved in politics. I formed the Family Republican Club. The idea was to get parents to bring along their teenage children to a monthly breakfast club meeting where political issues were discussed. I was elected its President. Dorothy would help me in putting out a monthly news letter and do the art work. One of our members was speaker of the House in Montana's legislature. Some of our speakers were the state governor, secretary of the state and state attorney general. Those vying for political office would also speak to our group.

I was elected Chairman of the Republican Party in Jefferson County and served two terms. When there was an effort to have a new national constitutional convention. To have a new convention needed only Montana and two other states, all other states had signed on to the new convention. My state chairman was after me to help pass this approval. I told him, "You leave my constitution alone."

When our nation's original constitution was drawn up we had true statesmen, very intelligent men. Today we don't have that quality of leaders. A new constitutional convention could destroy our original constitution and bring in heaven knows what type of government. In my opinion this was too much of a gamble to take. I also went to the Capitol and lobbied to have this bill turned down. We won. Other states then began recalling their votes.

At one of our state conventions I was selected to serve on the Human Rights platform committee. The chairman of this committee was a state senator. The vice-chairman was a state representative. We were to write the party human rights portion of the party's platform. It became a battle over pro-choice and pro-life. There was a Catholic lady on the committee. She was also a national committee representative. I tried to get her to go

306

along with my pro-life position. She became very angry, stating, "A woman has the right to choose what she does with her body."

I asked, "How many choices does a woman need?'

She said, "What do you mean?"

I told her that a woman's first choice is to not have an affair, if she doesn't want to get pregnant by that person. Her other choice was not using contraceptives. So, how many choices does a woman need? This lady hasn't spoken to me since.

Those of us who favored a pro-life platform debated those for pro-choice. A convention "floor fight" was averted when the state attorney general, Marc R. was contacted for advice. He advised our committee that to be successful in a pro-life stance it must allow abortion in situations of rape, incest and mother's life in danger. It was a good compromise, and a challenge on the floor of the convention was adverted.

Being active in politics and attending state conventions is interesting. One gets the feel of how things are done in congress. In politics I got to know the "movers and shakers" of the party, and they got to know me. One of our party senators had a great sense of humor. He would work into his speeches one liner quips. I really liked him and his humor—I would send him one liner quips. He sent me a beautiful set of four cocktail glasses with the gold seal of the senate on it.

Some of the quips that I sent him were: "You can tell when it's really cold. Congress goes around with their hands in their own pockets"; a quote by W. C. Fields—"If at first you don't succeed, try, try, try again. Then give up. No need to be a damn fool"; the art of diplomacy—"Saying nice doggy 'till you can find a rock" and the definition of an ingrate, "A person that bites the hand that feeds him, and complains of indigestion." I also gave the senator a published article about Davey Crockett, titled "It's not yours to give." It dealt with using government funds.

I believe that understanding government and how it should work is very important. Today voters vote for selfish personal desires when they should be voting for what's good for the nation as a whole. As long as this continues some politicians will use our tax dollars to buy their votes — giving large groups of people what they ask for. This practice will bring our nation down. A good book on how the founders of our nation determined the proper way to run our nation is *5000 year Leap* by Cleon Skousen. It gives the 28 principals that made our nation great.

Every February our party holds a Lincoln Day dinner. The purpose is to build up funds to help candidates in elections. County Republican ladies would bake pies and cakes to be auctioned off at the dinner. At our Lincoln Day dinner my auctioneer would be state Speaker of the House or U. S. Senator; pies were delivered to successful bidders by our state governor.

I also became an active member of the Christian Coalition. The first organizing meeting was funny. We met in a school classroom. I would guess there were around forty people at the meeting. The organizer went from individual to individual asking them what church they were members of. My seat was in the back of the room. Many denominations were present. When I identified myself as a Mormon you could have heard a pin drop. They soon learned that Mormons are also Christians. The elected chairman and I became good friends. We worked together on many issues.

Chapter 26

Life was good to us. My real estate appraisal business was run from an office in our home. It was quiet and peaceful. I could look out my office window at our front lawn and the forest across the street from our home.

Our front lawn slopped down to our dirt road. When our grandkids were brought for a visit, they loved to take cardboard and slide down our slopping lawn. In winter Ron, Dan or Larry would put a rope around Koyak's neck and get him to pull them on their skis. Other times Dorothy and the kids would take turns riding downhill on a sled.

One Easter we were fortunate enough to have both Susan's and Jim's kids. We hid Easter eggs for our grandkids. Our granddaughter, Meagan was having trouble finding eggs. Susan's children helped her. I was glad to see the good fellowship between the families.

At church one Sunday, a friend asked if we'd be interested in a Dachshund. He said he had sold the dog to a young couple and they had returned the dog. He told me he had too many dogs and would hate to have this one destroyed. I asked Dorothy if she was interested in having a young Dachshund. Happily, she said yes. That's how we came to own Penny.

We quickly learned what must have happened with the young couple. We shut up Penny in our laundry-room one time, when we left. She did a real number on the laundry-room door. After that we let her have the run of our house when we were gone. She was never destructive again. When we drove up our hill we could see Penny lying on top of our couch, looking out the window. When she saw our car, she'd jump up and race to our front door. She would happily great us when we opened the door.

Penny and our three cats got along together. The only exception was Simon, a Siamese. Every once in a while Simon would swat Penny, as she passed. The race was on. Penny angrily pursued Simon, teeth bared and barking, until Simon hid in a place where Penny couldn't reach her. The two would then become friends again.

During winter I'd scrape snow away for a place for Penny to use when going too the toilet. When she finished and came back inside, she'd run to our bed and get under our covers to get warm, eventually coming out to be with us. When she rode with us in the car, she rode in the back seat. I'd lower the windows enough for her to stick her nose out, to get the neighbor smells. When she wanted to see what was up front, she'd put her paws on the top of our seats, looking between the seat gap. She was a very personable little dog, and we loved her.

When we let her outside we had to tie her to a 100' length of small nylon rope. This gave her plenty of room to run and play. It also kept her from chasing after deer or some stray dog on our street. Between our lawn and the street was a shallow ditch, for water run-off. One day a strange dog came trotting up our street. Penny was so excited she forgot about the ditch. She ran to meet the dog and disappeared into the ditch.

A disgusted looking Penny soon appeared back on our lawn. The stray dog didn't pay any attention to her.

When we would leave her behind she would sometimes show her displeasure by taking Dorothy or my shoe and place it at the top of our stairs. We couldn't miss seeing the shoe. When we ate dinner, Penny would sit up on her hindquarters and petition for a bite.

The deer seemed to sense that Penny was our pet. They'd stay clear of her. However any strange dog entering our yard was met by the deer's sharp front hoofs.

Our place was cat heaven. The three cats loved to hunt and explore our area. Simon was weird in her actions. If a stranger came she would hid under a platform rocker and bolt out when least expected, scaring the visitor. Poncho loved to stand on his hind-legs and rub his whiskers on the side of our face. Newton was truly an outdoor cat, coming inside for only short periods of time.

Between ground squirrels and deer, I had a hard time having flowers. I'd plant bulbs and the ground squirrels would dig them up and eat them. The cats soon took care of this problem. Flowers that made it up were "mowed" down by the deer. I learned that I had to place black nylon netting over the plants to keep the deer away.

Being near the Bureau of Land Management forest we once had a black bear and mountain lion visitor. One night when Dorothy and I returned home, we heard what we thought was a scream from our neighbor's house, above ours.

I got my loaded M-1 carbine and drove up to check. I knocked on their door and looked through a glass panel. No one appeared to be home. I then heard the sound come from the darkness on the other side of their drive. I levered a shell into my rifle and took off the safety. I now knew the sound had come from a mountain lion in the darkness above their driveway, and I had to go there to get in my car. Any sudden movement would have received fifteen rounds as fast as I could pull the trigger. I told Dorothy when I got home.

One day our neighbor down the street from us was getting her groceries out of her car. A black bear came loping down our street. Our neighbor dropped her sacks of food. Dorothy watched from our living-room window the bear sit down and enjoy our neighbor's food.

One day a coyote and skunk got into a fight near Susan's room. It took hours and room spray to finally kill the odor.

Chapter 27

Larry wanted to take his mother and me to Europe, England and France. I had a backlog of appraisal work to do and turned down the offer. And, at that time I wasn't interested in going to Europe. Had it been to the Philippines, I might have gone. Dorothy and Larry went to Europe and brought back tales of their adventures.

Cousins of Dorothy, named Colin and Bridie, visited another cousin in Benton, Arkansas. The Thibault cousin is a doctor that Dorothy had never met. At the same time Dorothy and me was attending my class reunion In Warner, Oklahoma.

On the way to visit her cousins in Benton, Arkansas, we went by Mount Petite Jean. Dorothy wanted to visit Crystal Falls, where her father had taken her when she almost four. I was going to take her picture, with the falls as background. A couple comes forth to offer taking a picture of Dorothy and I. We leaned on the wood railing for the picture. When we got home and had the picture developed, there were the initials of her father and mother carved in the rail, between Dorothy and I.

We joined the cousins in Benton. It was a great get together of Dorothy's cousins in the area. In the doctor's garage he showed me what I thought was a 1954 MG. He told me it was a kit. He had taken a VW power train and installed the MG body design on top.

When it came time for Dorothy and me to return to Montana, Colin asked if he and Bridie could ride with us, that they hadn't been able to see much of America from the air. I let them know we'd love to have them along.

Colin asked how long will the drive take. I told him it'd take two days. He was shocked and asked how many miles. When I told him it was about 1,200 miles, he was again shocked. He then told me that in England it was about 500 miles to go coast to coast.

When we left next morning, I had to get Colin to help me get their luggage in the trunk of our car. Their big suitcase must have weighed close to ninety pounds. Colin, with his camcorder sat up front in the passenger seat. Bridie and Dorothy sat in the back seat. While they enjoyed chatting, Colin was busy filming some of the sights along the interstate.

He filmed the hardwood trees and waterway of Arkansas; the pumping oil wells in Oklahoma; the huge farm lands of Kansas. In Wyoming he had been filming its vast open ranch lands. Suddenly he lowered his video camera and said, "Smashing!" He couldn't get over the vast amounts of land, as far as the eye can see, and no houses. He then stated America has it all, pointing out the hardwoods, oil, farming and lots of open land.

Colin and Bridie had another shock after arriving at our home. I put a target upon our hill behind our house and let they take turns shooting at the target with my .22 Colt Frontier Scout pistol. They told me in England all firearms had to be kept in an armory and owners had to check them out. They took turns filming each other shooting the pistol, to show to friends in England.

Montana doesn't have a sales tax. Colin and Bridie couldn't get over how inexpensive things are in Montana, especially Jeans and leather good. I kidded them about being like Teddy Roosevelt, going from store to store saying, "Charge." They bought so much that they had to box up their purchases and ship them to England.

They enjoyed Helena. Since Colin was involved in English politics, Dorothy and I took Colin and Bridie on a tour of Montana's capitol building. Going by the Governor's office, Marc came out to greet Colin and Bridie. I let Marc know that Colin was an elected official in England. Governor Marc R. asked his secretary to use Colin's camera to take a picture of all of us, at Colin's request. Both Colin and Bridie enjoyed visiting with the governor.

We took Colin and Bridie to one of the sapphire diggings. We all bought a bucket of material and panned through the material. Colin and Bridie found some nice small sapphires, which he left behind to mount. This was quite an experience for them.

Next we took them to Yellowstone National Park. When we saw a buffalo near the road, Colin wanted to take a picture. When he got out I thought he'd take the picture staying near our car. He started walking closer to the buffalo. I warned him they can be dangerous and to go no closer. Later on, near the park exit at Gardiner, we stopped so Colin could film a herd of elk comfortably bedded down on green lawns of buildings. Again I cautioned Colin to not get close. The bull of that herd had a huge antler rack.

Colin and Bridie flew from Helena to our daughter's, and her husband's, home in Oregon for a visit. From there they flew back to England.

Colin and Bridie had visited Benton, Arkansas to do some genealogy research. I gave him Dorothy and my pedigree sheets. He let know that in doing some research of English records that my ancestor, Elizabeth Cowen, was a member of the Scottish Colquhoun clan. I checked this out with the Colquhoun society and found that it was true. They informed me that I was authorized to wear the clan tartan. I bought my tartan colors from St. Andrews, Scotland and had my kilt made. I have the whole Scottish outfit.

I now had a reason to visit Europe. I went with Larry and Dorothy to England. We flew into Gatwick airport. I had never before flown such a distance, without refueling. Our plane was a Boeing 777. On the back of the seat in front of me was a map monitor that gave a visual display of the plane's location, passing over a ground map. I found this very fascinating.

At Gatwick, Colin had sent a car to pick us up—the airport was about thirty-five miles south of where they lived. My having to walk using a cane allowed us to quickly be cleared through customs at the airport and got underway. The drive got my attention. We drove "on the wrong" side of the road.

Colin and Bridie lived in Hatfield, a few miles north of London. Their house became our base to trips to London. We would catch a train at Hatfield and ride into London, where it entered the underground subway system—the tube.

I found that the British people are very courteous to the elderly, which is what I am, at this time of my life. If the subway train seats were taken and I got on using my cane, a young person would get up and give me their seat. I hadn't seen such as this since my youth in Oklahoma. I used to do that for elderly people or ladies when I was young. It brought back good memories.

There was a long line of people waiting to tour Westminster Abbey. Again, my use of a cane helped us to get in quicker. The Abbey is like a who's who of history. Buried beneath the Abbey floor are such remembered individuals as poets Tennyson, Robert Browning and writers such as Charles Dickens and Rudyard Kipling—to mention a few that I knew from reading about them over the years.

Many of England's royalty are entombed there. Their tombs have life sized figures of them on the lid of their tomb. I found the tombs of Mary Queen of Scots and Queen Elizabeth I most interesting. They are entombed, one above the other. Elizabeth is located above Queen Mary. Elizabeth had felt threatened by Mary, Queen of Scots, and gave the order to executive Mary.

On another trip to London we went through Madam Tussauds wax museum. It has life size statutes of famous people. It had Princess Diane, Queen Elizabeth II, Ronald Reagan, Winston Churchill, King Henry VIII and his wives, Prince Charles and Sean Connery, to mention just a small portion of famous people being displayed.

I got tired and took a bench seat along the wall. I let my wife Dorothy and Larry know that I'd wait for them on the bench. I sat and watched people viewing the displays. When a young couple stopped, I turned to see what they were doing. The girl said to her escort, "He's alive!" I smiled and replied, "I sure hope so." They smiled and walked on. All the statues displayed there, look very much alive; that they could speak at any moment.

On another trip to London we toured the Tower of London. I took several pictures. King Henry VIII's suit of armor is decorated with gold. One could tell he had a big ego. I chided Dorothy that I now understood how they could they could get around with their heavy armor. Every time we turned around there were stairs to climb or go down. It would build up leg muscles.

Colin and Bridie took us out to dinner at Hatfield House. Whenever King Henry VIII got angry at Elizabeth I, he would exile her to Hatfield House, referring to her as Boleyn's brat.

Most of the original Hatfield House was destroyed by fire and was rebuilt. The surviving wing is used today for Elizabethan—style banquets. Being an appraiser, I took several pictures of the fascinating ceiling structure, a true work of construction art.

On a raised platform a red headed lady that played the part of Queen Elizabeth I, in regal costume. She sat on a decorated throne. There was a court jester that entertained and a ministerial group that played instruments of that time period. Some of "the queen's" court, dressed in costumes of the mid 1500s, performed dances of that period. The "queen" informed the diners if they enjoyed the music and dances, pound the table. When I thought of Knights possibly wearing chain-mail gloves, I understood her comment.

The meal was served to us by ladies dressed in peasant clothes of that period. After our meal the "queen" visited around the tables, talking to various individuals. I took a picture of her while she was talking to Dorothy. When she asked where we were from, I told her Montana. She replied, "Oh, our rebel colonist." I replied, "Yes, the ones who kicked you out." We both had a good laugh. Going to a banquet at Hatfield house is one that I'd highly recommend.

Next day Colin took us to the air museum close by. They had many type of aircraft. I was interested in the English spitfire. I had watched the movie *Battle of Britain* and how the Spitfire and their pilots saved Britain. Next I looked at our American P-51. I worked at North American Aviation, the company that made these planes —putting out a P-51 daily during WWII. Both the Spitfire and the P-51 use engines built by Rolls-Royce. I love the sound of those engines.

In the museum is a German Stuka dive bomber, whose screaming dive sound frightened many. There were many other planes that I don't remember.

Larry rented a car and drove Dorothy and me to visit Stonehenge. Along the way we spent the night in a cute bed and breakfast home. This was a new experience for Dorothy and I. Our upstairs room had a feminine feel as though it might have once been their daughter's room. Our hosts were friendly and kind.

Stonehenge is located in a rural setting, about two miles west of Amesbury, England, in open countryside. When we paid an entrance fee, we were given a hand-held audio tour player. We were told to stay on the walkway and not approach the huge stones. Following the walkway around the huge stones, we came to small numbered viewing sites. Pressing that number on the audio tour player, a voice told us what we were seeing.

Stonehenge is a circle of monoliths standing about twenty-feet tall and weighing about four tons. Some have lintels that probably weight a ton. The entranceway to the blue stones is aligned with the midsummer sunrise. Stonehenge is reported to have been built, or started, around 2100 B.C., and the stones quarried in Wales which is about 250 miles northwest.

The mystery is how they managed to get these large monoliths to its present location. How did they manage to upright these monoliths with the tools available at that time? How did they raise the lintels to cap the up-righted monolith? This is a mystery that still exists today.

Just west of Amesbury is an area called Collingbourne Ducis? There are a few beautiful old homes with thatched roofs in that area, well worth seeing and taking a picture.

The next place we visited was Bath, England. It probably got its name from the Roman bath that was built there. We took pictures of the large pool type bath. Water is supplied by underground hot springs. We were told that the temperature of the pool doesn't vary by more than one degree from its set temperature, and has been that way since it was built around 55 A. D.

Over time the roof that covered the bath has been destroyed, there is a scaled model of what it looked like when it was built. We had a nice lunch served in the restaurant overlooking the Roman bath. While we enjoyed lunch a pianist played beautiful classical music on a concert grand piano. Before leaving we had a glass of mineral water, supposed to be healthy and good for the body.

From Bath we headed for Scotland. Arriving in Edinburgh, Scotland we spent the night at Melville Guest House, a bed and breakfast house. Larry and Dorothy went to see Edinburgh Castle. I had a bad cough and went to see a Scottish doctor. It was very windy that day. The wind was so strong I had to lean into it. When I met the doctor I tried to mimic the Scottish brogue and said, "It's a wee bit windy today." She smiled at the humor. After checking me, she prescribed some pills and told me where to go to get them. When I picked up the pills I wasn't charged anything. After a nice breakfast at Melville's we left for St. Andrews.

St. Andrews is home of the world's oldest golf course. I was hoping to get to play the course. This golf course was built and used in the early 1400s. It became a popular sport. In 1457 King James II of Scotland banned golf because he felt it took up too much of young men's time, and not enough time for archery practice. The ban was removed in 1502 by King James IV of Scotland, himself a golfer.

I wasn't allowed to play the course. The course was being conditioned for playing the British Open next week. I did buy some golf balls showing St. Andrews on them, proof that I had been there. I also bought a golfer's tam with my clans' colors.

The Scottish landscape reminded me a lot of Montana. There are hills and neat wooded valleys, clear running streams. Many of the hills had lots of heather. We drove north on the main highway from St. Andrews to Inverness. From there we drove south along Loch Ness, stopping to take pictures of this famous body of water. From there we drove further south to Luss, Scotland, home of my Colquhoun Clan. It's a village of cute stone cottages, that all look alike, even down to their landscaping. The village sets on the bank of Loch Lomond. It had a very peaceful setting. I felt like my g-g-grandmother, Elizabeth Cowen, appreciated my visiting her village.

We left the next day from Colin and Bride's place. Leaving the rented car, we went by train to London and caught the high speed train to go through the Chunnel to Paris, France. It's about a 31 mile trip in a tunnel built under the sea. That thought troubled me. I was glad when we exited the tunnel into beautiful French farm land.

All too soon we arrived in Paris. We were confronted by rude cab drivers. We finally got a cab to the hotel where we had reservations, the Ambassade. It's a small hotel with some embassies nearby. Dorothy and my room were about the size of my present office room. It had a small bathroom with shower. They had excellent hot coco. Of all things, we walked a block and a half to a Chinese restaurant for dinner that night. It was raining slightly and I still had a cough, not a smart move on my part.

Next day we went to visit the Eiffel Tower. There was such a long line of people waiting to get into elevators that go to the top that I decided to wait on a park bench while Larry and Dorothy took the elevator to the top. People were crammed into the elevator like sardines. I noticed the presence of several armed policemen and armed soldiers patrolling with them.

We then went to see the Arc de Triumph and take pictures. We tried to see the Louvre, but, it was closed due to a strike. We tried some pastry near the Tuileries. We then took a stroll near the river Seine. On a bridge crossing over the river was a life-size statue display depicting the battle at Big Hole, Montana. It was interesting that such would be shown on a bridge over the Seine in Paris, France.

We then caught the high speed train back to London, spent some time with Colin and Bridie and then flew back to Montana. When we took off from Houston for Salt Lake City, Utah it was aboard a McDonnell-Douglass MD-80. A storm was going on at the time. I was concerned as we were climbing-out. We passed through an electrical storm with lightning flashing all around.

Doing appraisal work was becoming harder due to my increasing difficulty in walking and climbing stairs. I was also a diabetic and my doctor said I'd soon not be able to walk. Being 70, I decided it was time for me to retire. I had been doing appraisal work for 25 years.

We had visited Susan several times and fell in love with Oregon. The state had so many beautiful flowers. It was quite a change from Montana. Both Dorothy and I fell in love with the state. While Dorothy attended a special class in Medford, Susan, and her friend showed me several cities, as possible places to retire. I was really taken by Grants Pass. Its downtown part reminded me of downtown Helena. Both Dorothy and I fell in love with Grants Pass.

One year Dorothy and I went to the fair in Medford. It was a hot day and I decided to sit in the shade, next to a building. Veronica, about four, joined me. She was telling her "Papa" Joe a thing or two.

Ron and Susan, our grown children found a nice senior subdivision in Grants Pass, Oregon, called Willow Estates. It was a subdivision of double-wide mobile homes with mature landscapes. Dorothy and I visited Grants Pass, and with a realtor looked over what was available in the area.

One of the senior subdivisions had a pool. From my appraising experience I noticed the pool house needed lots of repair. That meant that there wasn't sufficient funds to keep up the pool house, meaning an increase was needed among those living there. Also the subdivision was a hodge-podge of different mobile homes. Some were small and could be towed behind a car; others were single wide. There were also some double-wide.

When shown Willow Estates, originally found by Ron and Susan, we loved it. It was a senior subdivision and all units had nice landscaping. The subdivision gave off an appealing sight that I knew would attract buyers, thus keeping property values high. We found a vacant unit. Dorothy's baby-grand would fit in its living-room. We hoped it would remain vacant until we sold our home in Montana.

Returning to Montana we put our home on the market. Larry offered to buy the mobile home we liked for us. When our home in Montana sold we would pay him back, which is what happened. When our house sold, we had a large garage sale and gave much to Goodwill and Salvation Army. Other items were taken to the dump.

Ron, Larry and church members helped us pack and load the largest rental truck we could find. It was loaded to the max. Ron drove the truck and had our yellow cat named Harry ride in the cab with him. Dorothy and I followed in our car with our pet dachshund. We spent the night in Coeur d'Alene.

Getting to Grants Pass requires going up and down several hills. The truck was so heavily loaded that Ron could barely get to the top of the hills. I had called ahead and several church members unloaded the truck for us, the exception was the piano. I referred to it as an 800 pound gorilla. The legs had been removed and it stood on its edge.

To get the piano in the truck in Montana had taken eight men. I called Grants Pass Chamber of Commerce and they recommended a man. I thought he would bring a crew with him. He was a guy of about sixty. He let Ron and I know he could easily move the piano in by himself. He had Ron back the truck near enough to our front door for the ramp to reach our deck. Ron helped him work the piano up on a furniture dolly. They then easily moved the piano down the ramp to our deck, and from there inside our home.

Each room in our house had stacks of boxes to unload. In the two front bedrooms there was only a foot of walkway around boxes stacked two layers, or more, high. Our living-room was basically the same. Susan and her husband's secretary helped us unload the boxes. Several church members came and helped get the piano up on its legs. We settled into our new home.

The previous owner of our new home had covered all but a small lawn in back with gravel. Dorothy and I went about putting in plants. Larry bought and planted a mimosa tree that would shade our master bedroom window. He bought and planted a red rose in front and a ground creeping evergreen. About a year later Larry and Ron put in a sprinkler system for us.

Things were going well until I had a heart attack, requiring triple bypass surgery on Thanksgiving Day in 2001. I was pleased to learn that both of my surgeons were members of my church. I felt I was in good hands. Due to my weakness following surgery, I spent twenty days in rehab at Royale Gardens, a rehab and nursing home. I was placed in a room with another guy. My bed was near the window.

The guy in the room with me was also a diabetic who had fallen and broke his hip. He was in lots of pain, if moved. He had the only TV in our room and he played it 24/7. He was an old ex-oilman and a character; he would try to sneak donuts from the kitchen.

A small bathroom, stool and sink only, were used by our room and the one next door. At first I was restricted to having a strong male worker helping me to the bathroom. He would place a wide web belt around my waist to enable him to keep me on my feet, if necessary. Later I was given a walker to use.

Each day I was taken to an exercise room. In the beginning it was in a wheel chair. My therapist's first name was Bart. I called him Black Bart, putting me through all the various exercises. The guy that would come get me for the exercise sessions was Scotty, a Scotsman. I owe a lot to those two and I'll never forget them.

From my room to the exercise room was quite a ways. It was a long hallway, then the nursing hub, then another long hallway, then through the dining-room and a short hall to the exercise room. In the beginning Scotty would take me in a wheelchair to the exercise room, then by using a walker with him holding onto the web belt. The time finally came when Black Bart told me to use my walker and, by myself, return to my room.

I learned I'd not like to ever be placed in a nursing home. All the commotion is disturbing. If you use the help button it seemed to take forever before someone would arrive. At night sound carries far, patients would yell out. Or one might I heard *code blue,* meaning someone has passed away.

I was finally released to go home. Being home felt so good. It was great having Dorothy nearby to talk to and learn all that happened while I was in the nursing home. I checked on my plants to see how they were doing. It felt good being back to gardening again. I began mowing and trimming my lawn, much to the chagrin of my doctor.

In November 2003 we received a call from Larry asking if Dorothy and I would be interested in going on an eastern Caribbean cruise, which he and Ron would help us. He told me that their sister Susan, her husband Dan and our grandkids Ben and Veronica were also going on that trip.

Every since I had that boat ride on USS Morton, going from Manila to San Francisco, and swearing I'd never go for another boat ride, I decided that Dorothy and I would go along. It meant paying a premium price to get our passports renewed in such a short time. We excitedly got ready.

We stayed the night before our flight at a Motel 8 in Portland, where our car could be left in a secure parking area, while we were on the cruise. Next day we caught our flight to Houston and from there to Atlanta, where we met Ron and Larry. We flew with them to Miami and joined the rest of the family. My having to use a cane caused some problems.

Next day we boarded M/S Paradise for the weeklong cruise. Dorothy and I had a cabin mid-ship, allowing for a smoother ride. It was a lower deck above the water line. Our small cabin had twin beds. I didn't know until we finished the cruise that we could have had the beds made into a double bed. It was made up each day by a person assigned our room. When they made up our beds they would leave a towel in the shape of an animal or fish. When we finally left the cruise, we left a tip of appreciation for that person.

To go to the main deck or topside, we took the ship's elevator. Walking down inside corridors was made easier for me, using my cane and their handrails. The cruise was very pleasant. There were snack places around the ship, we could choose what we wanted to eat, and the food was good. Their soft ice cream bar was great. I would select a cone and fill it with soft chocolate ice cream as high as I dared.

Dorothy and I would stroll around the Atlantic deck looking at the various shops, or the Promenade deck. I'm not sure which deck the Atrium plaza was on, I would guess deck 7. At that area you could see the railings for the decks about. I would guess there were about six decks above. When the rest of the family was enjoying the pool on deck 10,

Dorothy and I would relax in lounge chairs and watch. One day they had an ice artist do a sculpture. It was beautiful and he did it so fast.

On the Atlantic deck shops we bought a few souvenirs, pullover T-shirts. Things in the various gift shops were duty free and no sales tax. Along the promenade deck was the piano bar and carioca. We sat at the bar and sang along with the pianist. Setting at the bar, the pianist would hand each of us the lyrics of many songs. We could request the song and sing-along. Larry did a solo on some of the songs while we listened.

It was really neat looking around. We found a Fish & Chips, Pizza and Deli bars. There was a club for dancing to a small band, the huge Normandie show lounge, gift shops art gallery, casino and night club. On the decks above, near the pool area, was an exercise and massage room. On deck 11 were lounges with great views. I liked the area about the bridge. One was looking at what the ship's Captain was seeing.

My book Empire, now Ridderzaal, had just come out. A couple next to me struck up a conversation. I managed to work in the title of my book. To dine at the main dining-room was a formal dress affair, at least once during the cruise. I wore a white jacket, light-covered silver shirt with black bow tie and black trousers. Dorothy wore an elegant black dress. Her black jacket was a flimsy light-weight show through with long-sleeves. It showed through black embroidered sleeves. With her silver hair she looked great.

We took a guided tour of Nassau. Our guide took us to see the much talked about Atlantis hotel. What caught my attention was seeing a young couple come out of the hotel main entrance and get into a chauffeur driven limousine. Out of habit I tried to guess their profession. I saw several other limos parked in front of the hotel. To me that added up to an expensive hotel. I later learned that part of the hotel's attraction is being able to ride around in a chauffeur driven limousine.

The hotel doesn't allow non-guest tourist to wonder about. Our guide had a friend who worked in the hotel kitchen. Though this friend our guide got us inside to see the huge aquarium. The aquarium height must have been at least twenty feet tall. I have no idea the length. I think our guide said the tank held 20,000 gallons of water. The fish inside were all large, even the stingray.

Our guide then took us to a beautiful balcony that overlooked tropical trees and plants, and a good view of the ocean. The tour then took in the remains of Old Fort Nassau. On the road by the fort a lady sold souvenirs. Dorothy bought a woven reed fan. The lady wove into the fan, Laura, my favorite name for Dorothy, and Bahamas.

Boarding our ship, we sailed for Saint Thomas, U.S. Virgin Islands. The rest of the family went scuba diving. Dorothy and I took the tour to Sir Francis Drake's house, overlooking the beautiful blue-green harbor. Our driver guide apologized for St. Thomas' cold weather — it was 75 degrees. When I told him Dorothy and I were from Montana, and that one winter it was minus 66 degrees, with wind chill, he said, "Oh my God!"

On the balcony of Sir Francis Drake's home, I took a picture of Dorothy with the beautiful harbor showing below. St. Thomas has many tropical plants. I saw my first cashew nut tree. The tree has what looks like a round green orange with the cashew nuts attached below. The town has many brightly colored buildings of orange, cherry red, pinkish and various colors in between. For souvenirs we bought two T-Shirts with the islands shown on the front.

Our next port of call was the Dominican Republic. We went ashore and to the main city. I'm not sure where our ship docked at. We went on the tour. To get to Santo Domingo was a drive of about twenty minutes. We went through areas where the land seemed to revert back to scrub growth of all kinds. We then went through a poverty area. The homes in that area were narrow, about the width of a couple of boxcars. They were long and narrow, and many looked like repair was neglected. I couldn't help but feel sorry for the plight of these people.

Our tour bus took us to see Columbus' Lighthouse, El Alcazar de Colon, La Basilique, El Faro de Colon and the President's Palace, an icon of extravagance. Those with Spanish names were very old, dating back to Columbus Days.

I took several pictures of these structures. Our tour had lunch at a local restaurant. The food was okay. Food on the cruise ship was much superior. Before leaving the restaurant, I converted an American dollar into their currency, to have as a souvenir. I was shocked to see them give me large bills and some coins in return.

We were driven through a shopping area in an older section of the town. There were many small shops selling all kinds of goods. Dorothy and I looked through some of the shops, along with those on our tour. When we returned to our bus, young men trying to sell things hounded all of us that had returned to our bus. I was glad when all on the tour had returned and we headed back to the ship.

The Dominican Republic shares the same island with Haiti. The island has seen many blood struggles. Spain once claimed the island, then France. The Dominican Republic was also attacked by its neighbor, Haiti. The island still shows the effects of all the struggles.

Dorothy's Thibault ancestors had fled France, and purchased plantations in Haiti. Then had to flee an uprising there. It was interesting getting a feel for the area, and what they must have experienced.

When we had left the ship were told the time we had to be back on ship; that our ship would not wait. I became concerned that our tour guide wasn't going to make our departure time, due to the traffic and shopping time some of our tour members had taken. I think he broke speed limits when we were in the open area. We barely made it to the boat on time. My impression of the Dominican Republic was not too good. We really enjoyed St. Thomas.

Arriving back in Miami, we left the ship and left for home. When our flight left Houston it was during a storm. As previously stated, I had never flown on an MD 80 airplane, a pusher type. I was concerned as we climbed out with lighting flashing all around us.

It was great being back in Grants Pass. Our life was back to normal, until October 26, 2006. At 2 AM Dorothy woke me saying she had a bad headache. I ask if I should take her to the hospital. She said no, that she just needed an aspirin. I got it for her and we went back to sleep.

In the morning she couldn't see or put words correctly. I called our doctor's office, telling his nurse I thought Dorothy had a stroke, and took her to see him. He quickly diagnosed her problem as being a mental case and prescribed a strong mental altering medication. After taking five of those pills, Dorothy went "Ballistic." In the ER room it took several to restrain her. When we asked the doctor what could be done, he flippantly recommended a local psychiatrist. He came across as uncaring, writing Dorothy off. I, and family members, was not pleased with his actions.

We asked about having Dorothy's condition evaluated at 2N in Medford, where mental people were treated. His flippant answer angered me. Our son Ron managed to talk the admitting doctor at 2N into a five day evaluation of Dorothy's mental state. As an expert in mental disorders, he found that Dorothy wasn't "mentally disturbed." He said she just had a temper, and changed her medication. From there Dorothy was admitted to a nursing home, to allow the old bad drug to go away.

I felt so sorry for her. She was pinned with an alarm system to her wheelchair and to her bed at night. The place was noisy with patients yelling out. I would visit her daily, bringing seedless grapes and CD records.

Because help was limited in taking her to the restroom, she came down with two urinary tract infections, a week apart which almost killed her. One day in a pathetic voice she said, "Am I never coming home?" That tore me apart.

After four and a half months I found a way to bring her home, thanks to April our neighbor's daughter. I had a caregiver to help her during much of the day. She helped with Dorothy's bath and to get dressed, then fixed meals and washed clothes. Dorothy was still blind, with aphasia, but back to her old sweet self and now happy being in her own home.

When I took her for her appointment with her new doctor, one that had been our doctor before he had transferred to Portland, he was appalled at how much she had improved. He told me that when he saw her on a visit from the nursing home, he was concerned that she wouldn't last more than six months. He said the caregiver and I had worked a miracle.

The previous doctor that had almost killed her saw us in the waiting area for our new doctor. He made a slight remark about her present condition and went on. I forgave that doctor for all that he put Dorothy through, but, I don't like him. I kept a daily account of him and his actions. If Dorothy hadn't made it, I was determined to use what I'd written down to see that he never practiced medicine again. I don't like to sue people, but, this is one time I would have.

I consider the last five years as a blessing. To be able to take care of someone I loved dearly, in her time of need; to let her know she's loved, cared about, and protected against outside sources is very rewarding to the giver. A biblical statement says it well. It's found in Matt. 25:35-40. Christ said, "When ye have done this to the least of my servants, ye have done it for me."

I've tried to put myself in her "shoes." If I couldn't see, I would enjoy hearing kind loving words in a soft comforting voice, a hand to hold onto that offers stability, a kiss morning and night to assure me that love still reigns between us, and little things done or given for my benefit. As an older song states, "Little things mean a lot." I try to do all these things for Dorothy, and I know she appreciates them.

The End.

ABOUT THE AUTHOR

J. H. Ellison, a native of Eastern Oklahoma and graduate of Warner High, he received an Associate of Science degree from Connors College. After attending Oklahoma State University, he enlisted in the Air Force during the Korean War, became crewmember on SA-16 amphibian aircraft stationed at Clark Field in Philippines and flew missions in Korea. After discharge he worked in aerospace as an Electrical Engineer, working on F-86D fighter, Minuteman and Hound Dog missiles and as Senior Management Analyst on Apollo moon rocket. Attended creative writing class at California State Fullerton and studied at Longridge Writers' school, Connecticut.

Other books include: *Warner—The Next Generation*, *EMPIRE*, *Westward Passage*, *Tim's World And Other Short Stories*, *Wagons West*, and *Ridderzaal-Tea Plantation*.

14881144R00180

Made in the USA
Charleston, SC
05 October 2012